BEGINNINGS IN SPIRITUAL LIFE

1. Beginnings

BEGINNINGS IN SPIRITUAL LIFE

DOMINIC M. HOFFMAN, O.P.

WIPF & STOCK · Eugene, Oregon

Wipf and Stock Publishers
199 W 8th Ave, Suite 3
Eugene, OR 97401

Beginnings in Spiritual Life
By Hoffman, Dominic, O. P.
Copyright©1967 Western Dominican Province
ISBN 13: 978-1-62032-799-9
Publication date 1/1/2013
Previously published by Daughters of St. Paul, 1967

Nihil obstat: John Fearon, O.P.
  Nicholas Halligan, O.P.

Imprimi potest: H. F. Ward, O.P.
  Provincial
  October 4, 1966

Nihil obstat: John P. Sullivan, M.A.
  Censor Deputatus

Imprimatur: ✚ Terence J. Cooke, D.D., V.G.
  Archdiocese of New York
  November 18, 1966

The *nihil obstat* and *imprimatur* are official declarations that a book or pamphlet is free of doctrinal or moral error. No implication is contained therein that those who have granted the *nihil obstat* and *imprimatur* agree with the contents, opinions or statements expressed.

*To
My Mother and Father
Who Gave Me
My First
Beginnings in Spiritual Life*

CONTENTS

Introduction — 11

PART I
ABOUT GOD AND OURSELVES

1. God and Love — 17
2. Ourselves and Love — 23

PART II
PREPARATION FOR LOVE

3. The Obstacles to Love — 31
4. Sin: The Sickness and Death of Love — 37
5. Temptation: The Battles and Victories of Love — 44
6. Practical Suggestions on Temptation — 48
7. The World and Love — 55
8. Our Bodies and Souls and Love — 61
9. The Love of God and Our Sexual Nature — 69
10. Marriage and the Love of God — 78
11. Solitude and the Love of God — 86
12. Suffering: Abandonment to God's Purifying Will — 90
13. Love Conquers All — 96

PART III
PRAYER: THE LANGUAGE OF LOVE

14. Love in Asking — 103
15. Mental Prayer: Our Embrace with God — 108
16. God's Presence of Love — 114
17. Practical Suggestions on Prayer — 120

PART IV
THE MASS AND SACRAMENTS: THE LIFEBLOOD OF LOVE

18	The Liturgy and Love	129
19	Holy Communion: The Food of Love	136
20	Confession: The Healing of Love	142
21	Practical Suggestions on Confession	149

PART V
THE HEART OF THE TRUE LOVER: THE NATURE OF CHRISTIAN PERFECTION

22	"Be Perfect"	159
23	"If Anyone Love Me, He Will Keep My Word"	165

PART VI
THE CHARACTERISTICS OF THE TRUE LOVER: THE VIRTUES IN GENERAL

24	Love and the Virtues	171
25	Love Means Peace Means Change	176
26	The Second Chances	183

PART VII
THE COMPANIONS OF LOVE: SOME VIRTUES IN PARTICULAR

27	Loving One Another	191
28	Love in Thought	197
29	Love in Word	203
30	Love in Deed	211
31	Some Problems with Love	216
32	Immodesty and Our Love of Neighbor	222
33	Loving the Unloved and the Unloving	227
34	The Love of Friends	234
35	Doves as Serpents	241
36	Love and the Humble Heart	247
37	"Love . . . Believes All Things"	255
38	Love and Authority	262
39	"Love . . . Hopes All Things"	269
40	"Love Is Strong as Death"	275
41	"Love . . . Endures All Things"	282
42	"Rejoice in the Lord"	289

PART VIII
LOVE AND THE WORKS OF LOVE

43	Work and the Spiritual Life	297
44	The Apostolate of Love	302

PART IX
PERSEVERANCE IN LOVE

45	"I Am the Mother . . . of Holy Hope"	311
46	Guidance for Love	316
47	Reading and the Love of God	322
48	Daily Life and the Love of God	327
49	Unending Love	332

INTRODUCTION

This is a book written for those who are making a start in the spiritual life. It presupposes only the knowledge that is common to all who have had some small education in basic Christian teaching. Also it presupposes only a minimum of good will. Not everyone who makes a beginning is on fire with spiritual enthusiasm. Some will begin out of a grim sense of duty. Others may not want to make a beginning at all, but do so only as a vague hope in an empty life.

Furthermore, this is a book written principally for the layman. Perhaps at other times he has opened a spiritual book in hope, only to shut it in despair, or with a distaste based not on the spiritual life itself but on the manner in which it was presented. He perhaps reads advice given from the point of view of a cloistered life safely and hopelessly isolated from his own world. Penances and mortifications may be encouraged by holy examples for him who shrinks from the thought of penance. He is told the proper attitudes to adopt—for instance, that he must see joy in suffering. But he is not told that these attitudes were reached only at the summit of the spiritual life and not at the beginning. And so, perhaps sadly, perhaps with relief, he puts aside the book, and so puts out a small spark of the grace of God.

In the pages which follow, laymen will find themselves and their condition of life the center of attention at all times. Consequently they will not find a specifically spiritual vocabulary or an alien pious rhetoric. They will not find a long list of prayers, practices, and penances. They will not find a list of things to be given up.

Patiently and gently, however, these souls will open up to God. They will see that true peace comes with true love, and that love means an entire giving, and that giving means some changes. Such transitions are sometimes easy, sometimes not. But in the end what was once unwisely loved is now put aside, and what was once foolishly despised is now embraced with gratitude. Every man who has gone even a part of the way knows this. The purpose of the book, then, is to open the soul to the grace of God and to show some practical consequences of the love of God in a life that wants to find love and peace.

But in writing for laymen, we are not "writing down" to them. There is never condescension when teaching the principles and basic practices of a true spiritual life. These principles and basic practices are the same whether one is priest, brother, sister, or layman. But here the emphasis of application will be on those living in the world.

However, despite the attention to the layman and to the beginner, this book is intended for all who may read it. As we have just said, the fundamentals are the same for everyone, because God is the same and human nature is the same. Most of the counsels of the spiritual life are valid no matter how many years we have spent at it or how far we have progressed. We do not leave these things behind when we have ceased to be beginners. Besides, the lives of many spiritual persons sometimes become too spiritually complicated for the efficient action of the Holy Spirit. These will see in this book a way to lift the burdens which they need not have assumed in the first place and now may discard with safety.

This book, then, will not present a watered-down spirituality. It presumes that there is need for God in the world just as there is need for God in the cloister. It understands that he can become the absorbing influence in the world as it is expected that he will be in the lives of those who are more externally dedicated to him.

This is also not a book just for Catholics. Those outside the Catholic Church have come to see that we hold treasures which can be helpful to all humanity even when not prepared to accept all the teachings of this Church. There are, it is true, many things in this book which are specifically Catholic. But the overwhelming number of ideas and counsels will fit anyone who wants union with God.

It should be unnecessary to state why we are writing on the spiritual life for laymen. They are the largest part, and in that sense the most important part of the people of God. The bishops and priests exist for them, and not they for the bishops and priests. Also, laymen are expected more and more to do the work of Christ in a world which can only be remotely reached by even the best of priests. But because of this role there can arise an error of emphasis. One is apt to think of this book as primarily for the formation of apostles and workers. But the full truth is even greater than this. Above all, this book is written because God wishes to love everyone very much, and because everyone should love God.

But the idea of the layman as an arm of Christ must not be minimized. The good to be done has unending possibilities. Yet the opposite is true also; the harm that can be done by a zealous but unspiritual layman is incalculable. This is a book which modestly hopes to prevent much tragedy to the work of God and to the individual.

Only the layman with inner discipline will do the great things for God that are waiting to be done, not the zealot, not the pseudo-intellectual who must say something new because he is compelled to say something different, not the professional rebel. Through the layman, God wishes to do enormous good. But frictions and false causes, as well as true causes imprudently pursued, may obscure the dawn of a renewed earth. The layman must have solid formation. Seminary training is intended to give this to the clergy, but obviously we cannot send laymen to seminaries. So this book may indeed supply a reasonable and yet inspiring framework for dedicated lives.

Obviously not all things which could be written even for beginners can be written here. The spiritual life has enough imaginary terrors without giving a real terror by offering a very large book. But we trust that this selection will meet the needs of a great number, and we leave other things to be read in other places.

This book intends to do no more than to reflect in many words what our Lord said in few. We shall try to portray the spiritual life, insofar as it is possible, as it would have come from the Christ who, although at once kindly and severe, gentle and strong, loving and threatening, yet was much more kindly, gentle, and loving than he was anything else. It is a book whose basic idea was conceived years ago when the author was a young priest, the idea that the love of God makes the spiritual life a simple way. A simple way does not always mean an easy way, but a way in which love *in the end* makes the yoke sweet and the burden light and the cross a joy.

One might say that over half a century of living has gone into the production of this book, and half of that spent in the priesthood. But in truth many lives are bound up in these two covers, lives met as confessor, director, parish priest, retreat master, chaplain, and teacher. Yet experience by itself is never enough; life needs the basis of sound principles. These principles, it is true, are found in the message of the Gospels. But the message of the Gospels must be applied to life by another gift of God which is human reason guided by grace; God has not written down every step of the way for us. In the search for a firm basis to apply the teachings of Christ, we cannot do better than to use as a guide the summation of divine and human wisdom given us by the theology of St. Thomas Aquinas, the Common Doctor of the Church. Although his words will not often be directly quoted in these pages, the spirit of his balanced wisdom will guide every word that is written.

Finally, more than in ages past we have become aware that many of our spiritual problems have roots in the emotional side of our nature. Likewise it is also true that a sound spiritual life will do much to promote a sound mental and emotional life.[1] But the spiritual life is not for that reason a matter of psychotherapy, nor is psychotherapy a part of this book. Yet certain obvious conclusions can sometimes be made and much clarification can result if the emotional and physical roots are considered. Whenever it will be helpful for those for whom this book is intended, such analysis of our human nature will be attempted, yet never in technical language.

This is not a theoretical book but a practical one. Experience, science, and theology still have here only one purpose, to lead the soul to God in the simple way of the Gospels, following Christ who said, "I am the way," and who spoke of that way in terms of sweetness and light and the cross.

[1] See *Heroic Sanctity and Insanity* by Thomas Verner Moore, M.D., Carthusian (New York: Crune & Stratton, 1959).

PART I

ABOUT GOD AND OURSELVES

CHAPTER 1

God and Love

For us the great truth of the universe is that God wants our love. Clearly seen, this truth is more awesome than the glory and the vastness of the galaxies, or the blinding light of the countless suns that make them up. For, although God does not need our love for his happiness, yet he wants it so much that his desire is still for us the most important thing in the universe. It is so important that he commanded his Son to die and rise again to prove it. We are, if we could see it, almost engulfed by love.

Now it is required of love and lovers that each find in the other something to love. The friendship between God and man is not an exception to this law, even though the two beings are so greatly different. Each must see in the other certain things which draw forth love. But because we do not see him for what he is, more lovable and desirable than any other being in the universe, many of us do not love him, and all of us do not love him as we ought. Thus he is often only feared, when he is not merely tolerated or even hated. But none of these attitudes allow us to see the truth which God is and which he so much wants us to see, that he is love.

If we could see him as he is, face to face as a man sees a woman or a woman sees a man, we would not need to have this explained to us. We would see it more clearly than we can see the goodness or the beauty of any human person. But ordinarily he remains hidden behind the veil of his creation. God has no human features, no human voice.

Yet there are times in the lives of ordinary people when the veil has lifted for a glimpse of something of what God is like. Suddenly at the change from one moment to another, often when not in prayer or in a holy place, for ordinary people the world has stood still, and nothing was so important as the unseen, unheard, yet undeniable perception of him who is there.

Such an experience is perhaps not so limited to the saints, as some of us think. For many it never happens in a lifetime. For others it is so rare that it is almost forgotten in the passing of years. In any case it cannot be procured, cannot be merely willed, cannot be prayed into, cannot be repeated except by the will of him who made himself present in the first place. But if it was ever given, it was given not to be forgotten. It was intended as a seed to bear fruit. God has no intention that his love, such love, should be sterile.

Although this awareness of the presence of God is usually a rare thing for those who are beginning the spiritual life, it is a commonplace in the lives of many of the saints. And this is the main reason for bringing it up. We are here trying to penetrate to God as love. Even though we ourselves may never have this transcending experience of the closeness of God in this world, we have the undeniable testimony of reliable people, the saints, that it is so. Such testimony can encourage us; that is one reason why God has put it into the world. A woman who had lost her faith at a secular university was brought back by reading St. Teresa of Avila. St. Teresa sounded authentic.

God by his presence alone, experienced by these fellow human beings, has great power to attract and hold human love, love that in some cases had been unwisely given to the world in great abundance. So it was with St. Francis of Assisi. But later in life Francis found God so irresistible that he spent whole nights in the prayer of love. Sometimes men like this had to resist the attraction of this presence in order to do their duties. For instance, St. John of the Cross would drag his knuckles along the stones of the building as he walked, in order to force his attention away from God.

Once more, however, we must insist that this extraordinary attraction is mentioned only to illustrate what God is like, and not to promise an experience commonly to be felt in this world. Many of us must wait. The eternal destiny of all is to have this love forever, in far greater fullness than anyone has experienced it on earth.

But whether or not God manifests his closeness to us on earth, there are other ways in which we can all see him as one who calls forth love. These are the ways of faith and reason. They provide the same truth about him as do ways which are more intimately felt. For, the God we know by means less profoundly experienced can never be other than himself.

Human reason shows us this loving God very clearly in a very simple manner: it sees him through what he has done. There is a deep but easily understood principle that you can't give what you haven't got. As the saying goes, "You can't squeeze blood out of a turnip." This principle applies to God too. Even he can't give what he hasn't got. As a result, if there is anything of goodness, beauty, and love in his creation, it is there because creation is somehow fashioned after him who is uncreated Goodness and Beauty and Love.

For instance, we see much goodness in the world: goodness in the eyes of children, in the faces of people close to God, old and young. We see goodness in the many kind things that man does to man, and we view it in the earth settling down to rest at twilight. When things are as God intended, they are good. But he could not even have known how to make them so if he were not goodness too.

This reasoning has a deep meaning for love if we look at our human nature. Man is instinctively attracted by the good. Even when he does evil, he is forced by his nature to seek the good in the evil. He is deceived, of course. But even the pleasure he seeks is a good thing created by God, when we consider it by itself. Goodness in some form is what we cannot help seeking and cannot help loving. The conclusion now should be clear: since we can love only goodness, should we not love him above all who is himself all goodness?

This same way of reasoning can lead to a discovery of the love which is God, by way of beauty. All of us are attracted to beauty in one way or another, whether it is the beauty of nature, of the beauty of women and children, or the beauty of character. Yet all beauty has its beginning in God. Somehow everything has to be created after his own nature. His nature is the idea or inspiration for every beautiful thing, which nevertheless falls short of its inspiration and reflects the Uncreated imperfectly. Yet if we are drawn by the beauty of his creatures, how much more must we expect to find beauty in their maker and thus to love their maker. Even the veil which hides him reflects him.

But surely the greatest reason for seeing him as love is love itself. Mankind lives for love more than for anything else. Yet all that we have of love, whether used well or badly, is in the world because God has put it at our disposal. We have love because he who is love has put it here. And if the splinters of love, so to speak, are so delightful that they can so fill a man or woman, what must be the experience of meeting him who is the whole of it, as we will met him when we are at home with him forever.

As we can see, reason has carried us far, indeed from what we can see and experience, up to the cause of all things, and has shown us that this first cause is also love. But another and better way to establish contact with God in this world is by faith. By our reason we find out about him from the things he has made, by faith we find out about him from what he has told us. While his love is indeed manifested clearly in many passages of the Old Testament, it is in the New Testament that he has chosen to emphasize his love above any of the other aspects of his nature. Here we learn from his own word the unfathomable truth that "God so loved the world that he gave his only-begotten Son." (John 3:16) Any father or mother reading these words should understand something of what kind of love that must be.

Perhaps all our reasons for seeing God as love seem too abstract. After all, God is still spirit and we flesh and blood. But here faith gives us an insight that our nature easily accepts. God has made himself almost unbelievably close to us in our human nature through the God-man, Jesus Christ. Though it is true that we do not directly see the God that he is in his divine nature, but only see the human in his speech and acts, these are still the speech and acts of the Second Person who is God. We thus come in contact with the incomprehensible divine through speech which was heard and actions which were seen.

In Christ we know love and goodness beyond what even the greatest thinkers of old had told us we could expect of God. We have gotten so used to him that we take for granted that he should be this good, forgetting that the crucified Christ was "a stumbling block to the Jews and folly to the Gentiles" (I Cor. 1:23) precisely because they couldn't believe in that much love on the part of God. In Christ we find God bending down to us: love for all, care for all, the bad and the good, the old and the young, the repulsive and the healthy. To those who have the gift of a living faith, there is little need of reasoned arguments about the goodness and love of God.

To put meaning into our lives, there must be an essential order: our hearts which were made for love must find that God is love. We must be convinced that he is the only treasure which we must possess, and we must seek diligently until we have him. We must learn to respond to God's love in some personal sense just as we would to true human love.

Now if this were not a book written for a practical purpose, we would pass on to the next step in our explanation of the spiritual life. But perhaps someone is already asking, "How am I to get to know God so that I may love him?" It turns out that the answer is simple and can be answered by another question: How do you get to know anyone?

Although the other person is God, and although God most rarely talks to men directly, and cannot be seen, the process of getting to know God is not too different from the way we get to know our friends. We get to know our friends and to love them simply by spending time with them. We can learn much about God in this way, even though he doesn't talk to us.

For instance, we learn that he is willing to listen to anything we have to say, even our complaints. When we find someone like this, we know we have a friend. We learn that God is ready to help us; we ask so often and he responds so faithfully that we become sure of him. We thus learn that he is dependable. We can speak to him at any time, any place, and under all circumstances. We thus see that we mean something to him. We tell him over and over of our love. Then by the mysterious way that lovers have of knowing the love between them, we come to understand that our love is not one-sided. And we are right. The Scripture has a simple and convincing proof of this: "We love because he first loved us." (I John 4:19) We could not begin to love him unless he wanted our love enough to give us first the gift of loving him.

Practical Reflection

Have I always stopped at the thought of nature and human life, and never seen beyond them to the thought of God? Do I give enough thought to God? Take the time to talk to him? Do

I see him as the central figure in the universe and in my life? Have I not thought of him only as a master to be obeyed, or as an accountant to be reckoned with, and not as a father or a friend to be loved? Am I convinced that love is the aspect of his nature that he wants most for me to see? Have I now at least the beginning of a determination to think of him this way, and without losing reverence for him, to approach him with love?

CHAPTER 2

Ourselves and Love

When we speak about love, we are concerned with the greatest depths in our nature. St. Thomas wisely observes that we always act out of love, even when we hate, even when we fear. It is then no surprise to learn that this is what makes the spiritual life attractive and fulfilling.

Without love the spiritual life has little to offer. It won't fill your pockets. It won't fill your stomachs. Likewise it isn't something that tastes good, and it has no appeal to what is called our lower nature. Our Lord did promise in the Sermon on the Mount that when we "seek first the kingdom of God and His justice," many things will be given us besides. (Matt. 6:33) But he certainly made this statement with obvious reservations. Whatever gifts he intends for those who love him, he never meant that anyone should, so to speak, marry God for his money.

The great superiority of the spiritual life is clearly seen when, without great concern, it passes over the things which motivate so much of our life, and still tells us that it offers something better. In truth it is dealing in the only thing that in the end does matter. While not denying the value of these other things, the spiritual life makes its major appeal to that part of man which at once is most noble and most in need to be rescued from the merely natural world. This part of man is what makes him man, the part which enables him to know truly and to love deeply and wisely. Without full development here, he is less than what he should be as man, and sometimes even less than the animals. Unless he is at peace in this deepest and noblest part of himself, it will matter very little how full his pockets may be, or how full his stomach, or how successful his other satisfactions.

This peace with ourselves is what the spiritual life promises, though not without interruption, not without warfare. It promises on earth a relative fulfillment of our deepest life, and then, let us never forget, a perfect fulfillment hereafter. It does this by the love of God reaching to his most profound echo in our nature, that is, to our desire and capacity to love.

But on the other hand it is necessary to avoid an exaggerated kind of love. One must, so it is said, love without any self-interest. But such a love is not taught in the sacred pages or by our reason. Despite the illusion of superiority, the soul that attempts it will have a stunted and fragile growth. The high place which we must give to love does not deny all self-interest, even in our love for God. He has made us to act in the instinctive manner that we do, and a purely altruistic love is alien to that. The difference between true love and a selfish love is that we love the other *principally* for the other, and not principally for ourselves.

Wise and mature love must see in the other something that is worthy of the gift of self. This gift of self is the supreme gift of love, and it is given in varying degrees to those who are loved. Ideally this giving should be in proportion to the good seen in the other. And here, strangely, where we should find ourselves rushing toward God, is where the spiritual life has its greatest failures.

These are the failures who do not even start the spiritual life. They are convinced that God is worthy of all the love that can be given. But they are not at all convinced that he can see anything to love in them. They accept the fact that he may forgive them, tolerate them, and take reasonable care of them. But a relationship in which he loves them with any sort of personal intensity, this they will not or cannot allow themselves to believe.

There are many deep roots for this misguided self-abasement, some of them psychological in nature. But there is an underlying intellectual error also: to think that anyone is *by himself* worthy of God at all. The simple truth is that no one meets God as an equal. Even though by love we come closest to equality with him, still no one gives to God in the same way that God gives to him. In a mysterious but all-pervading sense we must receive from him whatever we would give to him. Consequently no one can give to God a self in any sense worthy of him or attractive to him, without that self and its endearing qualities being beforehand the gift of a love who is also first and universal cause.

Therefore in our spiritual insecurity we have a firm basis for hope. Our attractiveness ultimately depends on God, whose love and ability to give is boundless. It is he who still adorn the beloved soul with gifts that in turn will attract him. It is as if the bridegroom were to purchase the wedding gown for the bride, and then love her the more because of the new beauty she shows.

We can trust God to act this way simply because he is love. We can see enough of the nature of love on this earth to know that it has its own laws. A fundamental law of love is to want to communicate itself, simply to give itself. With God then all else follows because, being love, he is compelled by his own nature to give of what he has, of what he is, to others. In our essential human loneliness it is a consoling thing to understand that God has this kind of compulsion.

Yet even this may not convince those of us, most of us, who do not see much in themselves to attract God. For one thing he is free as to the bestowal of his gifts, and does not bestow them equally or in any exact pattern. To some, for instance, he pours out his gifts in unbelievable abundance from the very beginning, as with our Lady. For others he apparently saves an abundance until the last moment, as with the thief on the cross. To some of us it will seem that he has bestowed on us very little; and we don't have much hope for something better. We know that we have wasted God's gifts by the rejection of love that is implied in sin and carelessness. But this pessimism does a dishonor to God, and we can see this by considering the two ways in which (from our point of view) God loves us.

After all these words on God's love, it may appear to be a contradiction to say that some of us are loved *actually*, and some are not. Those who are here and now in his friendship (by being, as we say, in the state of grace), he loves actually. Those who have chosen to reject his friendship (by mortal sin), he does not love with an actual love here and now.

But this is not a contradiction, because God loves everyone with another kind of love, except those who have turned from him by an eternal choice. This other kind of love is based on *potentiality*. That is to say, God loves all of us, the good and the bad, not so much for what we are now, but for what we can become. In this kind of love he loves each one of us according to the way he has made us, and always endeavors to give each that abundance of love which will fill our particular capacity for love. Those who are not actually his friends he calls to make their peace with him. Those who are his friends he always wants to draw closer.

We have a great proof of this, one that we can never afford to forget though we may have heard it many times. There was once a woman who rejected God's love most completely, even though it was probably offered to her in great measure. She was so immersed in evil that she required more than ordinary help when our Lord came upon her. She is Mary Magdalene, "out of whom he has cast seven devils." (Mark 16:9) In her we see the truth of God's tenacious love. For our Lord does not just forgive her and then merely tolerates her. He apparently makes her his closest friend. It was she to whom he made his first public appearance after his resurrection, even before Peter and John, both beloved apostles. God surely saw and loved the potentiality for love in the soul of this sinful woman. Perhaps only one who could be so evil could also become so good.

But in placing our emphasis on the working of God in our souls, we must avoid an obvious misunderstanding. We cannot merely sit and wait for God to come and adorn our souls as one might put clothes on a small child. Though all things are the gift of God, in some mysterious way which no man has been able to explain fully, our free will enters.

God always respects the nature he has given us. Although in the parables our Lord spoke of gathering us in like a harvest, there is a necessary activity on our part. This means that we must somehow seek him who is always seeking us. With his help we must do things; his giving always implies our accepting and often our doing. What we must do and how to do it is in practical terms what we mean by the spiritual life. We must do, and yet because he must ever be the giver, we learn to look for his help and guidance at every step of the way. "The Lord's delight is in them who trust in his goodness." (Ps. 146:11)

Then too, although he gives us much without being asked, he gives us more when we ask. We must not neglect to pray. We must pray for what we need, and even for what we don't see that we need, especially in this beginning of our journey into the heart of God.

Practical Reflection

Am I deeply aware that everything God has made is good, in fact "very good," to use the words of Genesis? Am I convinced that God, therefore, sees in me reasons why he should love me deeply? Sees that these reasons have much more to do with my potentiality than with what I am at present? Am I willing to give of myself at least to this extent, that I will try to overcome any deep fear of rejection which keeps me from giving myself to a loving God? Am I willing to trust that he will continue to show me the way to become more worthy of more love? Will I perseveringly ask him for this?

PART II

PREPARATION FOR LOVE

CHAPTER 3

The Obstacles to Love

The way of love implies a certain freedom, for now we are no longer merely slaves or servants but freemen and friends. On the other hand love cannot live without discipline. The loving soul is not an irresponsible soul. It does not move upon whim, now here now there, as the butterfly appears to move from flower to flower. The failures in love, even in human love, are failures of those who did not live up to its requirements. True love prompts us to be worthy of love and to prepare, not only for love itself, but for more love and for the secure possession of love.

We should not be surprised, then, if we encounter some restrictions upon our lives. Human experience tells us that love imposes certain obligations toward the other, and that it is not true love if these are not recognized and fulfilled. We cannot therefore think of the spiritual life as an amicable, leisurely stroll about the countryside. Only the sentimental think that they can enjoy a liberty which is limited perhaps only by emotional repugnance for certain sins. If we want the love of God and the peace that comes with it, we must see obligation as a consequence of love.

This is a law binding upon every human friendship. Our best example of it is marriage which, as God intended it, is the most complete of human love relationships. For, our life with God is easily compared to marriage. Our souls are in a true sense experiencing a courtship. God the creator seeks us the creatures, seeks our love forever. We accept his interest and attention, perhaps with joy. God shall have our heart, we say. But as in every courtship, every marriage, there comes the time of adjustment or adaptation of one to the other. God adjusts himself to us in ways which show that infinite love is infinite understanding and patience. We on our part have the greater obligation to adjust to him.

God's love will not allow unlimited freedom any more than a human partner would allow it in marriage. In marriage a man may not loaf as much as he wants, may not be as thoughtless as he wants, may not neglect his family for others as he pleases. A woman may not attract men as she pleases, may not spend money on clothes as she pleases, may not talk or complain as she pleases. With God things are not too different. As we get to understand him, we get to know that certain things we do or want are not pleasing to him at all. And then also we see that there are other things which interfere with or delay the full possession of his love.

These things which are not at all pleasing to him we call sins, varying as they obviously do in their degree of guilt. These involve evil in one way or another. But there are other things, those which impede or delay our complete friendship, and these are usually not evil. In fact, considered by themselves, they are good. But just as a husband cannot spend too much money on recreation, or a wife on shoes, so we are required by love of God to certain renunciations, not only of sin but even of some undeniably good things. This kind of renunciation is often called by the name of detachment.

But now we have come into an area where many misunderstand the spiritual life. A certain image of it puts great emphasis on what must be given up if one attempts more than ordinary closeness to God. So the hesitant beginner expects that not only will his smallest vices be torn from his soul like the clawing of a bird of prey, but that every pleasure will also be taken away in the same irrevocable manner. The world, he fearfully understands, is to be treated with utter aversion, despite the fact that he must continue to live in that same world and, in some good sense, come to terms with it.

It isn't as if he expects the spiritual life to be pleasantly easy. He has no unrealistic dream that it is a gay, happy encounter with God whereby all sorrows, disappointments, and frustrations are lifted away as the sun disperses a morning fog. And usually he has no difficulty with the fact that he must give up sin, any big ones of course, and then steadily work on the smaller ones. His real difficulty is with the price he fears he must pay in respect to good things which he understands are incompatible with the deeper love of God.

To anyone who is frightened by this prospect of life on a lonely and endless glacier, this book is intended to give reassurance and courage. We must not crush the spirit in attempting to give it life. We must not overemphasize the letter of the law as against freedom of the spirit. The spiritual life is therefore not a series of minute rules and prohibitions for every phase of personal and public existence. Such an approach will chill the soul and put it beyond the warmth of God's love.

But never to the opposite extreme either. The spiritual life still implies rules, which liberate what is enslaved already. The letter of the law has rights of its own. Without the letter, no law. And if no law, then the order and tranquillity of the soul, and the deep possession of God, are impossible. Law is a necessary condition and safeguard for love.

The natural unwillingness to accept restraint is encouraged by some of the things we hear. We hear "our times" and "modern world" as if all things from the past are useless or harmful. But although it is true that some adjustments must always be made to conditions of the present world, there are some things which cannot be changed. Among these are the fundamental principles of the spiritual life.

The spiritual life is only incidentally changed by the times we live in. We easily admit that the past ages of faith cannot be an absolute model for ages which are not of faith. But the truth is that the spiritual life is not something essentially concerned with the soul and its world, but with the soul and God. Now these two do not, cannot essentially change. God is always God, and human nature will always be the same basic human nature. And besides, we cannot repeal original sin. All this is of course a truism, but it is one that the enthusiast for the ever-new often forgets.

Yet restraints are always restraints upon freedom. If the beginner feels that his freedom is already heavily burdened with the restraints imposed by the laws of God and the Church, he will hardly welcome further limitations on that freedom by the spiritual life. We dislike restrictions upon our conduct and desires, and furthermore we dislike to be told, to be commanded or prohibited.

3. *Beginnings*

No one easily surrenders any part of his freedom. In order to do this in the spiritual life, we must have an understanding of the nature of freedom. This precious human possession does not mean the right to throw off all restraints or to exist without limitations in conduct and desire. True freedom is a reasonable, not a tyrannical thing. It sees the reasonableness of certain restrictions, then accepts them freely, and makes them a free offering to God. In accepting these limitations, the soul finds that it has delivered itself from an unrecognized slavery. And it is a slavery that grows worse with the years, for our false needs are always growing deeper roots, increasing our slavery and unhappiness.

We are all relatively blind in the ways of God, and this blindness imposes slavery. Our blindness comes from the attraction of material things, from the pleasures of our bodies, from pride and self-will, and from certain false principles which we have absorbed. Freedom, on the other hand, means the joy of being free from the guilt of sin, of knowing the love of God instead of only useless and temporary pleasure, of finding peace instead of emptiness. We sometimes fear that restrictions will make us narrow, whereas their purpose is to make us like Christ. And Christ was not a narrow man. On the contrary, he is the ideal man who was free.

The principles and the rules of the spiritual life are the way to this freedom; they free as they bind. They destroy a slavery that is so familiar to us that we feel secure in it. But it holds us down and burdens us in our search for true happiness, for God.

In our inborn desire for what is comfortable, we cry out, "But isn't being good enough? Why does God want more?" There are several reasons why close friendship with God requires more than average goodness, and we shall discuss them as we go along. But for now it should be sufficient to mention the strongest reason of all: simply that God wants to give us himself in love. He knows that he cannot possibly gives us better than himself. The same love that did not let our Lord stop at half-measures in giving himself in his life and death will not let him stop now. He knows that we will be lastingly happy only when we have received that fullness of himself of which each is capable. His love will not rest until each of us belongs to him in the way he intended when he created us.

But he sees that we have only one heart, and that it has only so much love to give. In one sense he wants all of that heart; in another sense he doesn't. He must have it all in the sense that it be undivided, that there be nothing in it that is alien to him or draws it away from his love. But in the other sense, many things can be loved and wanted and enjoyed also, providing they do not draw us away from wanting him and his love first.

We can see this distinction more clearly by an example from the ordinary family. The family must be the first love and duty of the parents, no matter what the other interests. Yet, as in our life with God, there is room for other interests when they are not in conflict but are rather a help to the family.

To keep our balance, we must have our interests. Besides, we must do the work for which God has put us on this earth. And then too, we need many things besides the merely necessary, in order to live a human life. God knows all this too. He understands that material things can be a help toward him in a broad sense, such as a cup of coffee in the morning or a bath at night. In such cases he doesn't want the thing given up. But surely there are some truly useless things which fill our minds and hearts and interests so that there is little room for anything else. Because of these, God, waiting and loving, remains unnoticed in the shadows.

It is a part of the wise judgment to be able to distinguish between what is helpful and what is not, and also between what was helpful a year ago and a useless burden now. It will be wise judgment seeing with eyes of love. Love is often truly pictured as an embrace. But sometimes it is also a matter of the set jaw or patient anguish.

In the beginning we may not see the reason for this or that restraint. No one can be expected to like all the limitations imposed by God in the spiritual life. To accept blindly at first is asking much, but this willingness is at the heart of our ability to be led by God. Our Lord cured many blind men during his lifetime, but they had to trust him.

The truth is then that self-discipline, and the cross willingly accepted, are an inseparable part of all good life, and are an inseparable part of the spiritual life. He who said, "I come that they may have life, and have it more abundantly" (John 10:10) also told us, "If anyone wishes to come after me, let him deny himself, and take up his cross, and follow me." (Matt. 16:24) The road which we must travel may now seem narrow, but love will make it seem anything but narrow. Even if there were other roads, surely like all true lovers, we should want a direct road to the house of the beloved God.

Practical Reflection

Have I looked upon this world as if it were to be my home forever, instead of realizing that here I have "no abiding city"? Have I allowed my true freedom to become immersed in material wants as in quicksand, which only enmeshes me more and more? Can I now see that love and truth bring freedom, and that they are worth much more than what you as my God ask me to give up? Despite my fear of what you might ask, can I see that the spiritual life, like all life, implies growth? Do I trust you enough to believe that you will not place upon the branches of this growth a burden unequal to my strength? Will I now put my hand in yours and allow myself to be led?

CHAPTER 4

Sin: The Sickness and Death of Love

Although we are trying to explain the spiritual life in terms of love of God, we must not forget that there are other aspects of God which must be considered. Too great and exclusive concentration on the love of God, especially in the beginning, can separate us from other parts of his reality. God is love, but he is also many other things besides, and our relationship with him must take them into account.

For instance, reverence might justly be called the first law of creation. This reverence, or reverential fear, if you wish, is based on God's holiness and power. It is commended to us so strongly in the sacred pages that a spirituality without it would be defective. "The fear of God is a gift above all gifts. . . . Fear the Lord and thou shalt learn to love him." (Ecclus. 25:14–16) This association of love and fear is a profound truth. They should not be seen as two horses pulling in opposite directions, but really as a team, both pulling us toward the same loving God.

We are all familiar with another praise of holy fear: "The fear of the Lord is the beginning of wisdom." (Ps. 110:10) We need this beginning of wisdom very much. It tells us that God is serious about our lives. He is so serious about them that we are going to be brought before his Son to make an exact accounting of them. All his love for us has not prevented him from telling us this fact. In the New Testament, and indeed in the Sermon on the Mount, we hear quite as much about the punishments of hell as we do about heaven.[1] St. Paul also warns us emphatically on three occasions that those who do certain things, and his lists do not exhaust the possibilities, are not going to heaven.[2]

---
[1] See Matt., Chs. 5, 6, 7.
[2] I Cor. 6:9, 10; Gal. 5:19 ff.; Eph. 5:5.

Such a condemnation is an intolerable alternative, all the more if we are beginning to love God.

If we think of God only as love, we will fall into a sentimental attitude by which God adopts our way of looking on things just because we are favored children. We are leading God instead of his leading us. We are really indulging in self-love and self-will under a spiritual disguise. We make God an indulgent father, but God will have none of this. He loves us too much to spoil us. And then too, he cannot renounce that aspect of himself which is truth. Truth is as much a part of him as love, and truth never changes to suit our subjective outlook and wishful thinking.

But sentimentality is not the only intellectual blindness to sin. There is a partial blindness of those who are too practical. Sin is seen merely as a sort of debt which they have incurred. But since they are used to incurring other debts and paying them off with honor, they somehow figure that going to confession and saying the penance does the same with sin. Thus the real malice of sin evades them, at least of those sins which, they say, "hurt no one." In reality, however, without losing the idea of debt, we should see sin as God sees it, in that awful light as God sees it, as a betrayal of love.

Perhaps a simple example will help to see this. We can imagine that God is on one side of a very high wall. On the other side are various things, attractive to various people, which we will call mortal sins. We are at a crossroads leading to either side. We can go one way or the other, but we cannot go both ways. God tells us to come to him; only in him can we find lasting happiness. But he has given us free will and we can have these forbidden things. But if we do, we cannot have God. The horror is that we can refuse God who is the giver and lover, and instead try to fill an eternal emptiness with only the things he has made.

This is the choice that is mortal sin. It is always a rejection of love. It is always the death of love in the soul; two things cannot exist in the same soul at the same time, true love of God and mortal sin.

Venial sin, on the other hand, does not reject love in the same way; the choice of God or sin is not put to us in such absolute terms, one or the other. In venial sin we are in general on the road to God but we are loitering on the way or making side trips which slow our progress and may lead us to the other road if we get lost. Venial sin is a sickness in respect of love, and like any sickness, if it is left uncared for, will end in death. It is something less than worthy of the love God has for us, and it is less than worthy of ourselves as true and faithful lovers. It is a dallying with love, whereas love should want to rush into God's waiting arms.

We will want God in that way when we at last see the deep roots of his love in us. We are made for him just as we are made for food and cannot be happy without it, just as we are made for beauty and cannot be happy in ugliness and filth. There is need to be at peace with God, to be one with him if our lives are to have their deepest fulfillment. In other words we must be in the state of grace. This is the basic friendship with God. Without it he does not actually love us here and now.

Any attempt to see sin from God's point of view is best translated into things of our own experience. This is why we have called sin a sickness and death. These are things we understand. For instance, venial sin, as a sickness of the soul, is more repulsive in the eyes of God than leprosy is to us. But his love for us, like that of a true father or friend, draws us close anyway, draws us close to heal us. Mortal sin, on the other hand, is a death more terrible than any death we can think of. It is a death which could be a living death, without end or hope, unless God in his merciful love has not appointed this moment to be the last for this soul on earth. Our choices are made freely, and God can take us at our word.

Most appalling in the sight of God, the saints, and the angels is a soul in mortal sin. For instance, if on the street instead of a graceful body in fashionable attire, we could see through to the soul in mortal sin, then instead of admiration and greeting, strong men would turn aside, the weak would faint with horror, and children would run shrieking from this soul in mortal sin. But such is the way God sees it; that is how it really is.

The soul, as God created it, is an angelic thing; like the angels he made it in his own image: power to know somewhat as he knows, power to choose freely as he chooses freely the good, the true, and the beautiful. To this soul he even gave a sharing of his own life through adoption by the Father, gave us brotherhood with the Son, and laid away an eternal inheritance for which this Son gave his life because he loves us. But instead of standing with angels, we stand with devils, instead of children, brothers, sisters, friends, we are enemies, instead of heaven, we deserve hell if ever we choose the rebellion and ingratitude of mortal sin.

Why is it necessary sometimes to think in this manner? Why not always look on the bright side of religion? The reason for these considerations is that we must set our thinking right where it may have been set wrong. We must see the truth where we have been told lies. For, one of the secondary tragedies of sin is that many times it is the beautiful things of God's creation that are used to make mortal sin attractive, acceptable, and fashionable. We have only to look about and see what is praised by those who would guide our tastes or make money from them. Sin is often wrapped around, so to speak, by the veil of the beautiful. We are urged toward it because it is identified with freedom, with happiness, and with that human desire for acceptance degraded into what is called popularity. But all these things are from God: beauty, freedom, happiness, and human fellowship, and now they are being used to take souls away from him. Unless we think his thoughts about sin, we too may become blind. But spiritual death is brought about by such blindness.

There is a very concrete way to see how God looks upon sin. No argument that we can propound can be as convincing as his own action in regard to it. Quite simply, he died on the cross because of sin. The more we get to know of what God is, and what it means to die for sin, the more will we see its unalterable evil.

But there is always a tendency to suspect that any appeal to the sufferings of Christ will have too much emotion about it, and therefore is to be put aside by the thinking man. Two things are wrong with this. First of all, the emotions are an integral part of man. It is true that an appeal which goes no deeper than the emotions cannot produce lasting results. Still, if the emotions are on the side of good, we are at a much greater distance from evil than if they are not. We will go to God better if our whole nature wants to go, mind, will, and emotions, than if only a part of it goes.

Secondly, despite any possible exaggerated emotional appeal, these sufferings of Christ were there all the same. They still show what God thinks of sin, all sin, even the sins we like or excuse.

Our attitude to sin and our reaction in the face of it is a test of our love. Love must be deeper than mere emotion, and here is the way to prove it. Our Lord himself gave us this opportunity. "If anyone love me," he says, "he will keep my word." (John 14:23) He spoke these words at the Last Supper, but we can easily think of them as being spoken to each of us from the cross: "If you love, keep my word. I know your sins. How well I know your sins! They press upon me with the nails, with the points of the thorns, with the heat, with the flies, with the thirst. If you love me who am now so unlovely, keep my word.

"I know your past sins and I know your future sins, the sins you will commit if you do not stop. Even now you can add to this my agony, you do add to this agony. If you love me, *as* you love me, I who am soon to die for love, I beg you to keep my word."

In view of what God thinks of sin, we would have nothing but despair except for another thing about God and about the cross. This is the love of which we have been speaking. The cross is our best proof of that too. No matter how we may reason to love of God, or how we may see it in the vibrant earth at springtime, or even in the manger at Bethlehem, there is no proof so convincing as his love from the cross. We can trust such love; whether our sins are great or small, many or few, trust that such love will hold us to his heart.

We have said that there are two things which cannot exist in the same soul at the same time, true love of God and mortal sin. The great evil of mortal sin is that it drives out love. But the opposite is true also, gloriously and consolingly true. The great power of love is that it drives out sin. When a soul turns from sin to love of God, all sins are driven out immediately, whether they be great sins or small, many or few. Since sorrow and purpose of amendment is at least implicitly a part of true love, this process of spiritual renewal is called perfect contrition, sorrow principally for love of God. As we will explain later, a Catholic must have the intention of confessing mortal sin according to the teaching and laws of the Church. But here and now guilt is cleansed, and if there be enough love in the sorrow, the soul can be even closer to God than it was before the sin. All this is the miracle of love.

By our sorrow for sin and a determination to avoid it with God's help, we heal the wounds against God's love. Thus sorrow is an indispensable part of the spiritual life. Not that we are at all times sad and sorrowful; the predominant reaction to forgiveness is gratitude and joy. But there is always the remembrance in the back of our mind that we have sinned against God, against love. Even St. Paul, although he loved Christ as few men have, never forgot that he was unworthy of the call to grace because he had once persecuted the Church of God. This remote but firm hold upon sorrow will be a guard against the future; we are farther away from sin because of a remembrance of our past weakness. Our forgiven sins have many uses.

Finally there is a practical consequence of sin. In the last chapter we showed that love of God demanded certain restraints in regard to good things. Here we have another reason for these restraints, but now we give them the name of penance for sin. God usually wishes us to make some repayment for sin even though we no longer bear the guilt. We have used his gifts badly; we are embezzlers who have betrayed his trust. Since the body is in some way involved in every sin, even sins of thought, it is fitting that we penalize the body to some extent, and also patiently suffer the unavoidable ills of life, in order to make a repayment to love. In words of the beloved John XXIII:

"There are two gates to Paradise: innocence and penance. Which of us, poor frail creatures, can expect to find the first of these wide open? But we may be sure of the other: Jesus passed through it, bearing the cross in atonement for our sins, and he invites us to follow him. But following him means doing penance, letting oneself be scourged, and scourging oneself a bit too."[3]

Practical Reflection

Am I now able better to see sin as you, my God, see it, as the greatest of all evil things that can happen to me? Can I now see that I must examine my life to see how it looks from your point

---

[3] *Journal of a Soul* (New York: McGraw-Hill Book Company, 1965).

of view? Can I see that the best place for me to make this appraisal is beneath the cross? Will I now show you more love by sinning less? By trying to sin not at all? Can I see practical things I can do to lessen the possibilities of sin? Is there some practical way, easily possible to me, in which I can make amends?

CHAPTER 5

Temptation: The Battles and Victories of Love

No one can truly be said to love something unless he is willing to fight or endure for it. The first law of our nature, that of self-preservation, is based on a love which compels us to fight for our existence. Similarly in the spiritual life, if we would possess God and know his love—indeed, if we would save our souls—we must be prepared to give battle.

From the necessity to oppose sin, we can easily see that the peace promised in the spiritual life is a relative peace. It would be an illusion to think we are embarking upon a placid voyage across a calm lake. The spiritual life, like all life, involves battle. Only as the enemies are subdued, will we find an increasing peace. Yet even in battle there is a certain deep peace; we know we are fighting for the right and for the good.

Conflicts are to a certain extent unavoidable, and some of us have more than others. Their sources are all around us: our work, our recreations, our friends, our enemies. There is hardly a situation where some soul is not called to decide, on small or large issues, for or against the love of God. And not only do we have the world and the devil to contend with, but we also have against us those things which we would expect to find on our side since they are a part of us, our bodies and our thoughts. These struggles continue throughout our lives. In many ways they become easier, but never so easy that we can become careless or independent of the help of God.

The sources of temptation affect all of us in varying degrees. As we become aware of them, we not only meet them when we must, but we avoid them when we reasonably can. Not every battle is won on a field; many are won by diplomacy in what amounts to avoiding the conflict. This is an often successful way of finding peace, not peace at any price which is the peace of the cowardly, but the peace of holy prudence which is the peace of the wise.

Now there are various attitudes toward temptation. We shall select two false ones and then give the correct one. The first false attitude is one of servile fear. Victims of servile fear think that temptation automatically means sin. They would feel guilty if the devil were only to place them on the top of the temple and invite them to jump down. They go miles out of their way, so to speak, because they fear any temptation whatsoever, or rather because they fear a haunting uneasiness of perhaps having sinned. Avoidance of conflict becomes their goal instead of the love of God. To live in constant fear of ordinary difficulties is not human and is not the spiritual life. God has not called us to abjectness. The solution here is to act reasonably and manfully with great confidence in God's help.

The other false attitude is that of carelessness or bravado. The overconfident man listens to the devil and throws himself down from the temple and into danger. After all, God has promised to take care of him. Consequently many foolhardy people constantly find themselves in situations which would be difficult for a saint.

Thus we must distinguish what may be called honorable temptation from that which is not. We are hardly to be praised for a battle brought about by our rashness. Indeed, even when we are victorious, we are not without some guilt before God—not guilt for the sin we did not commit but for the sin against our common sense. The loving heart benefits much from a clear mind.

Aside from such cases of carelessness or presumption, we can see that the correct attitude on temptations is very simple: they are not sins. No matter how strong they have been or how weak we have felt during the battle, they are not sins unless we have somehow chosen the evil thing or willed the disobedience.

Here it is well to recall something we learned as children; the three things necessary for a mortal sin are valid all our lives. The consequences of mortal sin are so grave that a just God, a fair God, will not judge us differently than these three things say he will. They can be put very simply: Something big . . . I know it . . . I'll do it. Two out of three of these conditions do not make mortal sin, nor even two and a half. It must be all three.

The distinction between sin and temptation often is not so easily seen in practice as it is in principle, and there is a special difficulty with sins of thought. But most of these difficulties are not problems of intellectual judgment but reactions arising from emotion. In this case the emotion usually is fear. Fear has a way of paralyzing our judgment so that we cannot see clearly or correctly. Many are kept from the spiritual life by such a subjective and irrational thing as this fear. God and religion have meant endless inner torture, and so the less of them the better. Thus God loses friends because of something which is often a matter of immaturity or perhaps of abnormal psychology, but not a matter of their spirituality or morality.

There are of course ways out of this dilemma of scrupulosity. One is consultation with an experienced confessor. Occasionally in more serious cases professional psychiatric help may be indicated. But it would be wrong to ascribe all scrupulosity to causes like mental illness. Some causes are quite spiritual. A proud man does not want to leave anything to mercy, even to the mercy of God. Or he demands that his whole destiny be securely in his own hands. In any case he must tally all his accounts himself to the last penny, and probably no one is capable of the exactitude he demands of himself. Similarly an insecure and immature man will fear that God cannot quite be trusted even as much as we would trust a good human being. For those people and for others, this curse of scrupulosity is permitted by God to bring forth humility and trust.

Many of those who have these fears have them because they do not understand what God is, that he is a loving father and an understanding friend. Such a God is what a true spirituality tries to teach, a God who could not condemn us unless we knew we were making a clear choice. Here again the cross tells us more than words ever can. This God would never send any souls to hell unless they chose to go there. Once we understand and humbly accept this kind of God, many interior troubles cease.

God understands that our lives are filled with many temptations that cannot be avoided, or whose avoidance would require correspondingly grave difficulties. In his wisdom he permits these in order to teach us one of the first lessons of the universe, our dependence on him. Here again we learn true humility through our struggles, our weakness, and even through our failures.

However, he also permits temptations so that we may prove our love by making the choices which are forced upon us. Not only do these choices prove our love, but they make us stronger and they make our love stronger. It is a truth that we find hard to accept, that we are closer to God after temptation than we were before—no matter how attractive the sin, no matter how vile, no matter how much we would have liked to have it. Even his best friends, the saints, were tempted; they also knew the terrible, almost overpowering attraction away from God. And even if our victories have been won with some wounds of hesitation, or of less than determined rejection, God still honors us for these victories. And his love takes care of our wounds. In temptation, even survival is a victory.

In temptation there is truly no substitute for victory. In major things our very souls may be at stake as well as the love of God. In smaller things we are faced with either a strengthening or weakening process, often our preparation for some more crucial battle in the future. For we have not only been speaking of temptation to mortal sin. Our souls may sometimes be almost torn in two at the crossroads of some smaller matter. As we grow closer to God, certain smaller matters become important. There are many turns which we must make correctly on the road to God, and these sometimes are taken only after much struggle and anguish. Those who take them know that no price is too great for the possession of God. Our human hearts are really dissatisfied with half measures anyway. Only when we love wholly what we love, are our hearts at rest.

Practical Reflection

Have I neglected to consider courage as an important companion of love? Do I see that, even humanly speaking, I am worth only as much as I will stand up for, or fight for? Am I willing to accept the fact that peace and love have a price? Am I willing to pay that price, O God, for your love? Will I try to see that in choosing the right, I am choosing for love and choosing you?

CHAPTER 6

Practical Suggestions on Temptation

No practical treatment of the spiritual life would be complete without discussing some of the means of overcoming temptation. The reaction to temptation is a highly personal thing. To some extent each individual has to discover what helps him in his own case. Therefore many of the more specific means of overcoming temptation should be considered only as suggestions. The more general or remote means, however, have a wider application. We shall discuss these latter first.

It is a truism that the best preparation against temptation begins before you get into it. A good life with strong good habits will provide an automatic aversion to sin that any number of practical devices or remedies can never do. Just as a seasoned army wins battles by using its previous experience, so the soul continually trains itself toward future victories. A man cannot hope to be successful over the particular sin he wants to overcome or must overcome, if he is a weakling in sins he figures don't count. This strengthening process is one of the secondary but vital reasons for the spiritual life.

Closely connected with a good life is the discipline provided by a reasonable self-denial. The strength that self-denial gives against temptation is another motive, and often an impelling one, for the voluntary restraints upon our life, of which we have spoken previously. St. Paul, even a saint, had the same problems we do: "I chastise my body and bring it into subjection, lest perhaps after preaching to others, I myself should be rejected." (I Cor. 9:27)

In our confrontation with sin we are like soldiers in warfare. Much of their training, for instance, calisthenics and drilling, has no direct application on a battlefield. Yet it has great value in toughening the body and in training men to follow orders unquestioningly. So it is with us in the warfare against sin. A will made strong by self-denial is the best predisposition for the help of God in actual conflict. If we can say no to some good things, we can more easily say no to evil things.

It is said that our worst enemies are those from within. We often think that temptation is strong, whereas it is our own defenses that are weak. Certain states of mind, by weakening our defenses, are very much more dangerous to our souls than any normal thrust of temptation. One of the worst of these states of mind is discouragement, which can do more to weaken the will against sin than any other emotion. The paralysis of spiritual energy can be quite complete.

Here it is important to be convinced of God's enduring love. Even when the war is going badly, he still loves. Even though it seems that it will go on this way forever and ever, with only defeats to be expected, God still loves. He is always there with another chance, with more grace to be fitted to lessons learned even in failure. He never gives up with us unless we in the end give up with him.

Our wills are also weakened by another state of mind called boredom. More than one tragedy has come to man or woman because life appeared to be too empty. In eliminating this danger, a wise man will not attempt to solve all his spiritual problems by spiritual means. In the case of possible boredom he will try to keep his life interesting. He will try to keep free at least some corner of his life where he will be drawn with interest when his duties do not call him. He will find contentment within his own real interests. He will not invite a deep and perhaps unconscious boredom by being influenced by what others may find absorbing, or by what he is told he must find absorbing by those who are trying to sell their product through the various means of communication. The spiritual life presupposes a balanced life based on a scale of values whereby a man knows what he really wants.

We can be weakened also by too great a concentration on avoiding temptation. In this way sin is like a bodily sickness or death. We would not think that the best attitude toward sickness would be constant thought about possible contagion resulting in our death. A man so afflicted involves himself in many imaginary crises. Similarly the man who is constantly aware of

4. Beginnings

possible temptation will be tempted much more than if he gave his thoughts to more positive subjects. In this, however, we speak of an extreme. Undoubtedly some thought about temptation is necessary. In fact if we hope to overcome all our difficulties by prayer without thought, we are really asking for a miracle.

Another remote conditioning of the soul to resist sin has to do with our attitude of mind toward it. We are, after all, largely what we think. The human mind must be formed into the mold of God, and this comes about by habitually thinking God's kind of thoughts. In order to overcome sin, we must be convinced of the desirability and freedom of a life of high principles of conduct. We must acquire a deep and quiet conviction that these principles are the only way to the friendship of the only being who can fill us and give our life a lasting direction and meaning. To help form our minds and to keep us from feeling less lonely in our search for God, we can receive much assistance from the lives of many saints. The turning point in the conversion of Augustine the sinner was his reading the life of a saint. He reasoned that the saint was no less flesh and blood than he, and if this man could do it, so could he.

To be successful, we can have no better condition of mind than a deep determination of will. The sincere man will resolve to resist sin at all cost. The more absolute this determination, the better use will be made of the grace which God always gives. Grace can indeed substitute for a defect of the natural powers, but then it approaches what might be called a miracle of grace. It really does best when it builds upon the strength of a determined will. In cases where the battles against sin are particularly strong, this determination is best kept alive by a strong resolution for a limited time, not to take a drink for three days, for instance, or some period of time more practical in the circumstances. When the time has elapsed, the resolution is again firmly made for a similar or longer period.

So far we have not mentioned the purely spiritual remedies against temptation such as prayer, the Mass, confession, and Holy Communion. This omission is not for the reason that they are less important, but rather that they are sometimes proposed as if they were the only remedies. As a matter of fact, they are the most important. They not only bring on our side the power of an all-powerful God, but they help us in the use of the natural remedies we have been discussing. And these spiritual remedies often supply for a deficiency in regard to the natural ones. Sometimes also, because God permits temptation and even sin as the only way to get proud men onto their knees, he intends spiritual remedies to be the only effective source of strength and victory.

Prayer is not only a source of strength when we are outside the actual temptation, but it is one which we can easily and profitably use when in the grip of temptation itself. Thus we now come to the more specific means of overcoming temptation. Prayer really has two functions. One is, of course, the inestimable help it can bring from God, and this is the more important, as we have said. But another function is merely to distract the mind from the temptation. Temptation has existence only so long as our attention is fixed on it. If we break that cord, we are free from its grasp.

There are temptations in which our prayer will be as desperate as a drowning man pleading for rescue from the shore. But not always. It would be cowardly and exhausting to treat all temptations with this same intensity, as if the man were to cry out when he could easily wade ashore. If we choose to pray in time of temptation, our prayer does not have to be lengthy. A short, simple prayer (some aspiration like "Jesus, Mary, Joseph") may easily be sufficient to repel the evil.

We have indicated that in temptation an important thing is to distract the mind. The force of the attraction will usually dissolve when attention is drawn away, and peace will return to the soul. Extreme examples of forcible withdrawing of the attention occur occasionally in the lives of some saints, how they plunged into icy waters or rolled around in brambles to rid themselves of violent temptations. Some of the other terrifying penances we read about must be understood in the same light. The saying, "Any port in a storm" holds true in the spiritual life where the friendship of God must be preferred to any alternative. Our Lord, speaking metaphorically, was very emphatic about this: "If thy right eye is an occasion of sin to thee, pluck it out and cast it from thee; for it is better for thee that one of thy members should perish than that thy whole body should be thrown into hell." (Matt. 5:29)

But violent methods are rarely to be counseled. The exhaustion which results, and a deepening of an unhealthy attention on the problem, can intensify the situation. There are safer and more simple ways to distract the attention. One is by removing ourselves from the situation if that is possible. Also we can do something different, such as reading or hard work. We can watch or think about something interesting, about some problem, about our friends. We can distract ourselves by some bodily movement such as walking or even by something as unnoticeable as pressure on the arm of the chair with our hand.

As we said in the beginning, in this matter of temptation we must find a personal solution. What we find successful will differ with each person, but each person must know specifically what he is going to do. In that way a resourceful commander is not surprised by the enemy. Thought and planning are weapons in our warfare.

But despite the importance of distracting the mind, there are some temptations which disappear or are weakened by the attention of the mind. These are usually not those which are vehement or which tend to have a deep hold upon us, such as strong temptations against purity. Where there is danger of an avalanche, common sense tells us to get out of the way. And of course, other temptations are too trivial to be given extended treatment. Yet as we have said, there are temptations which respond to thought. We can reason out why the sin is a sin; we can look at the consequences for ourselves, for our neighbor, for society. We honestly face the sinful situation. Such a method must be recommended with extreme care, especially in temptations against faith, because not all of us are theologians. And besides, when we want to do a thing badly enough, our reason can unconsciously follow our desires. Yet if we can reason clearly on the side of God and the Church, we have put the determination of our will on a strong foundation, stronger than if sin is avoided only because it is forbidden.

The mind, however, plays one of its greatest roles when it counsels us against the near occasions of sin. More will be said about this when we discuss confession, but for now it is sufficient to remark that if we take care of the near occasions of sin, the sins will in great measure be taken care of too. Not only should we be content to avoiding dangerous situations, but we should surround ourselves with good ones insofar as it is practically possible: good companions for bad; good reading and entertainment for trash.

The secret of self-discipline, then, is normally not violent repulsion, but a firm, quiet, gentle disowning what is evil and embracing what is good. This leaves us in peace, in full possession of ourselves, and more open to the action of God's grace. In God's grace is our greatest help, and we can't emphasize that enough. Some problems can be solved only by abandoning them to the action of God's grace. While we see that we do not have to use means that are exclusively spiritual, still all of our techniques are only means which proceed from God's grace and dispose us to make use of it.

Our reaction to temptation and sin will be determined by our love for God. This love will become our most appealing motive, but it is often love under another aspect, that of holy fear. While fear of punishment may never be wholly forgotten, we can grow spiritually to the point where our greatest punishment would be the loss or displeasure of the one we love. "Fear is born of love," St. Thomas tells us, "since men fear the loss of what they love." (*Summa Theol.*, II, II; 19; 3) The more we love, in a good sense the more we fear. If God is our greatest friend, we can fear to lose him with a great reasonable fear.

Sin can be repelled in two ways. One is by an argued conviction that, while this rival to God has its good points and is undeniably appealing to some of our appetites, we can have it only at the price of punishment or of offending and rejecting God. The other way is by striking out against temptation by instantaneous aversion, as a mother would kill a dangerous spider near her child. In the first case we conquer the temptation with perhaps a touch of reluctance. We crawl away from it. In the second, sickened by the repulsiveness of the loss of God, we vomit out the poison.

Practical Reflection

Am I ready now to take thought as to how I can best meet temptation? Will I give the same kind of thought to my spiritual battles as, for instance, a businessman will give to his competition? Will I try to keep myself in spiritual fitness, even as an athlete in training for a contest? Do I have a determined and clear plan of defense for what I consider my most vital temptation? Do I have some way of handling small temptations? Will I in all these preparations trust in you, the God of armies, to be nevertheless the true source of my deliverance? Will I, after I have taken thought on these things, find my security and peace in the assurance of your strength?

CHAPTER 7

The World and Love

If sin and temptation were to be found only in some faraway place, few of us would seek them out and our lives could more easily be lived in love and peace. But the love of God encounters the widespread opposition of sin because an enemy has his encampment all around us. We can do little to remove his encampment, and only a few of us have the calling to remove ourselves from it. This all-penetrating enemy, favoring sin and temptation, is what our Lord called "the world."

The world in another sense, our earth or our civilization or our culture, has so many good, useful, and beautiful things that we are sometimes surprised at our Lord's emphatic rejection of the world as an enemy. "If the world hates you, know that it hated me before you. If you were of the world, the world would love what is its own. But because you are not of the world . . . therefore the world hates you." (John 15:18, 19) Our Lord who loves us warns us that there is a certain deep and irreconcilable division between what belongs to God and what belongs to the world.

In one sense this division does not and should not exist in respect to the world that God has made, nor to so much of the world that man has made either. There is, as we have said, so much that is good, useful, and beautiful. But in another sense the world is in rebellion against God. It is trying to become master where it should be servant. It leads us away from him, whereas it was intended to help us reach him. Thus our souls endure a continual siege from an enemy who has his camp all around us.

But "no man can serve two masters." (Matt. 6:24) Our Lord has told us that this is impossible. To our doubtful credit, however, it can be said that we try. On one hand we try to keep on the side of God, and on the other we are quite proud to march under the banner of the world with the best of them. We want God, yes, heaven and all that goes with it, but how dear to us are the world and its pleasures, its standards, its smartness, its sins, its admiration. Ah, if we could only have both. But we can try, and we do, despite the fact that God has told us that no man can serve two masters.

Religion becomes for many of us an attempt to get a cheap bargain. We give God as little as we can and stay out of mortal sin, if we are lucky. Then we take as much of the world as we can get, if we are lucky. The danger is that we may not succeed as we had planned. Instead we find that it is the false master whom we really serve, and the true and loving God whom we despise.

The world is so much around us and we have gotten so used to it that it is difficult to see it as an enemy. The things of this world are, after all, God's gifts. And surely God wants us to enjoy them. So why not enjoy life? The best people are doing it, or at least they are trying. Thus we may think, and thus we hear from the false prophets who through various means of communication counsel and persuade us to live as if nothing existed but this world.

The basic evil of the world is not that it leads us into sin at every turn of the way, for it does not. The evil is that it would concentrate our attention on itself as if no higher world or order existed. As a specific teaching or movement such thinking has been condemned by the Church under the name of secularism. But we are not so much concerned with anything as specific as that. Here we are dealing only with an attitude of mind which is opposed to God's way of looking at things. And we are not condemning the world in order to lay down numerous rules against it. We are only trying to make you think, to alert the mind to the dangers to the love of God, dangers in which all of us are unavoidably immersed every day.

Our Lord spoke of the false prophets as wolves in sheep's clothing. The sheep's clothing is the respectability and general acceptance of those who teach us the message of the world. Indeed, we might even say that the voice also sounds like the voice of the sheep. For the voice promises us happiness. And this is the secret of the appeal; we all want happiness and can't help wanting it. If we could see this clearly, we wouldn't be deceived. We are persuaded to think that we must have excitement, security, money, social prestige, the envy or admiration of our neighbors, glamor, luxury living, carefree living. And never far off is an undertone of appeal to the flesh. But what we really want all the time is happiness. The deception and the error come in believing and being made to believe that happiness is to be found only in the things that the world has to offer.

But God promises us happiness too. This is the root of the opposition between him and the world. He promises us peace, love, enough of this world's goods to fit his purposes in our lives, but with our greatest fulfillment hereafter, a matter of trust in his word. To all of us at times, God's promises seem distant and intangible, but those of the world have an immediateness that impresses us.

Now both promise, God and the world, but who produces? Our Lord has given us a way of finding out: "By their fruits you will know them." (Matt. 7:16) Will the world deliver what it has promised? We need only look about and see so many who serve the world diligently and are paid with disappointment. But not all. Some are blessed by the world with an abundance of its gifts, and these inspire hope for the rest of us.

But even in its abundance, the world cannot deliver the happiness that it promises. The root of its failure is found in our nature; we are not made to be filled by these things and they will not fill us. We sometimes hesitate in this judgment because we see so many of the world's servants apparently very happy. But you can also drive a car very well on cheap fuel . . . for a while.

The excitements of the world need constant replenishing. After several consecutive rides on a roller coaster there isn't much thrill in it. To keep up the pitch of excitement we need more and more different things, and in the end, like the palate of the aging gourmand, there aren't enough new things to interest us. Then there isn't much left except boredom and the loneliness that comes with it.

Wealth and its prestige won't fill us either. Obviously money can't buy love or friendship. It is at its best in providing things for our senses and the body, but sometimes it can't even do that.

The rich man may be in the most expensive hospital in the world, but it's still a hospital. And money can't buy comfort of soul either.

Glamor and popularity are like flowers that bloom for a few days and then go to seed. Even for the more successful at it, the colors become faded and finally perish along with the newspapers and magazines which have produced this popular figure only to follow with another. The end of life for those who have lived only for glamor or popularity, when not poverty or suicide, often isn't much more than living with the clippings of a past that the world they served has all but forgotten. In the end there are two people we cannot avoid meeting, Father Time and the Grim Reaper.

Knowing what God is, we expect that he will fulfill his promises. Our Lord has invited us: "Come to me, all you who labor and are burdened, and I will give you rest." (Matt. 11:28) Those of us who wholeheartedly accept this invitation know that his promise is fulfilled. We know love even though we do not see him nor taste him. Though he does not mean excitement, his love is ever new to us. Though he may not make us rich, the poor in spirit will inherit heaven and many of the deeper riches of earth besides. Though he does not renew the youth of our bodies, we ever remain young in the spirit. And the death of the body is blessedly a coming home. For witnesses we have the saints, those who have served God with the same earnestness that anyone has served the world. Even though many of these gave up much of the world to find him, there are no vain regrets of a wasted life, no final boredom, no inescapable disappointment, but that characteristic of the saints that goes beyond peace, the note of joy.

In a very true sense we can say that the world is not only an enemy but the worst of our enemies. It is not without reason that the world is placed first when our enemies are listed as "the world, the flesh, and the devil." We are told to fear the devil who, "as a roaring lion, goes about seeking someone to devour," as St. Peter has described him. (I Pet. 5:8) These are strong words. But the saints repeatedly tell us that the devil cannot harm us if we keep our eyes on God. Yet because the world confuses us, we don't keep our eyes on God. We keep them on the world, looking to it for our pattern of conduct, beseeching it for its admiration and approval. And so the devil finds us ready fools for his purposes.

But the flesh, is not this our greatest enemy? Certainly observing how so many occupy themselves so much in sins prompted by the flesh, we might agree—except for this: when has strong passion been an irremovable obstacle to God? There have been saints with stronger passions than most if not all of us. We know this because we know what kind of sinners they were. It is not passion that makes a person weak, but ultimately his principles. And whence the weak principles leading to weak determination? Our eyes and ears drink in the principles of the world all day if we are not careful.

The world spoils all that it touches. For instance, we sometimes see an inner beauty still in the face of some young actress, and then a few years later we would in gentleness not want to make a comparison. But the world spoils others than those who serve it; its usual and worst evil is done in children. The children, whose innocence in early years wins our hearts, should grow closer to God during adolescence and later life. Grace is always meant to increase, despite the increasing pressures against it. Yet how different the result. The principles of the world, the principles of the crowd are accepted instead of the invitation of the loving God. We have all seen dwarfish people whose bodies have not grown normally. This is the way God and the angels must see such souls.

But even though we may be convinced of the evil of the spirit of the world, quite obviously almost none of us can leave the world. There may be a few who are called to flee to the desert, so to speak, but it is not the usual vocation. We are told this by Christ: "I do not pray that thou take them out of the world, but that thou keep them from evil." (John 17:15)

There is great need for those who, as it is said, are in the world but not of it. These use and enjoy many of the things which God has made and many of the things that man has designed. But they use them in ways which agree with the designs of the creator. They are not ruled by what the neighbors think and do nor by what the advertising says they ought to think and do. They are ruled by a deep love of God and a firm conviction that what does not lead to God at least in some indirect way is worthless. They are needed in the world to redeem the times, to save the world from the anger of a God who sometimes must chastise in order to save what he loves.

As to how to live in this world and not be stained by it, there are few practical things to be said at the moment. The weaning away from the world, like the growing up to the full stature of Christ, is a gradual process. We see more incompatibilities with the world as we grow closer to God. But even now there should be some self-discipline, some discipline of the senses. We should not, for instance, listen to and look at the propaganda of the world for hours of the day. Also, while there are many things we may be interested in and legitimately curious about, and we do need recreation, still there is an idle curiosity which is an abuse of the senses and not a proper use of them. We can dissipate our energies in the many and fail to take hold of the One.

To the extent that the spirit of the world influences us, to that extent are we interiorly divided. We are under a deep, though perhaps unrecognized tension. And this is why many ordinarily good people are not at peace. Our souls are in some respects like our bodies. If some harmful germs enter our physical system, at once certain forces begin to oppose them. Until they are overcome, the body is in a state of sickness. Neither can our souls be at rest while holding one set of principles, if they are infected by a different set. Our free spirit has laws which demand a oneness or total dedication.

Practical Reflection

Are my eyes, like those of a blind man, now opened to see reality as you, my God, see it? Can I see that the world is in many ways an enemy depriving people of your love? Do I see that the choice of serving you or the world is ever before me? Have I honestly considered the returns from serving the world? From serving you? Is there not some way in which I can even now remove some dangerous or truly useless influence of this enemy to your love?

CHAPTER 8

Our Bodies and Souls and Love

Our attempts to live with some separation of the spirit from the material world must not result in a disembodiment of the spirit. We are created by God to be men and not angels; we are body as well as soul. In the spiritual life the body must be taken into account. If it is not, we will hurt the soul.

The spiritual life has to be a human life if it is not to risk being unrealistic and ineffective. But true human life means a balance between body and soul, not a balance in which each shares equally, but a balance in which each receives its due. And it is something that belongs to the soul, that it be in control. The body must serve the soul so that both may serve God together.

This subjection of the body is required for true freedom. We are thus freed from the excessive love that the body has for material things, freer to go to God. Any other situation would make the soul the slave of the body and, to speak metaphorically, put the angel under the domination of the brute.

Only when our souls are in control can we begin to experience the peace which God promises. Often we are troubled by the storms of our desires and our artificial needs, but only in tranquillity can we really find delight in the love of God. Yet as we have said before, peace must often come by warfare, and warfare is not always to our liking. But in this choice of warfare or enslavement, true men must choose to fight.

We sometimes try to avoid the warfare by rationalizing our way out of it. We give ear to a one-sided view of the Christian life which tries to do away with all mortification because it isn't "modern." We therefore emphasize the positive side of religion, which we should do, but we almost totally neglect the negative.

We are told to go to Mass or to adopt this or that devotion as a way to God. But these do not hit directly at the cause of the division within us, of the unrest of inner disorder.

The undisciplined man is neither a fit vessel to hold grace nor an efficient instrument to bring grace to others. The cultivated glutton or the amusingly slothful man is not likely to have developed the spiritual sensibilities for either. We have within us the spirit of selfishness which wishes to make a god of itself. While it is true that love of God will not tolerate this false god, the same love also will impel us to use the weapons that will kill it.

The fact that the body is the lower part of us does not mean that it is a dishonorable part, something to be despised and ashamed of. It was made by the same loving God who made our souls. The fact that it is somewhat unmanageable does not prevent God from loving it, nor should it prevent us either. While we must not love it in any sense in which it does not lead us to God, we still must love it and take care of it. The spiritual life must give it an honorable place as our partner in going to God, even though at times it is a difficult partner.

It is an interior discipline for some people that they must resist the scruple that this love and care of the body is wrong. We often find it easy and appealing to associate spirituality with sackcloth. Yet the soul is not always led by what is appealing in some spiritually glamorous sense, but by what is best according to right reason enlightened by faith.

This love is not a "giving in to the body," nor a materialistic fall from a higher life. It is the *way* to God for most people. These are not the great souls who can toss aside the physical as an encumbrance, or tame it violently like a wild horse. Wild horses can also be tamed by gentleness and patience. Love, it is said, begets understanding. We shall better understand how to deal with ourselves if we love our bodies with an intelligent love.

This way of love, however, has its own discipline. It is not the discipline of starvation or joylessness, but the discipline of keeping away from excesses, from vanity, from any form of uncontrolled indulgence. It is sometimes harder to be moderate than to be very strict. Our pride can delight in a glamorized or overly heroic image of ourselves as a spiritual person. A wiser, more sober moderation avoids being better dressed, better groomed, or more fashionable than is customary for those in our state of life.

A love and care of the body basically means to give it sufficient food and rest. More than one overzealous beginner has collapsed on the journey because he forgot that spiritual strength must have a foundation of sufficient physical strength. And sufficient strength does not mean the bare minimum on this side of exhaustion. The saints whose examples of penance we may perhaps admire are not to be followed here. They had their lights to guide them; our light must be our reason and perhaps some prudent trial and error, leaving a wide margin of safety in favor of health. In anything out of the ordinary, it is a universal rule to obtain permission from an experienced and wise confessor or director.

On the other hand we should not need to be persuaded that some restraint is needed in the matter of food and rest, even though these are necessities. We all have different requirements, but we must never think that the spiritual life is going to allow indulgence under the guise of need. For instance, not only must a man not injure his body by overeating, but he must not set his heart on eating. People who do, often neglect other duties. If it is a matter of quantity, we call them gluttons. If it is principally quality, we call them gourmets. And this is supposed to be more respectable. But the result is the same: the soul is kept from God, from wanting God. To be filled with God, the soul must be in some sense empty for God.

Here we see the wisdom of the Church in prescribing or encouraging limitations at times as to how much food we may eat and even what kind of food we may not eat. In the hurried course of our lives, she tells us to come to a halt: something, Someone if you will, is more important than this food at this time. We then must put God above something material, even though it is desirable, even though good. And in doing so, we find it just that much harder to become selfish, to make a god out of the appetite or out of ourselves. Being compelled to put God first is no small blessing. A great psychiatrist has said: "When God is not recognized, selfish desires develop, and out of selfishness comes illness."[1]

Restriction in some of our necessities does not, by a rigorous consequence, mean total abstinence in non-essentials. No truly

[1] C. G. Jung, *The Secret of the Golden Flower*.

human life is possible without some of these non-essentials. St. Thomas tells us that we cannot live without some pleasure. This applies both to the essentials, so that a man may surely enjoy the taste of his food, and it applies to the enjoyment of some non-essentials. It was St. Thérèse of Lisieux who taught this to an artificially spiritual age that had forgotten it. If she received some good thing to eat, instead of blotting out all pleasure in it, she simply thanked God for it and enjoyed it.

Therefore pleasure, or in a broad sense recreation, is an important part of mental and spiritual balance. The ways of obtaining this relaxation of the mind and spirit are various, and it would be foolish to make suggestions. What pleases one will not please another. But of course, our pleasure or recreation must be taken according to God's law. Scarcely does a reasonable man have to be warned about sinful or dangerous recreation. And he should not need to be warned about the amount, so much of it that he neglects his duties or that his mind is turned too much away from God. Indeed, it is expected that recreation will distract us from God; that is one of its divine purposes, to take the mind off serious things. But too intense or prolonged absorption in it may clutter up the mind for days and impair our spiritual vision without any proportionately compensating good effect.

With only these cautions as have to do with God's love, with his law or right reason and sometimes with charity to our neighbor, the choice of recreation can generally be left to the individual. A few special cases, however, might be mentioned because they appear to have an opposition to the mortification required by the spiritual life. These are the eating of things like candy, the drinking of alcoholic beverages, and smoking.

Of these perhaps the first has already been sufficiently covered in speaking of moderation in general. We may certainly sometimes eat for pleasure, not that pleasure is the end in itself, but because it raises the spirit. The universal human custom of celebrating even the holiest days, such as Christmas, with a special array of food is surely following an instinct placed in us by God. St. Thomas would call the opposite a vice, and he gives it the name of insensibility. Our Lord's miracle of providing wine for the marriage feast at Cana shows where the true Christian attitude lies.

The use of alcoholic beverages, however, is a form of pleasure with an obvious difference from that of food. One might perhaps overeat with little consequence either moral or spiritual. But overdrinking can bring consequences that are enormous in every sense. Not only is sin involved in the excess itself, and this is often mortal sin, but an atmosphere is set for other sins more serious or more shameful. These often would not be committed but for the drinking, sometimes not even drinking to the point of ordinary drunkenness. Moderation here is a very personal thing; each one must recognize and not exceed his capacity. And this capacity is not just this side of drunkenness, but well within the limits of complete rational conduct. Inability to achieve this limitation calls for some definite rules of at least limited abstinence.

It is not out of place in a spiritual guide such as this to speak of alcoholism or near-alcoholism. The founder of Alcoholics Anonymous first found his way back to sobriety through a spiritual experience, and many others have found similar help ever since. The spiritual life offers an orderly and sustained way of getting that help, understanding always the requisite abstinence.

What is said of smoking can in general be applied to other things such as cosmetics and fashions. None of these as such are obstacles to the spiritual life. Whatever physical evils there are in smoking, it may certainly be done moderately for lawful recreation, as St. Pius X did. What must be said about excess would seem to be the same as excess in almost anything else, except that here we may forget that excess is often based on deep psychological causes. These should caution the inexpert against any absolute demands for reform. The withdrawal of this psychological prop can bring greater evils than the excess.

Even when smoking ceases to be a matter of enjoyment but rather a matter of habit, an enslavement if you will, we have to advise a certain caution. Many people are discouraged from the spiritual life because they consider such a habit (and the same is true of cosmetics and fashions) to be unspiritual, and yet are unable to break the habit. It is, of course, unwise to hinge one's entire spiritual life upon something non-essential. The spiritual life is immensely more important than the habit.

Even such an enslavement can have a spiritual purpose. A man is thereby kept humble. God sometimes allows him to remain in

5. *Beginnings*

a minor slavery to remind him of his need through his weakness, so that he will not forget his need in more important matters.

Yet it is obviously true that those who do not have habits involving certain forms of material attachment should not lightly take them up. If we can conveniently live without a certain material support, we are then carrying that much less of a burden. Often too, the beginning of such a habit comes not from a freely chosen means of lawful pleasure, but from other less worthy motives. It is often begun because of human respect, following the crowd, or living up to some artificial image proposed by those who make money selling their products. We are wise if we question this symbolic meaning of so much that is pushed at us. Most often the product is a symbol representing something which is actually unattainable and unrealistic. An unconscious desire and acceptance of the unrealistic is ultimately incompatible with the call of Christ.

Although mortification regarding external things is important, even more important is mortification of the will. This does not mean anything so irrational as supposing that "my will" must always be given up and "God's will" chosen. The truth is that for sincere and normal persons, there is a presumption that their will is also God's will unless it is clearly otherwise. But our will needs restraining all the same, to remind it that it is a horse in harness and has a will above its own.

Our wills can be kept strong and yet under control by such small things as getting up immediately in the morning, being on time, walking and working without undue haste, and keeping on when things are difficult, as for example keeping on praying when everything is complete darkness or dryness. We don't really have to go shopping for mortification. It comes without looking for it; much is wasted because we are not attuned to it. The backache, heat and cold, itch—not relieving these at least for a while gives them the element of mortification freely chosen. But we should not rashly adopt such a complete mortification that we never allow ourselves to relax, as for example, that we never settle down comfortably in a chair.

The main point in the spiritual life is not giving up things, but growth. Growth in the spiritual life is like growth in our natural life. We first feed a baby milk. As the child grows older, we let it play and ask no work or relatively little work. We could hurt a baby by feeding it solid food. We hurt a child if we don't let it play. And so in the spiritual life, if we give up too much too soon, we kill the spiritual life because we kill the human being with its enthusiasm for good and for love.

But on the other hand, if things are to grow they cannot always remain the same. The baby cannot feed only on milk forever. The playing child must mature little by little into the adult who sees work as necessary, useful, and even enjoyable. And likewise in the spiritual life we cannot always expect that things will remain the same either.

But here at times a problem perplexes us. How do we know what God wants? Sometimes it is easy to find out. It's been there a long time. We know it by our thinking, our reading, and by the sound advice we have received. As we grow closer to God, we see that certain things don't fit. Instead of being a help, something now becomes a barrier. When we see this clearly, we are probably ready for the next step. When we don't see it clearly, it is time to pray for light and to ask guidance of someone we trust. But except in cases of emergence from a life of serious sin, we never conduct a terrifying examination of our lives to tear out all things at once.

The restraints upon our desires must be controlled by a holy wisdom, always considering our state in life, our physical powers, and our spiritual strength. But once determined on, and proved to be reasonable, our choice should be constant. Exceptions should be rare, and for a reasonable cause, with no danger that an exception will cause a collapse of the whole structure.

It is perhaps unnecessary to mention the ever-present need for God's grace. Our nature is such that it cannot see or achieve the way to inner freedom without his help.

Practical Reflection

Am I aware that I must love my body with the love due to a precious gift from you, its creator? But am I also aware that my body, despite its needs and the time I must give to it, is created to be subjected to my soul? Can I see that my love for you means that I impose practical controls to prevent my body from demanding more than its share? To prevent it from keeping me from you? Am I willing to consider that moderation and restraint are not just for special times of the year, but that some of it must be present every day? Will you always show me anything which is in my way? And will you help me to remove it?

CHAPTER 9

The Love of God and Our Sexual Nature

Our life is a love life with God. The pledge of this love is sanctifying grace, given freely by God, accepted and nurtured by us. By sanctifying grace the beloved soul is transformed into the lover insofar as this is possible. All our other loves, be they more appealing to our human nature, be they emotionally more attractive, must fit into the greatest love of our lives, our love for God.

Love of God means that we must love all his gifts. This includes, as we have said, a love of our bodies, and thus it also includes a love and respect for our sexual nature. This is no less a gift of God than the rest of our nature. It is a good work of our creator, and not an evil implanted in us by some other source.

Yet we do not have to be told that there is a disorder in this part of our nature, just as there is disorder in all of our nature as an effect of original sin. But difficulty of control and the sometimes enormous sins of those who fail in control should not blind us to the goodness of nature itself. Nor on the other hand should this goodness and the appeal of our sexual nature blind us to the potential evil.

This instinct is basically a love instinct, and perhaps that is one of the reasons why sins against it often appear so repulsive. Only the best things can become the worst. In controlling this instinct mankind shows its manhood, in the highest sense of being man. It controls one of the deepest, most impelling, most appealing of all our instincts, an instinct that so resists control that it is easily able to persuade us that it cannot or ought not be controlled. For these reasons this constraint is one of man's supreme challenges, and the love of God depends on it.

Perhaps because there are so many pressures on it, chastity is the most misunderstood of all the virtues. It is not easy for us to think clearly on it, and so its meaning has been distorted into something it is not. It is not, for instance, the same thing as virginity or celibacy. Married couples are chaste when they are living a full married life according to God's law. Chastity does not imply a non-use of sex, and even less, a horror or an exaggerated fear of it. Its purpose is to keep under control, according to our state in life, this very precious but difficult gift of God.

It will help us to understand chastity, as well as the evil of sexual sin, if we comprehend the precise terms under which God has bestowed this gift. It was given to be fulfilled in the state of lawful marriage and in that state alone. Therefore not only adultery, fornication, and perversion are forbidden, but any other deliberate use of the sexual faculty or any deliberate enjoyment of sexual pleasure outside of marriage. No matter how obtained, how attractive, or how rationalized, such deliberate use or pleasure is an abuse of the gift and involves sin. It does not matter whether this comes about by thought, word, or action, whether it be alone or with others. If the essential condition of the bestowal of the gift has been violated, man has preferred what he shares with the animals to the love he shares with God.

But man tries to justify his actions when he does not choose to control them. He creates a philosophy of life which says that he must have sexual pleasure in this or that unlawful manner in order "to be normal," or because "no one can control these instincts anyway." But against all the arguments and all the allurements are the uncompromising words of the Scriptures: "If you live according to the flesh, you will die." (Rom. 8:13)

And more dies than the love of God, as if that were not enough. There is often a death to honor, to many kinds of responsibility, and to the careful love of another. For how can one say he loves another when by sinning with the body, he has brought spiritual death to that soul? If instead, he knowingly gave a disease to the other, would he still call it love?

Were it not for the enormous pressures within us and without, everyone could see for himself that the use of sex outside of marriage brings disorder to man and to his world. If God did not place eternal punishment in the balance against it, only the very few would use his gift for the fruitfulness of married life and married love as he intended. Man instead would seek various sexual satisfactions for pleasure alone in an attempt to find temporary forgetfulness. But there always is an end to these. Satisfaction is not the same as happiness. But man would not always learn this lesson with practical results. At the next call of the flesh, he would be off again to seek the happiness he again will not find.

Emphasis upon the evil of sexual impurity is necessary because of man's fallen nature, but perhaps even more because of the kind of world so many of us have to live in. However, such emphasis must never obscure the beauty of the gift or make us fear it unreasonably. For mankind, it is raised as far above the union of animals as our souls raise us above them in dignity. Not only is it principally intended by God to bring forth other human life destined for a glorious immortality in his love, but it is woven in and out with human love patterned after the divine spiritual love of the three Persons in the Trinity. Love tends to union, union from the tenderest touch of the hand to the full marriage relationship. In giving sex to the world, God has in a true sense shared some of his own uncreated happiness in the spiritual union of the three Persons.

So we must look upon sex with a delicate balance, without a horror or unreasonable fear of it, and yet always in such a manner that it does not lead us from God. We can perhaps imagine ourselves at a flower show, with all the varied beauty that the creator has allowed man to create with him. Since the flowers are not ours, we may not pick them, or even handle them, except the one that may be ours. They are for us to admire, not in vain longing of a possession we may not have, but in the kind of admiration that leads to the creator.

Therefore not only in action are we commanded to be chaste, but also in our thoughts, our eyes, and our words. Our Lord spoke of our thoughts and our eyes: "Anyone who so much as looks with lust upon a woman has already committed adultery with her in his heart." (Matt. 5:28) St. Paul, his ever-faithful witness, spells it our further for us: "But fornication and all impurity, or lustful desire, let it not be even named among you . . . nor obscenity . . . nor scurrilous jesting." (Eph. 5:3, 4)

Though sinful sexual actions are usually a matter of some privacy, sinful sexual talk is not. This is one way in which weakness is spread from person to person, reaching down eventually to inflame the imaginations of the young. When the suggestive phrase or story is ready on our lips or ready to our ears, how can we say that our own resistance to sin is being kept at a high level? And what about the resistance of someone who is weaker, for whom Christ also died? We can become without being immediately aware of it, not our brother's keeper, but his destroyer.

Then too, in order not to have our spirit immersed in the flesh, we must integrate our sexuality into our full nature which is basically spiritual. If we see sex as a gift of God and a thing of beauty, we raise it up to a spiritual level. It is not spiritually degrading for those who use it lawfully, and they are unashamed before God and each other in this very physical manifestation of their mutual love.

But if sex is lowered to the vulgar by dirty talk and allusion, this complex of beauty and wholesomeness is destroyed. A barrier is placed to their deep love in the spirit by which the physical love leads them to the love of God. Common filth and the sophisticated innuendo alike will lower the inexpressible dignity of fatherhood and motherhood. And how can a low attitude on sex not affect the respectful love for the children who came by this way?

As to the tendency of unwanted sexual interest to occupy our thoughts, perhaps enough has been said in the chapters on temptation and the remedies for it. Yet these thoughts not only disturb us in the form of temptation but sometimes are even more troublesome because of uncertainty over our guilt. For some reason fear is apt to confuse us in regard to unchaste thoughts more than for any other kind of sinful thoughts. So the distinction between temptation and sin must be clearly drawn again, even at the risk of repetition.

In the first place, thoughts about sex are not sinful when there is a good reason for thinking them, a good reason such as legitimate information as opposed to an itching curiosity. But even good thoughts about sex can become occasions of sin if we become careless, and therefore we cannot think about them as freely as we can other good things such as honesty or bravery.

Such necessary care, however, should not make us so fearful that we imagine we have sinned if we think about sex at all. The precise evil of all impure thoughts lies in taking pleasure or in desire. If we were to desire to enjoy here and now something which is forbidden here and now, we will have sinned. Likewise if we were to take pleasure in the feelings or enjoyment aroused by the thoughts or desires, we will also have sinned. Sexual pleasure is reserved by God to the married state, and only there is it a holy thing to be enjoyed as his gift.

When we see that the evil of impure thoughts consists in unlawful sexual pleasure or desire, we can see through a whole maze of confusing attempts to assess the sinfulness of our thoughts. For instance, the time element is sometimes unduly stressed. But the simple truth is that length of time is not a standard to judge our conscience. A man, for instance, may find that he has been thinking and enjoying a mental sexual image for some relatively long interval, but only now does he avert to its sinfulness. Not only is he not guilty of sin, but he hasn't even been tempted during this time. Only now, when he must make the choice of acceptance or rejection, has temptation really begun.

When he puts the image out of his mind, even though with great effort, and even though it returns again and again, the man has won a battle. He is closer to God after the temptation than he was before. Even the saints were tempted thus.

If, however, he consents to the sin, realizing that it is grave matter, he commits mortal sin. We repeat that this is true only if he has given reflection sufficient to know that he was doing a serious evil, and was able to give it the full consent of his will.

But sometimes there is not a clear awareness of the evil nor a full consent of the will. He half-realizes that there is something wrong about his thoughts, but does nothing about rejecting them. This can easily happen in daydreaming or when somewhat under the effects of drowsiness. In such cases the man would be guilty of venial sin only.

And finally, sometimes he isn't sure. He is unable to decide clearly how far his awareness or consent has gone. In such cases he does not spend time in fruitless, confusing, and even torturing self-examination. He simply tells God of his sorrow in the best way he knows, trusts himself to a loving mercy that will condemn only those who wish to be condemned, and tries not to be disturbed. As to confession and Holy Communion in such cases, we will speak on this later. Obviously, not only unchaste thoughts but the question of any kind of sinful thought can be solved by these same directions.

In regard to impure thoughts, it may be noted that the problem arises differently for the man and for the woman. The man's attraction to sexual pleasure is apt to be more direct, being brought about by an image which is sexually appealing. In the case of a woman the temptation is more likely to arise from uncontrolled thoughts of love and affection, often the result of loneliness. But the result is the same. We must all learn to control the thoughts and desires by controlling their occasions, internal as well as external.

In these temptations as in all sins of thought, we can imagine our minds to be like a motion picture projector. What is projected on the screen depends on the will of the operator. Similarly in our thoughts, we have free will and God's grace. With these we can change the pictures. In extreme cases when we cannot, we can refuse our consent, looking at them with unseeing eyes, so to speak.

While the world that we see is in many ways more of a problem for men than for women, both are still affected by it, though in different ways. The world worships at the shrine of physical beauty. Such beauty is not wrong, except of course, in obscenity and immodesty; it is the emphasis that is wrong. Too much for the mortal body; too little for the immortal soul. Yet it is still true that for some of us a certain amount of our difficulty will disappear if our awareness of the opposite sex can have the aspect of beauty or handsomeness. These are God-given qualities, and if we can see them in this light, we are to that extent removed from real temptation.

Yet we must not expect too much from this. Although the aesthetic sense is basically a spiritual thing, and the beautiful is not different theoretically from the good, other forces are at work besides the aesthetic. Our sexual instinct is all too ready to occupy the first place. It will not allow unlimited contemplation of the beauty involved in sex and the sexes without exerting an influence against the moral good. This instinct of man will not be controlled by the goodness of beauty, of sex, or of the body alone. Beauty must here give place to the good, to the higher good, the good of a man as a whole, spirit as well as body, to the goodness of mankind as a whole as designed by God.

When man's attention focuses unduly on the objects or pleasures of the senses, he cannot so easily focus on the higher things of the spirit. This is not only true of the grosser sins. It is true also of situations where the sexual instincts have been allowed to become aroused outside of marriage by a lack of control of the eyes or, more especially in the case of women, of the affections. We lose the fine edge of contact with God. We destroy a higher beauty and a higher good by too much emphasis on what may be lawful but lower.

We do not want to admit that our beautiful feelings can do this, and they do so more unconsciously than consciously, but it still happens. We can test ourselves to see if too much pleasure of the senses is drawing us from God. If we have been living under some excess of the senses or affections, we will sink back into a dull, mechanical fulfillment of duties, into a state where we doubt the validity of the spiritual life, if we do not give it up altogether. But caution is necessary here. The same effect may arise from other causes; indeed, wise discernment or direction may find that it comes from not having enough of the external world, in the sense of recreation. But it is still true that in being drawn too much toward the things of the senses, we are in direct proportion being drawn away from closeness to God.

Therefore whatever definite restrictions are necessary, these must be a matter of the individual who will face himself in unblinded honesty. In certain situations and for certain people this control of the eyes can approach the heroic. Perhaps this is the reason our Lord spoke so emphatically: "If thy right eye is an occasion of sin to thee, pluck it out and cast it from thee." (Matt. 5:29) If we would find inner peace and if we would find God, we must take care about the wandering eye and the eye which fixes itself on the outer world to the loss of the attraction of God in the inner world.

Lest some of us become discouraged at this point, it must be emphatically stated that an ardent, passionate nature is not necessarily an obstacle to God's love, and it is not a thing to be ashamed of either. It will be the cause of many temptations, but it will therefore be the cause of much merit before God also. If we have the necessary determination and wisdom, with the grace of God this ardent nature can be a sign that God is calling us to close union. Such a nature may indicate a great capacity for love. St. Augustine confesses that once he could not bear to spend a night without a woman. A man or woman who could love deeply in a human sense is thereby fitted by God to love greatly and deeply in the divine sense.

In any case we cannot erase this instinct out of our nature as if it didn't exist, or so suppress it that we can believe that it is no longer there. But we can firmly hope to control it with God's help. While control is principally in the will, the will must operate along with our intelligence. The will controls the exercise or non-exercise of our instincts, and the intelligence judges what may have a determining influence on them.

In the matter of occasions of sin the practical intelligence makes an enormous contribution. Indeed, it enables the will to operate effectively when the will is not particularly strong. We honestly know our own limitations or wisely accept the warnings and judgments of the Church. And we build a pattern of life on the basis of our limitations. This is a necessary exercise of humility. Whereas the proud man courts certain tragedy by taking on all comers, the truly humble man is victorious by adhering to definite self-imposed rules inspired by wisdom.

Man has been entrusted with these two treasures; one, his sexual nature, and the other, far greater, his life with God which is sanctifying grace. Sanctifying grace is given so freely that we forget it came hard. It came because our God died on a cross. This fact urges our careful control of our sexual nature too; he suffered in his flesh for the sins of the flesh. Our love therefore will impel us not only to oneness with him through grace but also to whatever is required of us in the oneness of the cross. "They who belong to Christ have crucified their flesh with its passions and desires." (Gal. 5:24)

Practical Reflection

Do I now see that my sexual nature is not a matter of shame but the honorable bearing of a gift from you, the creator of all things? Do I see that the difficulty which I inherited with original sin presents me with a challenge to prove my love for you? Will I be more careful in speech, so as not to give help and comfort to your enemies? Will I guard my affections and my eyes, insofar as I can, from all that would draw me away from you? Will I keep my thoughts such that I can always face you with them, who are always looking at me anyway? Will I examine my life honestly to see how I can reasonably eliminate any serious danger to your love and my own peace of soul?

CHAPTER 10

Marriage and the Love of God

This is not going to be a discussion of marriage in general, nor an attempt to give advice on how to live the married life. There are whole books written on this subject. This chapter is not trying to summarize them. Besides, the spiritual life is not so different for married and for unmarried. For instance, things like charity, patience, and sacrifice will be discussed later in the book and can be applied to one's state in life by reflection and prayer. And as for the love of God and the other things already discussed, these apply to everyone also.

We shall instead discuss marriage as a segment of this part of our book where we are concerned with fitting ourselves to God's love and preparing ourselves for more of it. Marriage brings up some special problems here, and one of them is the comparison with another kind of life, in itself more austere, the unmarried state embraced for love of God. Many times married people feel that the spiritual life is a reserved area for the unmarried, especially for those in the religious state. A look at the catalog of the saints is enough to discourage them. They somehow feel second-class in relation to God, and often because of this feeling of not being wanted, God's invitation to special love is never seriously considered.

It would be relatively easy to answer this discouragement by applying all that we have said about the love of God. But our understanding is sometimes clouded by an opposite opinion. We hear occasionally condemnations of the unmarried state, even when it is chosen for God and the works of the apostolate and charity. To eliminate any confusion, it seems better to discuss both states of life here, the unmarried first and then the married state. But the principal hope is that the position of the married state in the spiritual life will be seen more clearly when compared with the other.

St. Thomas speculates that if Adam had not sinned, mankind would live only in the married state. The imperfections would have not gotten into the system, and the reasons for the freely chosen unmarried state would not exist. Perhaps some people dream at times of such a situation, where they could have all that it means to have God close, where they could do all the work he wants done, and still have the happiness of marriage and family besides. Any such wishful thinking is at once brought back to reality by a reading of the New Testament. In this we have the central fact of Christ himself, unmarried, who spoke with praise of those who are called to renounce marriage "for the sake of the kingdom of heaven." (Matt. 19:12) He spoke of leaving all things, including wife and family, if we would be perfect in our following him. The last book of the Bible praises those male virgins who "follow the lamb wherever he goes." (Apoc. 14:4)

It would be tedious to quote other passages from the New Testament, notably in St. Paul, which prove the same point. But in one place St. Paul does give us a reason why the unmarried state is the preferred state in regard to the spiritual life. This reason has to do with the division of soul of a man or woman in marriage. "I would have you free from care. He who is unmarried is concerned about the things of the Lord, how he may please God. Whereas he who is married is concerned about the things of the world, how he may please his wife, and he is divided. . . . Now I say this for your advantage, not to cast a noose about you, but to direct you toward what is becoming so that you may attend upon the Lord without distraction." (I Cor. 7:32–35)

The essential perfection of remaining unmarried for God is not that it is more perfect, naturally speaking. Marriage is a natural fulfillment and therefore a perfection of a man and woman in many ways. The spiritual perfection of remaining unmarried consists in having chosen God alone to the essential exclusion of the help one may have had in life from the love and care of others in the unity of the family. We are all made for God, and these dedicated unmarried people have chosen him immediately and directly. More than any others they can say, "*The Lord* is the portion of my inheritance." (Ps. 15:5)

But despite the emphasis of the New Testament upon a certain ideal, the fact remains that God wants the souls of everyone, married and unmarried, wants to love them with great love and to bring them to the perfection of the full spiritual life. If married people are confused about the words of Christ and his apostle, or have feelings of rejection or inferiority, they can see a way toward light and security by means of a simple distinction. The unmarried state chosen for God is *objectively* the higher state. *Subjectively*, that is, for this or that person, marriage may easily be the better or higher state. It is a matter of vocation, as our Lord told us: "Not all can accept this counsel, but only those to whom it is granted." (Matt. 19:11) St. Paul is honest about it: "I would that you all were as I am myself [that is, unmarried], but each has his gift from God, one in this way, and another in that." (I Cor. 7:7) Furthermore he warns those who would take his Lord's words too literally and leave an actual family for more spiritual freedom: "The Lord commands that a wife is not to depart from her husband. . . . And let not a husband put away his wife." (I Cor. 7:10, 11)

It is then ultimately a matter of personal calling by God. While God does not everlastingly condemn those who miss their vocation, it would obviously be more difficult for them to reach perfection in a state for which they were not personally designed. Yet God's invitation to deep love is open to all.

We must never think that everyone who is in the unmarried state is more pleasing to God than everyone in the married state. This would be an absurdity. We might, for instance, like San Francisco better than we like Los Angeles. But it does not follow that we like everyone in San Francisco better than everyone in Los Angeles. No one will be closer to God either on earth or in heaven just because he has chosen to remain unmarried. We are close to God in proportion to the amount of love we have for him, and love is not limited by our state in life.

The very things which in marriage tend to divide man from God are used by him to bring these souls to him. The many cares tying them to this world will also bind them to God. One of the spiritual reasons for entering marriage instead of merely remaining unmarried is that it is harder to be selfish in marriage.

The unmarried person who is also undedicated can have much of his own way and therefore much self-will. But not so the married. They must always think of the other and of the children. Marriage demands much sacrifice and many strong virtues. From the point of view of the spiritual life it is indeed a school of perfection.

If at times married people are busier than they would like to be, with little time to give to God directly, like all of us they are by that same pressure of work kept from many temptations. And they will perhaps appreciate the little time which they have fenced off for God, more than many religious who fail to appreciate the hours of prayer at their disposal. God, we must not forget, does not count our actions. He weighs them.

The responsibilities of the married keep them close to God in a fundamental sense. They have to pray well simply because they have no choice. The welfare of others, temporal and above all spiritual, depends in great measure on how well they pray. If our needs are the firm basis of our attitude toward God, the married are made conscious of this basic humility in ways they are not allowed to forget.

The absorbing involvement with natural things does not indicate that the spiritual life is impossible to married people, but only that it may be harder. But if harder, then certainly in that sense more meritorious. Many times they must make submission to God's unfathomable ways. But many times also their heart will overflow with an appreciation of his goodness when they look into the eyes of their children and into the eyes of each other. This love between husband and wife is the basis of their way to God; they do not go alone but together, often one more than the other, and occasionally one bears the burden of both. But the reward is worth the labor, for they do not build marriage for this earth alone, but also for heaven. There all will be forever in perfection of soul and body, and the love of God will be known more fully because of those who have been brought to heaven through self-sacrificing love on earth.

All this is a God-given ideal and married people must try to live according to this ideal in following Christ in the spiritual life. But sometimes, even when the idealistic side of marriage is understood, there is still a confusion and hesitancy in seeking God. We find an apparent opposition to a life of the spirit that is implied by the physical side of marriage and the joys or pleasures that go with it. Something so material does not seem to fit into an intense spiritual effort. It surely does not fit the austere image of sanctity pictured in paint, plaster, and word. To speak plainly, it is simply hard for us to imagine a saint in bed with a married partner.

Yet here we come to a need for adjustment in what true spirituality is. It is not a thing totally of mortification, suffering, and hardship. It has room, as we have said, for many joys, and some of these are material joys under God's benign will. And if material joys are a part of every spiritual life, then there is no reason that the joys of married life should not be embraced wholeheartedly according to the will of God who created this holy state and therefore these joys. In fact a man or woman might be culpably rash to attempt the more spiritual life of high virtue without the support of this physical love and pleasure. The spiritual life, because it is a striving, brings its own tensions. If God's natural remedies for releasing these and other tensions are not used when at hand, no one can expect that he will always supply for this misguided rejection.

But we must not dwell unduly on the material element of marriage relations; they are intended to have a spiritual meaning far deeper than the physical union. This union, so close that God speaks of it as two in one flesh, should be a means toward an equally close oneness in the spirit. In fact the physical union and the other intimate physical expressions of love are intended as symbols of the deeper love that should exist between husband and wife. His manhood being buried deep in her womanhood, and her womanhood lovingly accepting and surrendering herself to his manhood, the two souls should also find themselves one, and one in God. For, God should be brought into these sexual relations, like children in the sight of a loving parent. And he should be thanked for his gift. Who, if not married people, will return the gratitude he deserves from mankind for this complete kind of love?

This very personal aspect of married love is ruled by the general directives of the spiritual life, just like everything else about our lives. For one thing there is the matter of basic obligation. St. Paul speaks of it plainly enough: "Let the husband render to the wife her due, and likewise the wife to her husband. The wife has not authority over her body, but the husband; the husband likewise has not authority over his body, but the wife." (I Cor. 7:3, 4)

Yet cold obligation would not be an attitude for guiding any human life, let alone the spiritual life which should be motivated by generous love for the other. The spirit of love would indicate a wholeheartedness in this delicate relationship. And the relationship is delicate, not only because of the entrance into so personal a domain, but more because of the psychological makeup of the married partners. The wife, for instance, needs to be loved much in this relationship, to be loved, in fact, into the complete giving of herself as a woman. But the man also must find his manhood appreciated, wanted, and at times at least implicitly asked for. In general, being a man is often a far more delicate thing than many women realize, and this is true also of his fulfillment in the marriage relationship.

Those seriously entering upon the spiritual life do not have to be cautioned that their sexual relationship must be in conformity with the law of God. And it goes without saying that what is displeasing to the other should whenever possible be avoided as a part of love for the other. But sometimes certain aspects of the sexual life, while they are admitted to be lawful, are looked upon as imperfect as far as the spiritual life is concerned. So it must be emphasized that whatever is necessary for lawful sexual relations, and for the lovemaking that should surround married life, is not contrary to spiritual perfection, providing that it can be brought under human love, true charity to one's partner, appreciation of God-given beauty, lawful release of tension, and happy companionship. This applies to intimate caresses and other manifestations of endearment and to the nude body. For, the whole woman is lovable and the whole man is lovable. Married people should not be ashamed to see and caress and love what God was not ashamed to create.

But if we would have a truly human life and a true spiritual life, the use of all things must include the caution against excess. If some restraint is necessary in the pleasures of eating in order to keep a balance, it is at least equally so in these pleasures which are more absorbing. St. Paul has given us a spiritual motive: "Do not deprive each other, except by agreement for a time, that you may devote yourselves to prayer, and then come together again." (I Cor. 7:5) This is not to indicate that sexual intercourse and prayer are incompatible. But rather that the division between spirit and flesh by original sin can dim our view of the higher by becoming too absorbed in what is good but lower. A false shame should not come between married people and God, but neither should a false belief that whatever is lawful may be taken without limit, as a glutton would take his food. But a certain discernment may be necessary here, for the idea of excess varies with persons and circumstances, as in the case of food. And a certain charity of judgment is necessary also, for the needs of one's partner may be very different from one's own.

Certain prudent restraints likewise reassure the dominance of the spiritual love between the partners. Each is then more certain of being loved for oneself rather than for pleasure or release of tension. This restraint is often demanded by physical circumstances such as the recent birth of a child, illness, or absence. Voluntary abstinence can prepare for the more cheerful acceptance of what is necessary. We repeat again that a part of true manhood is self-control. A woman once wrote that she never appreciated her husband's love so much as she did when they were young and the doctor advised total abstinence for a year because of her physical condition.

Therefore, though one may love and desire the sexual relationship, and within due control recall and anticipate it for good reasons, one must not so use it that it leads away from God and not toward him as he intended. The difficulty of acquiring a balance between an excess of otherwise lawful pleasure on one hand and a neurotic or a misguided withdrawal from it on the other must not discourage married people. Some of those in the same holy state of life have walked this way successfully, and they are now declared saints; and there will be many more.

There have been saints who have loved their partners deeply and others who had difficulty living with theirs. But the same result was worked out by God, spiritual perfection according to his will. St. Louis IX, King of France, was the father of a large family. And surely St. Thomas More, who was married twice, was a saint before he went to the block. And in more modern times: Blessed Anna Maria Taigi, in spite of the preoccupations and duties of a mother of a very large family, was raised to a kind of sanctity we tend to associate with the cloister. "Her heart was under the spell of superhuman attractions which, in the Church, belong only to the greatest contemplatives. . . . This woman, poor and ignored, but faithful to grace, became the rival of St. Teresa, St. Bonaventure or St. John of the Cross. . . . When she began to pray, rapture was as natural to her as a simple prayer is to us, and her soul was so absorbed that it seemed to leave her body."[1] Of course we cannot expect that God will bless every sincerely spiritual married person in this manner. He has a different way with each of us. But such an example does show that he has no repugnance to a soul living a full married life with the body.

[1] Fr. G. Bouffier, *La Ven. Anna Maria Taigi*, quoted in *Mystical Phenomena*, Farges.

CHAPTER 11

Solitude and the Love of God

There are probably few people who have not at some time passed a monastery or other religious house and felt a desire for the quiet and peace that such a building represents. Even when we know we have not been called to a cloistered life, there is something in our nature that demands with greater or less frequency that we be alone. It is true that there are people quite the opposite, who cannot bear any silence and seclusion whatsoever, but these for the most part are less than ideally human. They will always live outside the boundaries of any deep grasp of the reality of life, and most of all they will not find inner peace, they will not find closeness with God.

Solitude is not just something for the cloister or for the spiritually inclined in the world. On the contrary, it is something demanded by our human nature. Nor is it something particularly for women, on the grounds that they are more religious by nature. There is much to be said on the greater need for solitude in a man, perhaps because he spends so much time in a world that is too noisy and hurried. But probably it is also simply because he is a man; he needs time to think his thoughts. Many women do not know of this deep need to be alone, that is a part of the enigmatic male.

Now, the need for solitude does not imply that we should all become hermits. Very few of mankind can live such a life and find God at all; it would be too much of a good thing. Aristotle long ago told us that he who does not associate with others is either a beast or a god.

In our times with the many devices for invading our solitude, we have unwittingly lost a secret source of freedom and power bequeathed to us by the ages. Formerly when all forms of entertainment had to be sought out, the great thinkers as well as the great saints had a freedom for their minds and hearts that we surrender at the turn of a switch.

It is sometimes thought that the discipline of silence in religious communities is a form of penance imposed by the founders. It is sometimes that, of course, as well as an efficient limitation of opportunities for sins of the tongue. But the principal reason for silence is to give solitude, to give time for thought and thoughtful work, and most important, to produce an atmosphere where it is easy to find God.

Solitude must not be conceived of as something necessary only for prayer. It is equally important for self-knowledge. For in solitude alone does man get to know himself. Self-knowledge is not the same as prayer, although it comes about best by being adjacent to the state of prayer, that is, God not being very far away.

Self-knowledge does not come about by too active a life nor, strangely, by long hours of prayer in church. When we are in church, we are apt to be saying our prayers, in some manner being in converse with God. Marvelous though it is to have God that close to us, it is not sufficient in itself to bring us to spiritual maturity. For that reason it has always been a part of spiritual discipline to insist on spiritual reading. Prayer is not considered to be enough without some time spent with ideas. Similarly, in order to reach spiritual maturity, or any kind of maturity for that matter, we must spend some time in thinking.

Now of course it is not easy to go to some quiet spot and just start thinking. Usually we need a prod, something to set us off. This can be a book we are reading thoughtfully or a problem we have been waiting to think through. We may just want to be quiet and let our thoughts follow their own path as we relax. Indeed, the most fruitful kind of thinking is what comes spontaneously, when we weren't particularly planning on it at all. This kind of thinking cannot be forced. It has its own times and seasons. But when it comes, all else as far as possible should be interrupted to let the thoughts come out. Even prayer must take second place in this time of unfolding of our thoughts.

Perhaps in speaking of this need for time to think, we are speaking of a luxury unattainable in many lives. For most people solitude will be a time, perhaps the only time, in which they can be with God in prayer. And this is of course the highest use of solitude. An excess of thinking without prayer would end up in comparative uselessness and spiritual sterility. But on the other hand, prayer without any thinking will not produce spiritual growth either.

Since solitude is a precious gift, we must take care to see if it cannot be preserved in our lives and, within reason, increased. The treasure is to be found in many unlikely places. One, for instance, is driving. In many cases driving is an automatic process, and traffic is not a problem. Some people pray and think during these otherwise wasted hours. And there are times when this is possible around the home. One mother had her numerous family asleep in the afternoon. One half-hour of this time was her own. The hours of the late evening can be discovered, and the time while we are waiting to go to sleep. For there is no required position or posture for praying and thinking.

While it is a more complex thing to arrange than time, the place we live in can be a help to solitude. A house, even an old house, with an attic and a basement will give all the members of a family an opportunity to be alone with their thoughts, their interests, their moods, and their play. This need for solitude applies even to children.

Not only do we have to find a place, but figuratively speaking, we have to build a wall around it. We cannot go out from it too readily through idle curiosity or meaningless activity. When something is without usefulness, without even the usefulness of recreation for ourselves or others, we must with determination have none of it.

And then we must not continually make holes in our wall by bringing things through it. There are many devices for doing this, some so apparently innocent, but subtly dangerous for the spiritual life as music, even good music. While it is one thing to enjoy music for recreation or for a lift to our spirits, it is another thing to live with it all day long. One will not find himself or God while half-listening to a continuous flow of concerto, sonata, and symphony, much less to the endless torrent of popular songs. Of course there are some kinds of music that do indeed at times help us in prayer. This is a proper use of the emotional and physical side of our nature. But we must beware of a certain emotional sentimentality that music can bring on.

We can confuse these pleasant feelings with deep prayer. Even though God uses our pleasant feelings in dealing with us, we must eventually find him in a deeper manner, and this will be in the companionship of silence.

The need for solitude is something which grows in us as we grow in love of God. This increasing need can cause problems in regard to those around us. We are required to be patient and understanding of them, and often we cannot expect them to understand us. Often a walk on a quiet street will be our best solution, or a visit to a church. Indeed a walk, whether alone or with a companion who respects our mood, is an experience in solitude in itself.

Solitude is something to grow into a little at a time, perhaps for highly nervous people a very little at a time. But at least that, and consistently that. This aloneness is necessary to draw out of us what is in us, to enable us to see ourselves and our lives clearly, to see what is good in us and what is not, to see our life in the past and present and what we can hope to make of it. But this aloneness is not loneliness. It is all done in the closeness of God's presence. He is always there to be talked to whenever we choose—or he is there to be found without talking at all. "Be still and see that I am God." (Ps. 45:11)

Practical Reflection

Have I allowed the world with its pressure of entertainment, sound, and noise to encroach upon my duty to be a man who knows my own thoughts? . . . a man who knows you, whose presence within me will not be found by tumult or distraction without? Have I used care, considering my duties and true charity to others, to try to keep a part of each day quiet for myself? . . . if not each day, then some time each week? Have I invaded or made impossible the private world that others have a right to enjoy?

CHAPTER 12

Suffering: Abandonment to God's Purifying Will

All of us would more readily give ourselves to God if it were not for the fear of what it will cost us. Here we are not considering the cost that we know already, the Commandments and the duties of our state in life. We are likewise not considering certain things which we have under our control, such as mortifications and penances. In all these things God's will is spelled out for us, and we can make our decisions with the cost roughly totaled. But what disturbs us is the unknown, the costs we can't see because we can't see the future, the costs that God may ask to be paid in the coin of suffering or the cross.

Besides being something we are afraid of, suffering is also a puzzle to all mankind. At least as far back as the Book of Job, the problem has been discussed in great detail: What is there about God that he allows suffering in our lives, even sometimes fills our lives with it?

We can understand suffering when it is punishment for sin, and we can be content with it. The law has been broken and the penalty must be paid. We do not even have too great a difficulty in seeing God's love in this. At least he loves us enough not to let us go away from him.

We can also understand suffering when it is used as a lesson. God wants certain souls even when they don't want him or want him very much. If he were to shower them with blessings as they would like, they would continue to resist his call of friendship. So God permits or imposes on the proud, the lukewarm, and the wicked the lesson of suffering to bring them to their knees. And he does this because he loves, just as a father or mother would love the child in giving it bitter medicine. His love must remind us that there is another world besides this, and that only there with him can we find perfect happiness. In some sense God thus uses suffering on all of us. To some extent we all have earthbound hearts.

But what about suffering that is not to atone for sin or to teach a needed lesson? When it comes to good people, even to very good people? God surely should love his friends. And if they are obeying his law and even adding other mortifications besides, why should he want still more?

We spoke earlier of the need to be disciplined in order to be freed from our own fallen nature and the world, so that we might find God. All this would seem to depend on our intelligence, on our insight as to what is necessary if we are not to be burdened on our journey. But the truth is that we don't have the kind of insight that will do the job thoroughly. Our intelligence is limited both by what it can't see and by the fact that sometimes we unconsciously don't want to see. We don't always have the courage to look honestly at what we need. And so God, who in his love for us is also wise, makes things happen or allows things to happen which will purify us for his love. In this way we will be able to come to him better because the real burdens we carry will be taken away.

In this sense suffering is a purgatory, and it can well be our purgatory here instead of hereafter. We are told about heaven that "there shall not enter into it anything defiled." (Apoc. 21:27) In the next life therefore, as well as in this, we must be cleansed in order to come close to God. And the closer God wants us and the more he personally wants our love, the more we must be cleansed. Not only do we have defilement because of our sins, but we also have the defilement of our imperfections. God longs to give us his love and doesn't want to have us wait for a long purgatory in order to make us completely happy. So he purifies us here, but with an added advantage. On earth we can still grow in love while he is doing it. Once we die, our degree of love is fixed forever.

Another thing, suffering is closely connected with love. This is a realization we must expect to arrive at slowly, even though the saints are always saying it. We tend to measure love by our feelings, and yet we know that this is an unreliable yardstick. Our feelings come and go, and yet surely we do not continually lose and find again our love for friends, married partners, parents, or children. A more reliable measure is not what we feel, but what we will do for others, or what we will sacrifice or suffer for them.

In the spiritual life suffering has its greatest value in thus drawing forth greater love and purifying it. If we have to keep on loving and keep on going in sorrow or pain or fatigue, our love will become stronger and purer because it is less self-seeking. We become more one with God because we put our will in his, even under great difficulty. With the acceptance of suffering our love is deepened; God has come to mean much more than our own will, our desires, and our comfort. God wants some of us to be closer to him than others in the next world. But the only way we can be closer to him either in this life or the next is to love him more in this life. Thus God often asks some of us to suffer more.

But there is always the tendency to think that God does not love us when he permits suffering. Our earliest experiences tell us that those who do not love us hurt us. But suffering is one instance of how the spiritual life is also a reeducation. We need only two examples to prove the relationship between suffering and love. One is Christ himself. All of the Father's immeasurable love did not prevent his giving the beloved Son over to suffering. And this Son in turn asked suffering of his mother beneath the cross. There is a mystery to suffering and we cry out "Why?" to the all-powerful God who is able to prevent all of it. But we solve the riddle not by demanding an answer but by accepting a fact, the fact of Christ on the cross and Mary beneath it.

We also solve the riddle in the practical order of things by observing the good effects of suffering in our lives. This takes time, like most satisfactory solutions, but after years we can see God's wisdom in allowing our hearts, our plans, and even our lives to be broken. We pound our fists on the doors of heaven demanding that our talents be recognized, whereas God sows many seeds whose blossoming must be known only to him. We demand our health to do great things, whereas he wants us to serve him, as we are told by a poet gone blind, by only standing and waiting. We demand that all obstructions to our happiness, to our peace, be removed, whereas God wants us to find that he is our peace. We complain that his laws are obstacles to our happiness, but he knows that there is no real love without law.

Our Lord not only taught us the lesson of suffering by his

example, but also left us in no doubt by his word: "He who does not take up his cross and follow me, is not worthy of me." (Matt. 10:38) Not to be worthy of Christ, not to know this deep love of God for which we were made, this is the unrecognized loneliness of the selfish, of those who, no matter what, must have their own will or their comfort.

How much better to endure with patience, or embrace with love, what often is unavoidable anyway. For, it is not only the good people who have sickness; the bad and the indifferent get sick too. The good have accidents and the bad have accidents. Suffering is as universal as life ever since the Fall. The secret is not to waste it but to use it. This takes only an act of the will. The pain of our sickness may be no different whether we curse it or endure it for the love of God, whether we pity ourselves or use it as a prayer for others, as a prayer united with Christ's sufferings. But how different the result. For those who love him God has promised that "all things work together unto good." (Rom. 8:28) Suffering is an element in his loving purposes for our lives. But even in its acceptance our suffering is lessened. A treasure of many of the religions of the world, and not only of our own, is that his will is our peace.

We sometimes feel that in order to merit from our sufferings, in order to come closer to God through them, we must endure gloriously, riding into the battle on white stallions with banners flying. But "what an illusion," one of the saints has told us, Thérèse of Lisieux. Her life has shown us that sufferings are not always borne, even by a great saint, with a joyful song on the lips, but often with the grimness of mere endurance. Our Lord himself, lonely in the Garden, is not singing praises of suffering either. He is almost begging that his sufferings may be taken away, and he sweats blood because they will not be. If we are sometimes discouraged by the praises of suffering coming from some of the saints, let us take comfort from the example of Christ, conformed by his own will to our lowliness.

We can lose much of our fear of suffering if we do not anticipate it, but live each day for itself as our Lord advises in the Sermon on the Mount: "Be not solicitous for the morrow." (Matt. 6:34) The Scriptures also promise his careful consideration of what our particular nature can stand. "A bruised reed he will not break, and a smoking wick he will not quench." (Isa. 42:3)

God who made us does not forget the weakness of our nature; God who is fair will not try us beyond our strength; he who is love will be our comforting strength.

What is God asking of me? You only need to look around you. This is your answer. As to the future, try to make some moderate provision for it, and then leave it to God. He does not ask every possible suffering of us anyway. Experience tells us that what we most fear never comes. What must come to those who love and trust God will mysteriously find them ready and prepared.

Nor do we have to accept all the suffering that comes. A certain wisdom called common sense must cover this as it covers so much in our lives. Therefore we will not push ourselves beyond the strength of our bodies. Instead we will consider our duties to God and to others—and we will consider our own spiritual strength too, that in our weakness we do not endure beyond what we can endure in peace. There are many situations where it is the better thing to accept the remedies which hopefully will relieve the suffering. Here we have the example of some of the saints too, St. Bernadette, for instance, in her painful last illness.

While sometimes we may be allowed to endure physical suffering without seeking relief, mental suffering may never be encouraged or sought, or even endured without striving for the relief of restored peace. This deepest of all suffering may be endured, in union with our Lord's agony in the Garden, only when there is no acceptable relief at hand.

In general, however, not only are we to be encouraged to bear the cross but to abandon ourselves to God's purifying will, to his purifying love. We place ourselves in his care, in his arms, and then tell him that we trust him enough to allow him to do what he will with us. All things then have a purpose, God's loving purpose. His will is seen in everything. Then we are in constant communion with him: everything is from him, not only the difficult things but also the pleasant things. For it is an insult to love to say, "Thy will be done," and think only of pain and sorrow.

God would mold us like clay, but because we are hard he must sometimes pound us like iron on an anvil until he can shape us as he wills, as we need. Or perhaps he means to mold us from something finer than clay—gold or silver, which must be pounded or melted. "For whom the Lord loves he chastises." (Heb. 12:6)

And if he loves much, he must perhaps chastise much in order to bring us to the degree of love with which he wants to love us.

Where is the despair and futility of the soul that is truly God's? There is none of it. All things have a purpose, God's loving though sometimes unseen purpose. And when others embitter their lives with the waste of fruitless complaint, or take their lives as the end of all hope, the man who loves God enough to trust him goes through life in peace. And even if he must lose all that life seems to offer, he finds Life itself—or rather he finds Love itself.

Practical Reflection

Am I honest enough to admit that I have sins that are still in need of the atonement of suffering? Is my heart still so bound to earth that I would not really want a next world with you, my loving destiny, if this world were not unpleasant because of suffering? Can I see that suffering and sacrifice, rather than only emotion, are the way I can best measure my love for others and for you? Am I willing to seek in love a practical solution to my frustrations, pain, and sorrow? Seek it beneath the cross of your Son? Do I give you credit for what you are, and therefore trust you enough to abandon myself to your will, giving you a freedom to do with me as you will, and knowing that your will is ultimately my only peace?

CHAPTER 13

Love Conquers All

In the second part of this explanation of the spiritual life we have been considering the preparation necessary if we are to have the love of God and to have more of it. Thus we have considered sin, the struggles against sin, the dangers from the world and the flesh, mortification, and now finally suffering. Anyone looking at such a list would surely be inclined toward a common impression, that the spiritual life is a thing of quite undiluted privation and gloom. All the things that make life worth living, as it is said, are taken away. This is perhaps how it looks from the outside. From the inside it is different. The spiritual life is not a gloomy thing simply because love is not a gloomy thing.

Love is the heart of the spiritual life. Even if our difficulties were many times what they are, love is the way to make them lighter. Man will always have suffering and crosses anyway, but love bears them more easily. Merely by loving God, many of our sufferings disappear, our disappointments, for instance, because we have seen the truth about life from the viewpoint of the possession of love. Besides, many difficulties will be taken away by God who now sees that he need not punish nor remind a soul which now is filled with love for him and his will. Nor will he now have so much need to purify by suffering because love is the best purification in itself.

There is an old saying that love conquers all. The meaning is that love will find a way if we love enough. Life is full of examples of this, so common a one as marriage, for instance. Love makes young people grow into maturity and responsibility, forgetting the freedom of their previous lives and choosing instead the routine duties of adulthood. On the other hand, life is also full of many failures that could have been successes if there had been enough love.

Those who are struggling against the call of God cannot understand the hidden secret of wholehearted turning to him. How, for instance, can one *want* to give up near occasions of sin? How can one *want* to practice self-denial? Sometimes the answer is found in so practical a thing as the desire to save our souls. But beyond that, the answer is more clearly found in love.

We often hear people say, "Well, I'm no saint." But if we are different from the saints, can we then say we are so different from the sinners that many of them once were? Perhaps many of us who hesitate with the struggling Augustine—"Convert me, O Lord, but not yet"—will come so to fall in love with God that they will repeat his eventual complaint, "Late have I known Thee, late have I loved Thee, O Beauty, ever ancient, ever new."

We can, all of us, see within ourselves old enemies against which we once took up the battle hopefully, where now we have given up the contest, largely by default. But through love of God there is a way to begin once more and this time to win, to find a freedom and peace known only to those who give themselves to God. The more complete the love, the more complete the victory, the more complete the freedom, and the more complete the peace.

Now it would be wonderful to be able to promise that love will at once bring victory or that it will make the battle easy. But we must not overstate the case. What we have said about love is necessarily an oversimplification. Love by itself is never enough, and to say so would be a false spirituality. We must still overcome bad habits and acquire new ones. We must use the common-sense means of overcoming a fault. And we must ask the help of God through prayer and the other great means of grace which are the Mass and the sacraments. But it is love which will make us take these means, and will make them successful now where they were not successful before. Taking them will be less bitter, even sweet, the more we are in love.

Any greater degree of love will bring a greater degree of victory and will make the battle far easier than it would be without love. Here again the lives of the saints can help us, not as examples to be imitated, but as **examples of the** power of love. We must not

7. *Beginnings*

imagine that St. Francis' nor St. Dominic's body was any less flesh and bone than our own when they prayed all night. Or that St. Catherine of Siena didn't have a body that craved sleep, for the same reason of long prayer. We must not think that Father Damien liked leprosy, or lepers as lepers. Or in more ordinary things, we must never suppose that we could get for mere hire the hours of work, the care and devotion that an average family gets from a mother out of love. It is a characteristic of love that it changes us. Its transforming power is freely available to all who can love.

And who cannot love? If, in order to come close to God, he were to ask you to fast, you might answer, "I can't do it." If he were to ask you to pray every night all night, you could say, "I'm not able." If he were to tell you to take a trip to the Holy Land, you might object. "I can't afford it." But what man would want to say of himself the most terrible of self-condemnations, "I cannot love"?

Again at the risk of oversimplifying, we can look at our lives another way. In becoming close friends of God, it doesn't matter essentially to him how intelligent we are, how handsome, how beautiful, how active, how healthy, or how rich. But only how much we love.

Love and happiness are so close they are almost one thing. For a woman there is usually no other real happiness. For a man love is one of the most manly things about him. But for a man there is also his work. Yet even his work fails to fill him completely as a man. There is the example of a Russian writer who said he would give all his works if he only had someone to whom it made a difference that he was home for dinner on time. And what a waste of love if we do not love God. What a waste, since we are always loving anyway: ourselves, others, things. What a waste and a tragedy, if we shower love upon the things he has made and have none left over for their maker.

How do we learn to love God? At least how do we make a start? How do we then grow in love? Again the answer is simple and to a great extent easy. We begin to love, we grow in love, we can even burn with love . . . by loving. Love is the most natural thing we do. We tell God of our love in the moments we think of him. For this we do not need a prayer book or the ability to fashion sentimental phrases. We only need a heart. And then, admitting that our love is a poor thing, we ask him to show us how to increase it. What man or woman cannot do this?

Love then is the way to God. If we persevere in loving and if we are honest in our love by making the choices of love, we will come irresistibly closer to God and to our true self, wherein we find peace. We will think differently, we will act differently. Our thinking and acting will become more and more what God wants us to think and how he wants us to act. This is because in our deepest nature we are made to respond to love. And love indeed conquers all.

Practical Reflection

Am I determined now that love shall be the way I see God and seek God in my life?

PART III

PRAYER: THE LANGUAGE OF LOVE

CHAPTER 14

Love in Asking

Many in the long history of the Church have attempted to trace out the path by which the Christian should find God. Whether all have done this wisely need not concern us in our times. For we have this good fortune, that the Holy Spirit has outlined, in terms that every man can understand, what are the principal and essential means to union with God. The Second Vatican Council has told us that these "consist in the use of the sacraments and in a special way the Eucharist, frequent participation in the liturgy, application of oneself to prayer, self-denial, lively fraternal service and the constant exercise of all the virtues."[1]

One of these, self-denial, has been sufficiently explained already, and we shall see all the others in due time. In this present part of the book we will now discuss what is most actual in our relationship with God, the way in which we come closest to dealing with him as a person. This is by the converse of prayer.

Prayer means different things to different people, and as we grow closer to God, it will mean something different for us than it does now. But there is no prayer which does not in some way fall under the easily remembered definition: the lifting up of the mind and heart to God.

By this simple definition we can see that prayer has a wider meaning than perhaps we had thought. It is more, for instance, than asking for things. We also raise the mind and heart to God when we thank him and when we tell him we are sorry. We also lift up the mind and heart to him in things somewhat removed from self-interest, like telling him how good cool water tastes on

[1] *Constitution on the Church*, No. 42.

a hot day, or what a good job he did in creating the woods, the lakes, the sunsets, the beauty of children and of men and women. In short, when we praise him for his works or praise his works to him, we are praying an excellent kind of prayer. But even better, we are praying and praying best of all when we just tell him we love him. In general he wants to hear nothing from us more than he wants this.

But just because one kind of prayer is higher or better, we must not therefore neglect the lower, especially if it is often the more necessary. All our lives, no matter how close we get to God, we will be asking him for things we need. And we find God through our needs because, after all, his power is himself. "The Lord is near to all who call upon him, to all who sincerely call upon him." (Ps. 144:18)

Indeed, more than any other reason this closeness to God requires that we ask for what we need. God does not make us ask merely because he is rich and powerful and wants us to be groveling before him. He is a considerate and loving father. Nor does he make us ask because he doesn't know our needs. He knows all things, even the needs we do not know ourselves. Nor is it because he lacks love for us and is not disposed to give us things unless we wring them out of him. On the contrary, by making us ask, he is showing his love for us.

He makes us ask so that we will not forget the first lesson of creation, our dependence on him. This dependence is an unalterable truth. God sees it, and we must see it. Because we are creatures, we have nothing which is not in some way from him. God is the only one who doesn't need anything. Even though he gives us many things without our asking (light and air are elementary examples), still he makes us ask for some things so that we do not forget who we are and What he is.

If we did forget it, we would become like spoiled children who become ungrateful to the parents who have unwisely given too much. At the worst, this could end in rebellion as did the pride of Adam and Eve who surely had all they ought to have desired. But even if not rebellion, then the result could be an indifference to God. But God cannot tolerate indifference to the basic dependence of creation. His love for justice and truth demands our recognition of his position as origin and giver. And further than that, our indifference or rebellion would mean that we had drawn away from him, put ourselves at a distance from his love. And so, because he loves us and wants our love, he makes us ask for some of his gifts.

When we deeply realize this dependence, while of course not forgetting our favored place as his children, we say we are praying with humility. This is an essential requirement of prayer. It brings help to the less worthy who have it, whereas help is denied the more worthy who don't have it. The familiar story of the Pharisee and the publican or tax-gatherer is our Lord's way of showing this. The situation is set up to show in an astonishing way the importance of knowing how to ask. All the Pharisee's undeniably good works avail him nothing because he is a proud man. All the publican's great sins do not prevent him from being heard because in his prayer he deeply recognizes what he is and what his relationship to God is.

This brings us to another point, one that keeps people from praying and getting what they ask for. This is a false humility that will not let them ask because they don't think they deserve to be heard or answered. Not forgetting the fact that God most surely is more generous in his own way to those who are closer to him, the deeper truth is that our prayer doesn't essentially depend on what we are at all. We are not appealing to God because of what we are (the Pharisee tried that), but because of what he is. We are not appealing to his justice whereby he must give us what we deserve, but rather to his mercy whereby he may give us what we do not deserve.

There are, of course, other ways in which God gives us help besides through prayer. One way is by our merits, what we have deserved by our good works. In this sense we are paying for what we get. If we give a hungry man some food, God rewards us, as he has told us he will. (See Matt. 25:31 ff.) But in prayer we are not proposing this kind of exchange. We are not asking God because we are good, but because he is. And there is no one who cannot ask on this basis and be heard, even as the publican, a sinner, was heard. In this sense we can always go to God with the confidence of a child to a wise and loving father, for after all he is that kind of father.

We can also push God away from us by a feeling that he is not interested in the same things we are. And for this reason we don't ask him for what we really want. We can learn a lot about God by our prayer of asking. He does not demand that we ask only for exalted spiritual things. "Our daily bread," which our Lord taught us to ask for, includes many things which are just that ordinary. Indeed, the gamut of our prayer can be as wide as our legitimate desires. We may trustingly ask God for whatever we can lawfully desire.

For a lot of us a difficulty arises from the fact that many times our prayers are not answered. This discourages some people from asking at all. Or else, even the urging of Christ, "Ask, and it shall be given you" (Matt. 7:7) fails to bring them before God with anything but a perfunctory halfheartedness. They interpret the non-answer as a lack of love or interest on the part of God, whereas he does not answer true prayer precisely because he is loving, or rather, because he is both wise and loving. Except in the cases when our prayer itself is deficient or it involves the free will of another, we may safely say that if God doesn't give us what we ask, he gives us something better. In this sense surely, we may say that prayer is always answered.

Our trust in him proves not only our fidelity to him but also our spiritual maturity. It is easy in many cases to say that God does not give us what we ask because he sees it would harm us. We cannot reasonably say that we are asking in our Lord's name, as he confidently told us to do, if the request is for something harmful to us.

But such an answer, although it will cover a majority of refused petitions, will not cover them all. Some others must be laid at our own door; we have not given him much gratitude for gifts already received; we have not prayed well enough or perhaps long enough. God sometimes has a reason for wanting many prayers over an extended time: our deeper spiritual life or the great value of the gift he intends to give, as it was in the case of St. Monica's years of prayer for her son Augustine.

But some other refusals must in a sense be laid at God's door, not in the sense of accusation but in the sense of mystery. Why the father or mother of a family must be taken by death despite prayers for recovery, or why the prayers for other Augustines do not result in conversion, things like these remain painful mysteries. Sometimes, as we have said, it is a matter of God's respect for the free will he has given his creature, a thing mysterious enough in itself. In other cases we have no immediate adequate explanation. Time often brings one, but not always. Sometimes we must wait for eternity for an explanation from God himself. And this is not unreasonable. God, like any father, is not obliged to an immediate accounting of his actions to his children. Besides, we have enough examples of his goodness to make us trust him in what is not apparent to us. Again, his love from the cross may have to be our answer. There is nothing unreasonable in blindly trusting such a God, even when we have no other reason than our knowing what he is.

It is important for us that we pray, not only as some need arises, but as a part of our daily life. In a broad sense some prayers each day are a matter of obligation, not because God has commanded us to pray each day, but because it is fitting that we recognize his supremacy over this day and ask his help in living it. Besides, we live by our habits, and if we do not form a habit of prayer, we may unnoticeably end by praying rarely or not praying at all. Then too, God can make many harmful things not happen, things of which we are not aware and will not be aware until his full goodness is revealed in heaven. Daily prayer insures this kind of spiritual and material protection. Thus we should consider some minimum of daily prayer as a daily duty.

Practical Reflection

Can I not see that in the very act of asking I am acknowledging your dominion over the world which you have created? Am I not thus kept aware of this most fundamental truth, that all things must come from you, even though you often hide your hand in giving them? Shall I then be reluctant to acknowledge the truth by sincerely asking? Since you are a loving father as well as a provident giver, shall I not ask with confidence in your love? But also with respect for your wisdom? Must I not persevere and learn patience, even with God, when the answer I desire is long in coming? Or never comes at all? Is it not then that my love has found a measure in my trust?

CHAPTER 15

Mental Prayer: Our Embrace with God

Despite the simplicity of prayer, when understood as the lifting up of the mind and heart to God, a stumbling block for many in the spiritual life is mental prayer, or meditation, as it is sometimes not too accurately called. Prayer which sounds so easy and natural when called a lifting up to God is somehow transformed into an earthbound drudgery. While it would be too much to promise that mental prayer will at once become a delight or that it will always be like a flight into heaven, still there is no reason why it cannot become that part of our life that brings us into intimate terms with God. After all, mental prayer is, in most of its aspects, merely talking to God.

We can talk to someone in three ways. First of all, we can prepare our words with great care so that we say precisely what we want to say. Or we can talk after the manner of close friends who never have time for all the things that come to mind when they are together. Or if they are friends and lovers at the same time, there are fewer things said but these are said more often. And there are times when not talking at all brings the closest communication of mind and heart.

Mental prayer can be understood simply but clearly if we see God as this other person. Adjustment, of course, must be made for the fact that God does not openly talk to us. But once we are convinced of his love for us, we know we have someone who is interested in listening to us. And this should be enough for us. Also, God is, by his grace, giving us the power to speak to him and love him; our own love is really a pledge of his. This interest is not usually just an abstract theological conclusion. God sometimes makes this very plain. He is not limited to the ways of human speech, and in his resourceful power he is able to make us know that our words are understood and wanted. We often leave prayer with an inner assurance of that. But on the other hand it would be a mistake to think that he is not interested when he does not do it. His ways are different at different times. Many times he will want us to believe in his love rather than to feel it. In fact we will know how he is going to deal with us in prayer only by giving ourselves to prayer each time. Like conversations between friends, each time of prayer can be like a new and different experience.

By not losing sight of the fact that prayer is simply the lifting up of the mind and heart to God, we avoid putting our spiritual life into a straitjacket of "methods of prayer." The central fact about prayer then becomes evident: we may pray as we wish. There is simply no "better" method of prayer which earnest souls must practice even when it becomes a wall between them and God. No one can legislate, St. Thomas tells us, about the inner converse of the soul and God. Barring of course the bizarre and the heretical, we experience the essential freedom of the Christian nowhere more vividly than in the life of interior prayer. Consequently all that is said here, or by anybody, about ways to pray must be understood as an attempt to be helpful, and not as a rigid imposing of rules.

It is undoubtedly the more formal kind of mental prayer that causes most of the trouble. We often have no difficulty in finding ways to talk to God when alone or in church just for a visit. But in attempting to take up formal prayer, we tend to think that, because such or such a method is printed in a book, it is the irrevocable way to be followed. Yet for many the very atmosphere of formality freezes the spontaneity which should be a dominant factor in all prayer if it is to be a personal and fulfilling experience. But instead of spontaneity, one kneels or sits down solemnly, one solemnly invokes God and this or that saint, and then solemnly settles down to a very detailed way of getting at some truth or getting at God. This, of course, suits some people, but just as surely it does not suit others. Besides, the prayer for the man or woman in the world must usually be approached more informally than prayer for monks and nuns, even if this formalized prayer were greatly successful for monks and nuns, which it is not.

But as we have said, each one is free. And if some desire a

formal approach to prayer, there are many good books on the subject of formal meditation as well as many books where they will find excellent meditations thought out for them. There are, however, a few cautioning words to say on this.

In the first place one should be selective of the meditations, at least after a while. At first, when one is a beginner, it is well to see the whole picture of the spiritual life. A series of meditations well thought out can do this. But as we grow in self-knowledge, we can more easily prescribe our thinking and praying to fit our needs. We should no more go through a book of meditations starting at the beginning than we would begin at one end of a medicine shelf to take all the remedies in turn. Much valuable time can be wasted in some good, but relatively useless, meditations.

Then too, in these prepared meditations we read of this or that step coming first, then something else second, and so on. We assert our legitimate freedom, and we remain more open to the influence of the Holy Spirit, if we freely depart from the order of the printed page. In a living situation our thoughts do not follow such a rigorous pattern anyway. The principal purpose in mental prayer is not to think in the same mold as another, but to find our own personal way of reaching God or some truth which is important for us.

However, not all mental prayer need be this formal. For many, any such formality will weigh down the spirit. Yet we must avoid an opposite error of the overly ambitious, who would do away with all meditation just because other kinds of mental prayer are higher. For one thing meditation involves thinking, and beginners usually should do much of that. The truths of faith have to become something more than mere abstract propositions in a catechism. They must be seen deeply and seen as applying to our life in practice, seen so as to strengthen the determination of the will to accept right as right and true as true at all cost. To consider these truths, then, and to think them over slowly with much repetition, can transform a theoretical Christian into a practical one in the highest sense of the word practical.

Another advantage of meditation, that is, of the thinking and considering portion of prayer, is an increased self-knowledge. This knowledge is an indispensable element in the spiritual life. Basically it means seeing the difference between ourselves as creatures and God as creator. But this is only a good beginning. Self-knowledge also involves information about our weaknesses, and yet it is incomplete if it stops there. A knowledge of our good qualities is also essential if we are to find the particular way God is leading us or drawing us. And in relation to our good qualities, a love of the self, based on the truth of what we are, makes us more certain, emotionally or psychologically, of the love of God. The true measure we get of ourselves is the identical measure God has of us.

A part of the difficulty with meditation is that the word itself is sometimes not understood. It is often thought to be akin to the leisurely reflectiveness we might have in the evening before an open fireplace. Or it is considered to be the preaching of a sermon to ourselves. Still others might fear that it involves long years of specialized training, as with adepts in Buddhism, in positions which are quite uncomfortable to Western man. Quite truly meditation is none of these.

Meditation involves much use of the mind and the imagination. With the imagination we can, if we wish, picture ourselves face to face with various events in the life of Christ. Or we can bring Christ into the situations of our own life. With our mind or intellect we can analyze, consider, and reflect. To approach the spiritual life without some such thinking is to risk the weakness of not totally integrating ourselves with the Christian message, and thus risk losing our course in time of temptation or crisis.

But thinking, even though greatly important, is not prayer. Prayer is the lifting up of the heart as well as the mind; our will and its movements, such as love, praise, or sorrow, are even more important than the thinking. In fact, our thinking should lead us on to the acts of the will and of our feelings. Our thoughts of Christ on the cross, for instance, should lead to love or sorrow; or the realization of a fault should lead to a plea for help.

An example may help to explain the difference between meditation and prayer as such. A seminarian who is studying his theology books is using his mind and is thinking about God. But he is not necessarily praying. The heart, or better, the will has to be in it, moving him into personal contact with God. Prayer is so little a part of our thinking mind that we can pray very well without using it very much. Good prayer does not depend on great knowledge or great intelligence. A theologian does not necessarily pray better than someone who knows only that there is a God. The use of our mind, then, while important for the knowledge of the situation between God and ourselves, and important for self-knowledge, is not ordinarily so important in prayer as our will and its movements. With these we love God, thank him, praise him in himself and in his works, trust him, and tell him we are sorry for our sins—there are almost endless ways in which we can raise the heart to God.

Although both mind and heart are in some manner in every prayer, the degree of their involvement will probably vary each time. At times it may take many considerations to bring us to a particular attitude toward God. At other times the heart might move immediately to God. If it does so, it should not be forced to retrace the steps by which it would otherwise have had arrived there. Such well-intentioned, but unwise, tyranny will end in frustrating the free movement of the spirit. The end and reason of our prayer is God, and not the following of a method or reading the whole page in a book.

There are some people who will never need the help of a method and who would find it a hindrance. But most of us will profit by some simple method if for no other reason than to fix the attention of the mind and to bring it back when it wanders. Such a simple method can be outlined in three paragraphs.

It is good to have a book, but a crucifix, a picture, or a statue may do just as well. In church we have the Blessed Sacrament. We do not have to be kneeling. So great an authority as St. Teresa advises a comfortable position, and that is a matter of choice. If a book is used, we choose it with some care for our particular needs or desires.

We then ask God's help and put ourselves mentally in his presence. If this satisfies us and we want what this brings, we need go no farther with the book. If not, we read a bit until something causes us to pause in order to consider, reflect, or go directly to God with spontaneous acts of the mind and heart. We stay with these as long as we wish, or break off into any other acceptable train of thought as we wish. And we come back to the book when the cup of our thoughts and feelings is empty.

Many times we will be able to form a distinct practical resolution as the result of our prayer. But we should never neglect to ask God to help us carry it out. Thinking and resolving without asking God's help is almost expecting the impossible. We can often compress the essence of what we have received from our prayer into a sentence, or better, a phrase that can be easily carried throughout the day, such as "Thy will be done."

But even such a simple method must not make us lose sight of the foremost purpose of mental prayer, which is to bring us into contact with God. We can use methods effectively only if we do not lose sight of mental prayer as simply talking to God or, more simply, just being with him without talking.

Practical Reflection

If there were someone I loved very much, or wanted to love very much, or were worthwhile loving very much, would I be satisfied with a perfunctory good morning and good night? Would I not seek a time and place where I could be alone with this person, some time every day, or as often as practical even if not every day? Would I not so arrange my whole life that I would be sure I would not miss the opportunity of this desired meeting?

8. Beginnings

CHAPTER 16

God's Presence of Love

Sometimes, what we don't like about God becomes one of the things we like most of all. For instance, most of us don't care very much to think about God as being just; we fear the consequences of this divine attribute. But when we get to know him better, we begin to appreciate his justice because it also means that he is fair. He is not capricious; he does not judge men by what doesn't count. He will not fail to give us our due; if we have worked for him, we will receive our wages and not have them forgotten. A just God is in the end the only kind of God we can respect and love.

Now it is similarly true that some of us don't particularly like to think of God's all-embracing presence. Before we have come to give ourselves to him wholeheartedly, we feel uncomfortable about having him that close. Some part of us would like to be able to get away from him because we would rather not have to obey him, and we don't want to have to account to him.

This, of course, is not always true. We want him close when we are in need. Then we even plead with him to observe the circumstances of our life and involve himself in them. But how much more shall we want him to be always present when we have begun to see him as a friend, when we get to see what he really is.

Perhaps one of the most tragic things about a life dedicated to pleasure is what it has missed. No doubt many a man so dedicated has congratulated himself on his ability to provide himself with so much. And surely he has been the envy of many who are not so fortunate. But the growing loneliness of the years and the increasing boredom with the things that money buys become evidence of the tardy truth that it was a life of emptiness. Man is built on a larger scale than anything material can fill. Somewhere hidden away in each of us is a great emptiness that can be filled only by God.

In this emptiness our souls are like our bodies. If we keep our bodies empty of food, they will die. For a while we can do well enough without it; we will work energetically and be alert mentally. But soon there comes the necessity of eating. Now we can quiet our hunger by various means. We could, for instance, give it poor food, food that tastes good but does not nourish. And we could quiet the pangs of hunger by alcoholic drink. With all these subterfuges we could again become energetic and reasonably alert. But not for very long. A sustained diet of non-nourishing food will bring an end to good health and eventually cause the deterioration of body and mind to the point of a diseased or painful death. This, in terms of the natural, is what happens to our spirit if we feed it on other things but never on God. Even though our lives would apparently be filled, we would be the really empty people.

Most of us can also see this emptiness of soul if we consider that we are made for love. One of the greatest tragedies in any life is that it be without human love. But even human love is not enough; everyone finds that out sooner or later too, even though in the beginning there may have been much protest that this love was all-sufficient. St. Augustine, who had more than a taste of human love, has pronounced sentence upon such shortsightedness: "Thou hast made us for Thyself, O Lord, and our hearts cannot rest until they rest in Thee." To learn to live with God is really to learn to live. We have him close all the time, he who is love, goodness, beauty, strength, and who cares for us as a friend.

Perhaps we sometimes think that our love or desire for God is one-sided, that although he did die for humanity, he has very little love for us individually. But this burden of loneliness should be forever lifted by the knowledge of his presence in our souls. This presence is not precisely the same presence by which he is everywhere and in all things. He is everywhere, especially by his knowledge and power. But his presence in our souls has an added quality; it is a presence of love. He is within us by the sharing of his life (see II Pet. 1:4) in some created sense, and we give this sharing the name of sanctifying grace. For most of us this presence came very early in life with our baptism and received an added note of strengthening when we were confirmed. St. Paul never tires of describing it by a figure of speech that indicates the reverence we should have for so great a gift: "Do you not know that you are the temples of God and that the Spirit of God dwells in you?" (I Cor. 3:16) God's personal presence, then, in the soul of each one of us is a pledge of his love and his care for us.

Although this presence is usually identified with his love, we must not forget that the whole of God is within us. This applies equally to his wisdom and power. We thus find it easy to look to him for guidance and protection according to his loving providence over us. Similarly all three Persons are within us, Father, Son, and Holy Spirit, though we often name only the Holy Spirit, the Spirit of love in the Trinity, to emphasize that the presence of God is principally one of love.

This availability of God is a testimony of his love. We do not have to seek him in some faraway heaven, or make an expensive pilgrimage to some distant shrine in order to find him. We find him within. We do not even have to go to a church in order to be with him; our soul and body is indeed a temple or a church, made a church by his living presence.

And here we see another reason for a good life. We must not treat God's presence with indifference or neglect or worse. We must not cast his presence of love out of our souls by mortal sin. It is a part of the enormity of mortal sin that it is something like throwing the sacred hosts out of the tabernacle, or making the church a place for obscene shows. The fact of God's presence calls not only for the holy familiarity born of love but also for reverence, lest we offend him who honors us above all honors by dwelling there.

Being able to be with Christ before his presence in the tabernacle has advantages too obvious to need mentioning, but we cannot be in church except intermittently. God loves us so much that he wants more than only sharply divided segments of our lives. He wants to be close to us always, and within us we have him no less than we have him in church. God is indivisible and we cannot possibly have less of him than all of him. All of God, then, is available to us on the street, in a quiet hour at home, in a moment or two at work, at night while waiting for sleep, or if we awaken.

One of the popular misconceptions about holiness is that it consists in a great number of prayers. The truth is in a sense to the contrary. It is possible to put things between ourselves and God. Some people put their sins in the way. Others put too great an attachment to good things, such as clothes or food. But still others put very good things between themselves and God, very good things like the many prayers or special devotions which they must crowd in. When we think of holiness for what it essentially is, oneness with God, we will not let these pious pressures keep us from him.

In our ordinary prayer, even at Mass, if we wish to turn aside from the course of our prayer and give ourselves to the presence of God or our own thoughts in his presence, we should be assured that this is most pleasing to him. To make God wait until we are finished, when he is pulling at our elbow, so to speak, would be like a husband making his wife wait for a welcoming embrace while he stood at the door giving a factual account of his day.

Perhaps some people living in the world have wished for the training in prayer which is given in religious life. But the presence of God is a gift far greater than any course of instruction can provide, no matter how brilliantly taught. In fact, speaking to those in the world of the presence of God is proof that in this book the spiritual life is not being watered down for the laity. Granted that the layman does not have the time at his disposal to keep working at any complicated system of prayer, it is still blessedly true that the presence of God is incomparably better than any "method" of prayer. And it does not take long learning or cleverness, or youth or age, or a special state of life.

And do we suppose that God wants to be loved only in churches and religious houses? Does he not surely want love in the very world where his love is so much rejected? Indeed, it was to all men that St. Paul was referring when he told the men of Athens that mankind "should seek God, and perhaps grope after him and find him, though he is not far from any of us. For in him we live and move and have our being." (Acts 17:27, 28)

God's presence within does not mean that we will always find him in the same sense that we would by knocking on the door of a friend who is waiting for us. While it is true that God sometimes makes us aware of himself, and this can even happen at times when we are not religiously occupied, most of our grasp of him must come by faith. We have his word that he is within us, and we must accept a certain lack of response as a part of our earthly life with him. It is much like writing to a dear friend who receives our letters happily but for some good reason does not write back as often as we would like.

But even with this limitation of only apparent one-sidedness, the presence of God is a companionship which will grow more and more in meaning as we live with it. We don't think of him all the time, but our mind learns to gravitate toward him when it is free. How much better than wasting time in daydreaming as many of us do. After all, this is reality; God is Reality. And his presence can help us, whereas idle thoughts cannot. We have a companion to share our joys and to console us in our sorrows. We have a companion to prevent the loneliness of later years. And no one need fear death. Having lived with God during life, we will find death to be like walking hand in hand from a dimly lit room into the bright daylight where we will see the greater beauty and love of the one we have lived with so closely in life.

Some of us, of course, feel inadequate in talking to God because we are inexperienced in this sort of thing. We perhaps have grown so accustomed to using other people's words in prayer that we think all prayers must be masterpieces of grammar and rhetoric. Living with God is really only another way of doing one of the most common things we do. Which one of us has not thought about someone we love? We did not have to learn love, nor how to speak the language of love, out of a book. God is with us as a friend, and a true friend is one to whom we feel free to say anything. He is even that kind of friend whom we can have close to us without feeling compelled to say anything. Getting closer to God does not mean that we find more things to say to him but rather that we have fewer, so great is the mutual love and understanding.

God's majesty would make him inaccessible if he were only majesty. But he is also love, as we have said so many times before. Yet his love is not contradictory to his majesty, in that he requires that we make certain choices if we are to have him as a close companion. The choices against sin and especially mortal sin are obvious. But obvious by now also should be the choices to be made against the servitude to the world, as well as the choices by which we acquire the treasure of inner solitude. Many times, of course, our duties, even in the broad sense of duty, will require that we put him out of our mind. But an ideal to be aimed at is never to put him out of mind deliberately unless there be such a reason. And of course even our needed relaxation can be such a reason.

One of the Pharisees once asked our Lord when was "the kingdom of God coming." By this he meant a Jewish kingdom which would free the chosen people from the Romans. Our Lord took him up in a much deeper sense, a sense which shows us that men can be free even when under many kinds of duress. He answered, "Behold, the kingdom of God is within you." (Luke 17:21)

Practical Reflection

Can I now see that I can no longer hide from your love in a belief that you are not interested in me personally? Do I not now see your unbelievably great desire to be close to me, to have my love? Is it not also clear that even my sins cannot keep you away, that even great sins find you on the doorstep of my soul waiting to come back after only a word of sincere love and repentance? Do I not now recognize you as a friend for my whole life, that I no longer need feel undiluted loneliness or discouragement? I ask you, my Lord, to stay with me forever.

CHAPTER 17

Practical Suggestions on Prayer

The general outline of prayer in the preceding chapters, while adequate in giving a clear picture, falls short in dealing with certain practical situations or difficulties. One of the foremost is the problem of distractions. These are like thieves that steal from us the moments we would give to God and leave us with a poverty of frustration instead of the riches of peace we had counted on.

This frustration can to a great extent be lifted if we consider the principal reason for coming to prayer. Despite all that we hope to get from it in peace, love, and help, the main reason for entering into communion with God is to please him and to honor him. All else, no matter how desirable, is secondary to this. Thus if God wills to permit our time to be filled with floods that carry us far out to sea without our knowing it, or storms we have to wrestle with, or at least with raindrops that spoil the sunshine we had hoped for, we will still have honored and pleased him by our efforts to remain at prayer.

Thus we may think we have gotten little from prayer that is mostly absence of mind when it is not struggle. But God sees it differently. Each time that we bring ourselves back to him, we are making a choice of him instead of the absorbing thing that was distracting us. Surely such prayer, even though filled with nothing but these choices, is prayer that God understands and fully accepts. In fact he often chooses this way to keep us aware of our weakness. The grand manner of technically perfect prayer can produce pride of spirit. So a careful God allows our poor nature to keep us close to him.

There are several other things to be said about distractions. In the first place they are not sinful unless they are deliberate. They are a part of the unavoidable weakness of most of us, including some great saints, and therefore should not be confessed unless deliberation somehow enters. However, this deliberation can sometimes enter by permitting an unnecessary cause of distraction. If we were freely to choose to say our accustomed prayers at a time or place where additional distractions are almost certain to come, we have acted with some disrespect toward God. This is the same kind of disrespect we would show if we were to choose to engage a friend in conversation where we could hardly be heard above the noise of the street, when we could easily speak to him inside. Such ordinary human courtesy we should show to God. And here it is not out of place to recall that the discipline of our senses, of which we have spoken earlier, will generally eliminate many unnecessary and disturbing distractions.

St. Thomas consoles us by telling us that prayer said with involuntary distractions is entirely valid. It has just as much efficacy before God as if it were said with attention. The reason for this is that our *intention* has persevered; it has not been lost through involuntary distraction. Therefore we should never make the mistake of starting our prayers over. If we do, we will make an impossible burden out of them and deserve a reproach from God because we have failed to comprehend his love and understanding of our nature.

Nor should we think we must make violent warfare against our distractions, with battle-ax flying as if we were slaying dragons. Instead we bring ourselves back to God firmly but gently, not with harsh self-incrimination but with a patient acceptance of ourselves as God sees us and loves us. We can even make our distractions a part of our prayer; at times we can bring some problem before God for solution or for pleading for peace from it—providing that it is not the kind of problem that is better kept out of mind.

In general, however, we leave our distractions rather than look at them. By taking away the attention which gives them life, we will find that they will more easily wither away into oblivion than if we try to conquer them by open assault or by diplomatic reasoning with them.

A far more deadly frustration than distractions can come from an emptiness in prayer that goes by the name of dryness or aridity. In the case of mere distractions, it is possible to find God very close in between the distractions. But in this emptiness of spirit one finds exactly that, nothing. The danger then is that, since there is no visible enemy to contend with, we make up our own. We consider that God is not pleased with us, or think that the spiritual life is not meant for us. And so we go off to a more active life, the works of God without the close friendship of God. Or we go off to a world which has been calling with a persistent attraction, whether we are conscious of it or not.

There are several reasons for this emptiness or dryness. A very obvious one is a life that is too much intermingled with the world. If we find that we have no interest in prayer and at the same time are filling our lives with enthusiastic involvement with the world, we need not seek much further for the cause. And the discerning of the cause of the disease brings with it recognition of the obvious cure.

On the other hand the causes of this dryness may be quite blameless, or even meritorious. These, for instance, can be physical causes, such as a headache or a bad cold. Then too, the consolation or fervor which we sometimes feel in prayer is a human response to our contact with God. We feel this human response partly in the emotional side of our nature. Our emotions are, of course, good and are not to be suppressed, though at times they may require control. They provide encouragement in the spiritual life and help us to grow away from pleasures which would lead away from God. But since these pleasing emotions are of a physical and psychological nature, the condition of our body and mind can affect and even suppress them. This involuntary suppression, then, is something to be borne with patience as we would any suffering or trial. It goes without saying, however, that we must take the obvious care of mind and body, and not do the imprudent for the sake of some imagined merit.

But even when there is no apparent physical or psychological cause, there will be many times, and perhaps long periods of time, when we will not find God in prayer but rather emptiness. This is not a small trial and it is one about which we cannot do much more than endure. We endure in faith and trust and in the kind of love which loves with the will when it cannot love with much else. We make our mere presence before God our prayer if such a situation of spiritual dullness becomes extreme.

Trust is perhaps the most important thing now. Instead of seeking causes by a torturing self-questioning, we see in this emptiness a purification on the part of the loving God who wants us to love himself instead of his gifts, even instead of the gift of feeling his love. Or as it is often said, we must be taught to love not so much the consolations of God but the God of the consolations.

Such dryness can already be a sign of spiritual growth. God sees that we do not need the help of the emotions and would draw us by faith and trust to the kind of love that loves him for what he is. However, this trial has an end, and usually we find a closeness to God afterward which was unknown before.

Sometimes our difficulty in approaching God comes from not knowing what to say. But if we can find nothing else to pray about, we can surely beg him for the gift of perseverance in his love. But here we come up against a common error that compels us to go to him with only a part of ourselves. We somehow think that he is interested only in the spiritual. Except when necessity presses upon us, we leave out of our relationship with him the less spiritual part of our life in which sometimes we are more personally involved. This side of our life may include things like our work, our ambitions, and even our social life. We must not expect to go to God by the exclusively spiritual. If we meet him where our interests lie, where a good part of our heart is, we will have a better chance of a relationship with him that is deep and lasting.

And then there is the manner in which we should speak to God. We have perhaps been exposed to prayers whose rhetoric is so far removed from our own way of speaking that we would be adopting a false personality if we were to pray that way habitually. Granted that praying in public must be different from praying when we are alone, and that we cannot impose a style of expression on anybody, still we should try to follow the advice our Lord gave in the Sermon on the Mount. He urges us to avoid ostentation and to speak with simplicity: "In praying, do not multiply words." (Matt. 6:7) And then he goes on to give us an example of a straightforward approach, by teaching us the "Our Father." So we should not seek to overwhelm God by many words, but rather let our approach be quiet, close, and direct.

It is surely not the purpose of this book to advise what prayers to say. We are all made differently, and this difference will show itself in the means we use to approach God. Yet there are some words to be said about the many prayers and devotions which are often recommended by sincere authorities and well-meaning friends. Indeed, the multiplicity of these prayers, and often their unsuitableness to our personal way to God, can bring about an unconscious aversion to any kind of life of prayer.

This matter of private devotions can even be a trap. By private devotions we do not mean the liturgy, such as the Mass or any of the sacraments. Nor do we mean mental prayer as such. Rather they are things like the rosary, stations of the cross, various litanies, novenas, etc. The entrapment does not come from any one of these, all good in themselves, but in the danger that we may acquire too many of them. By their excessive number alone they can lead us away from God who is the center of the spiritual life. We become involved in too many prayers and so must leave God by the wayside in order to get them all in. Thus we have no real interior peace.

Many of these prayers and devotions have indulgences attached to them. Yet we must not allow the desire for this particular spiritual advantage to clutter up our life of prayer and draw us away from the directness and simplicity that should be an ideal. Indulgences concern only one very narrow side of the spiritual life, the generous remission of temporal punishment for sins already forgiven. They are ratified by God only in proportion as he sees in us the proper interior dispositions. Then surely they will avail us little if they are allowed to interfere with the heart of the spiritual life which is union with God through love.

The important thing about these private devotions is that we are free. All of them are means to an end, and the individual devotion may be a means for one person but not for another. So each person is free to take them up or not, as he is drawn.

We should be careful anyway about any permanent addition to our prayer, whether it be the number of prayers or the time given. Under the influence of enthusiasm it is easy to add, and then feel burdened when the glow subsides, and guilty if we retract. Beyond a reasonable minimum of time for prayer we should not feel obliged to continue what we have taken up in moments of fervor.

In the spiritual life it is an observed phenomenon that as we progress in it, our devotions become more and more simple. But, of course, not too soon. The point is that we may abandon some of these devotions as a result of clear insight, and know that this is what God wants us to do. The opposite would be to smother the divine spark within us by the compulsion to continue as an obligation, regardless of our revulsion to it, what is by its nature a matter of choice and freedom.

Practical Reflection

Do I see prayer for what it is, primarily a duty of creature to Creator? Do I see that it is a duty of love, and that I show my love for you by persevering in prayer despite the difficulty and even distaste I sometimes experience? Have I enough trust to accept the fact that my prayer may be very pleasing to you even when it is not pleasing to me? Do I see it as a door through which I come into your presence, many times by faith alone, but eventually with an experience much more vivid?

PART IV

THE MASS AND SACRAMENTS: THE LIFEBLOOD OF LOVE

CHAPTER 18

The Liturgy and Love

In placing our consideration of liturgical prayer after the discussion of prayer in general, we do not indicate that it is less important. The liturgy is the worship of the whole Church, of the whole people of God. It is the Mystical Body of Christ offering public prayer to the Father. But the reasons for placing the liturgy in this particular place are practical.

The ordinary layman has probably been engaged in some form of liturgical prayer for some time. He has been going to Mass, to confession, to Communion, all perhaps without much good. So if we were to place the liturgy first according to its dignity, he might become discouraged under the belief that he has tried this already and it doesn't hold much promise. On the contrary, our hope is that through a general understanding of prayer, he will be better disposed to receive the great spiritual good that the liturgy can bring him.

But there is another reason also for placing the more personal kind of prayer before our treatment of liturgical prayer, which is public by its very nature. We have intended an emphasis on private prayer in order to offset a certain harmful influence upon the spiritual life. Some of those who have written on the liturgy have at times become too exclusively enthusiastic over it, even to the point of rebuke by the highest authority in the Church. While man is a social being and therefore is bound to worship God according to this side of his human nature, some have forgotten that he is not just a social being, a member of creation, but also and more basically an individual with an individual soul. To say otherwise is to distort the clear meaning of the word of God.

These men sometimes consider the personal side of the spiritual life, and if we may say so, the more demanding side, the interior life, as relatively unimportant compared to public or liturgical prayer, whereas this is not so. God's grace is unlimited in the variety of ways it can come to us. Indeed, if it does nothing else, personal prayer will dispose us to receive more transformingly the manifest graces of the Mass, the sacraments, and the rest of the liturgy.

We can, if we will, think of these graces as if we were approaching the altar to get water. Our supposition is that water is very precious. Some of us will come with large containers to carry the water; others will come with small ones. Some will come with large containers having small openings; others will come with containers tightly capped. Obviously some of us will come away with large amounts of this precious water and others will not.

If we think of grace in terms of this water, we will see that the example applies to the Mass and the sacraments. Even though we all attend the same Mass and receive the same sacraments, some of us receive much grace so as to become strong in the Christian life. The saints, let us not forget, had no better Mass than we, no better absolution, and no better body and blood of Christ. But there are others who receive no apparent benefit. These souls, which are shrunken or closed by selfishness, by affection for sin (for instance, for sins of the tongue), will receive very little of the torrents of grace that are offered, even though they go to Mass and Holy Communion every day. But those souls which are opened by love of God and neighbor, by trust and humility, will find that the Mass and the sacraments are truly what we have so often been told they are, the great channels of God's grace.

But such a preparation for greater graces is an important purpose of the spiritual life. Besides bringing many graces of its own, the spiritual life prepares us to receive with great abundance what God has placed at our disposal in great abundance in the Mass and the sacraments. And without the spiritual life this will not be done. We must not forget the lesson of the Pharisees. They were very meticulous in their liturgy, that of the Old Law, but received little profit. Our Lord did not condemn them for their liturgical spirit, but basically for their proud and unloving hearts.

But the lack of a spiritual life is not the only difficulty. Sometimes a lack of wholehearted love and participation in the liturgy comes from a certain distaste. The prayers of the liturgy, it is said, are not personal enough, or they are not "devotional." While we must in the end leave everyone to his own taste, there is something to be said about this objection. It would not be true to say that liturgical prayer is exclusively objective, whereas the more personal prayer is subjective and that this accounts for its appeal. The many sentiments expressed in the Mass, for instance, do echo our hearts. As day follows day, we will hear or speak all of our deep emotions in language that is expressive and beautiful. But we don't have syrup; the prayers don't drip. Yet despite this dubious lack, we have expression of a true piety of great intensity and depth.

For instance, the prayers of the liturgy constantly remind us of who we are. We are the needy. They thereby put God in his rightful place, first. Also, there are indeed days in which the liturgy sorrows with the suffering Christ. But we are not allowed to forget that this suffering God is also a strong God, a God who eventually wins, as we too are meant to win by hope in his strength.

In fact, one of the great achievements of the liturgy is that it keeps our attention centered on God, where it should be. We do not risk having God suffocated by the many devotions which are so ready at hand. These, of course, are not wrong. A full liturgical life still has room for personal preferences in prayer. But these preferences should lead to union with God. Yet sometimes this great lover of our souls can become an afterthought, or someone to be approached in too great a reverence, only after we have approached everyone else. The liturgy does not make this mistake, and thus it is some sort of standard by which to judge the effect of our private devotions.

The liturgy not only asks God for things and thanks him, both excellent ways of keeping him first, but it also praises him. This is a part of our duty as creatures and quite a natural thing also. We are always praising excellence, whether it be in work, in sports, in beauty, or in any form of true art. How much more then should we praise him whose excellence is without limit. Since "the heavens declare the glory of God" (Ps. 18:1), we should not fail to do so as well.

The desire for a more personal approach indicates only that there must be a balance in each individual between liturgical prayer and personal prayer. The liturgy by its very nature is not intended to satisfy on demand every facet of the heart of every human being. Religion must always in some way be organized. It has to be established externally so that it can teach. If it were not, the wonderful message of God's love for us would soon be forgotten by many, and we would be men without hope, irrevocably discouraged because of our sins.

Religion must not only teach; because of the nature of man, it must worship God with certain rites and ceremonies—in other words, by external, group worship. Even though group worship may not always appeal to us, it is an obligation flowing from our human nature. As human beings we are social beings; that is, we live by co-operation with others. We depend on the co-operation of others not only for food, clothing, and protection but also for our advancement in knowledge and culture. This need to co-operate is the way we are made. Therefore, since we cannot neglect to go to God according to the way we are made, we must worship him at times in co-operation with a group.

Another thing, our worship must be different from that of the angels, who do not have bodies. God is the creator of both sides of our nature, spiritual and physical, and should receive worship in a similar manner. Therefore, we publicly worship him by voice, by various postures of the body, by ceremonies, and by visible symbols—all because we are human and are conducting our external worship according to our full human nature.

Yet public worship has difficulties, sometimes even a deadening effect. We can come to look upon religion as so ordinary a part of our life that we see it only as a given set of obligations to be fulfilled, often interfering with other, more appealing plans. Sometimes also it is merely something very dull, when it is not annoying. But we can obtain a clearer view of the liturgy by looking at the basic reason why we go to church. Various people would give various reasons why they go, most of them worthy reasons. But we can never forget that the principal reason always is to give worship to God, publicly with our fellow men and externally through our bodies. So whether we are consoled by the service or not, whether we like the sermon or not, whether the singing is good or not, whether the people seem devout or not, all this is very much secondary to the fact that we have fulfilled a duty to God as human beings.

Not that we should look upon the liturgy solely as a duty. Like everything else in life, and in this more than most, we act out of love. Love is not so much found in the words of the service as in the heart that uses the words. So we don't go to Mass or to confession or to Communion just because we have to. We go because we will meet and will please Someone who means much to us. Liturgy without love in the heart is liturgy without life.

Likewise a necessary emphasis on the externals of worship should not cause us to allow the Liturgy of the Word to overshadow the Liturgy of the Eucharist. It is possible to be very careful in our participation in all the prayers and ceremonies and still assist at Mass unintelligently. The Mass is not only a meeting of the people of God where we pray and are instructed. It is even something more than the occasion on which we are fed by the body and blood of Christ. The Mass is above all a sacrifice. And too much concentration on the externals, or even on the marvel of Christ's sacramental presence within us, can weaken our grasp of this great truth.

The Mass, as we all know, is essentially one with the sacrifice of the cross. The same victim is being offered up by the same priest, Christ the Lord. This is true despite the obvious differences, that the Mass is an unbloody sacrifice, and that Christ now offers himself, not directly, but through the ministry of a man who speaks in his name when he says: "This is my body. . . . This is my blood." It is at this point in the Mass that we should be most attentive to what is happening, for here precisely we "proclaim the death of the Lord, until he comes." (I Cor. 11:26) This is where we should be offering the victim to the Father, and ourselves along with him . . . and not only ourselves but all our needs, all the love and honor we have to give, all our gratitude and all our guilt. How poorly we will have assisted at Mass if we have done all else and have failed to achieve a crescendo of awareness here.

Here at the consecration the layman finds his highest dignity. He is not only one of the people of God joining in group worship. But each man and woman is fulfilling the priesthood given at baptism and strengthened at confirmation. St. Peter calls all Christians "a holy priesthood . . . a royal priesthood." (I Pet. 2:5, 9) This is of course not the priesthood which Christ conferred on the apostles at the Last Supper: "Do this in remembrance of me." (Luke 22:19) But it is still a priesthood and a true sharing in the priesthood of the one high priest of the New Testament, Christ the Lord.

Only the priest at the altar actually acts in the name of Christ to offer the sacrifice. In offering the victim to the Father, the people must also in a true sense offer him through the priest. But the essential subordination of the priesthood of the layman to the priesthood of the priest does not detract from the dignity the layman here possesses. By reason of this priesthood he not only offers Christ to the Father but he also offers himself as being one with the victim, and he offers his many daily sacrifices in union with this victim also.

A climax, therefore, is reached in the life of the layman when he offers to the Father through the priest, with the priest the unbloody sacrifice of the Son. His attendance at Mass is therefore something alive. Instead of the merely bowed head at the consecration, or only the adoration of "My Lord and my God," instead of the superfluous (for him) repetition of the words of consecration, he too in the silence that is intended to be a part of public worship renews the sacrifice through the Christ at the altar with the Christ on Calvary. He does it not only for personal needs but even more so that God will have mercy on the sins and needs of the world, that God will see our gratitude superlatively expressed, and will accept with even greater willingness the honor and love from our hearts.

Practical Reflection

Do I understand that, besides giving love to God, I must give him worship also, worship that acknowledges what he is and what I am? Do I see now that in church we do not worship together merely as a matter of convenience because of numbers, but because we are obliged by our nature to give God public worship in an external manner? Will I try to see myself, not as a mere observer nor only as an active participant in the words and ceremonies, but as having a special dignity before God and an acceptable part of the sacrifice itself? Will I try to make myself more worthy of this dignity? Will I make the Lord's day something belonging to the Lord as well as to me? Will I try to see this worship, as I will try to see everything in my life, as a fulfillment of love of my God?

CHAPTER 19

Holy Communion: The Food of Love

The spiritual life is occasionally presented as if it consisted solely of the Mass and the sacraments. You go to confession, to Mass, and Holy Communion and you automatically become better. Many people have tried this, however, and have found that spiritual progress isn't that simple.

On the opposite side, the spiritual life is sometimes presented without much reference to Mass and the sacraments, as if great spiritual perfection were possible without much attention to these channels of grace. But while God can indeed make exceptions for those who are in good faith outside the Church or for those Catholics whose circumstances make any frequency at Mass impossible, still he will not compensate for indifference or neglect. He intends that our salvation and our closeness to him come about by the divine, life-giving graces which come to us under the coarse veil of the material. Just as we have a more certain and fruitful contact with God because a divine person took upon himself the material by means of a human nature, so the flow of the divine life of grace within us is given more certainly and comes more abundantly because of these material signs which are the sacraments.

In the case of the Holy Eucharist this abundance is one more example of the urging of love that impels God. Our Lord was not content merely to come on earth, nor even to do the almost unbelievable, to die for us. He wanted this same sacrifice always to be available so that we might more easily and fruitfully share the benefits it has won for us. These, if we think of what the Mass is, must be very great. A sober calculation of these blessings for time and eternity should impel us to be present at the renewal of this sacrifice as often as circumstances honestly permit, even every day. No man likes to think he is losing a fortune by a lack of shrewdness or energy. But here is a spiritual fortune often missed.

Our Lord's love is so great that he was not content with bestowing gifts upon us. He would give what is always love's best gift, he would give himself. This he does through the marvel of his presence under the appearances of bread and wine, by the interdwelling of himself and us: "He who eats my flesh, and drinks my blood, abides in me and I in him." (John 6:57)

The number of people who attend Mass but do not receive Holy Communion will always be one of the practical mysteries in the Church. It has all the incongruity of a hungry man sitting down before an inviting Christmas dinner, saying grace, and after a while giving thanks, but eating nothing. Perhaps such a man is sick, and if so, he needs medical help. In spiritual terms this means mortal sin and its cure, confession. Yet surely mortal sin is a deterrent for only a minority of the many who stay away. The apathy must be laid to other causes. It will help to look at some of them.

One of the reasons for the neglect of this union with Christ in Holy Communion is a sense of unworthiness. In a way this unworthiness will always be there, as it was even for the saints. But there comes a time when too much of "Lord, I am not worthy" becomes an insult to God, to his mercy. But there is in this excuse of unworthiness also a misconception about what this sacrament is. Our Lord said, "The bread that I will give is my flesh for the life of the world." (John 6:52) But if he called it bread, it is therefore a food, a spiritual food, food for the soul. Now if it is food, it is not a reward. Receiving it does not imply perfection: it implies need. And who does not need? We should, of course, go to our Lord because we love him, but we should also go to him because we need.

Besides, our Lord did not say, "I am giving my flesh as food for my special friends." He said, "for the life of the *world*." Not only then is he meant to be the daily food of those who, for instance, are consecrated to him by special vows, but food for everyone he loves, food—if they will take it—for the whole world.

Food has various effects. One of them in particular shows the unreasonableness of those who stay away because of a special kind of unworthiness, the fact that they have committed venial sins. The truth is that Holy Communion actually forgives venial sins. Just as the effect of food is to repair the damage done to the body by daily living, so Holy Communion is a food that renews us. Or, to look upon this sacrament as the union of love that it is, venial sins disappear on receiving our Lord just as the wounds from ordinary impatience and thoughtlessness disappear at the embrace of a loving husband and wife.

Another reason for apathy in regard to Holy Communion is a lack of awareness of our need. To cure this, God sometimes makes us aware of it, painfully. But a reasonable man should be able to see that we always have great need of spiritual food. In the spiritual life we are called to do what is essentially hard work. There is no vacation from this and no unemployment. Like every worker we need food.

Food has another effect in that it nourishes and strengthens us, and thus enables us to grow. There are indeed other sources of strength than this sacrament. But if we refuse this, we are like those unfortunate men who refused to come to the wedding feast. We can expect little closeness to God, and perhaps not much strength at all, if we refuse the food that love is so eager to provide. Yet for those who are not able to have much of this, God can give as much in one Holy Communion as he ordinarily would do in many.

We can find another reason for apathy in regard to Holy Communion if we consider still another aspect of food, that it gives pleasure. This pleasure has been put in our nature by God so that we will more readily fulfill our duty of eating. Such a plan on the part of God is true of our spiritual food also. Our meeting with him in Holy Communion can be a repeated experience of inner peace, consolation, and even joy. Here we are in a tangible relationship with love itself. The search which fills so much of our lives comes to an end, the search for a completely understanding friend. These feelings then, the result of contact with our Lord, are partly intended to induce us to have more of this food so that we may grow more like him and closer to him.

But although for many of us there will be Communions which will be the most moving moments of our lives, quite surely there will be many others which are not. Despite God's great goodness in this sacrament, this is still earth and not heaven. But this lack of feeling is sometimes a reason for staying away. Some may decide that God doesn't want them and that this lack of feeling or of former feeling is a proof of it. But as we said in speaking of dryness in prayer, this is no proof of God's rejection. If it were, he would have been rejecting many saints also at certain times in their lives. The truth is that he sometimes wants us to grow by the kind of love that is based on faith rather than on feeling.

There are others also who will interpret this barrenness of emotions as an indication that the sacrament is doing them no good. But since it is a food, we do not have to feel pleasure in order to receive its deeper effects, just as it is not necessary that our food should taste good in order to nourish us. In daily warfare, as well as in fierce battles, it will be our experience that the strength from Holy Communion, strength often without any emotional consolation, will bring us through better than anything else we can do.

Another excuse closely connected with pleasure keeps some away from Communion; they fear that it will become a routine as colorless as eating the same kind of food day after day. This is perhaps a way of admitting that one fears to lose the pleasure, whereas pleasure should be something secondary. It is quite true that if the husband were away for long periods, his rare meeting with his wife might bring extraordinary joy. But what man or woman who loved would want to exchange an occasional overwhelming experience in preference to the support of daily love, counsel, and strength? Such overly cautious fear would make Holy Communion a narrowing self-indulgence instead of the broadening and freeing effect of wholehearted giving. Routine is one of the necessary risks of the spiritual life. A refusal to risk it is failure before we start.

Instead we must fight the battle against routine. We can get used to almost anything if we are not careful. Even the apostles seem to have become used to Christ; at least they quarreled in front of him. But there are ways to fight the effects of routine, and we must use them in the spiritual life just as we must use them in other parts of our life. We can keep reminding ourselves of what we are and who our Lord is. We can remind ourselves of what is going to happen and what has happened. And also we can love. If we love, we really never get used to the other. But love must be more extensive than one short period in a day, even as it would have to be in a successful marriage. This is another way of saying that the spiritual life must be broader than daily Mass and Holy Communion if we are to draw all the good from them.

It may happen that we go to Holy Communion in great dryness of spirit, are distracted before, during, and after, and still receive a great abundance of grace because our souls in their hidden depths are open to God, to his love, and to his will. Even some of the saints had to become saints in this manner.

It is therefore not so much the prayers we may say directly before Communion, but our lives, that are the best preparation for our Lord's coming and for increased graces. The sacraments give grace infallibly, as baptism does to a sleeping infant, unless we place obstacles in the way of them. This presence of obstacles accounts for another excuse to remain away from Holy Communion. This excuse is the ever-present scandal of some few who are always in church, so to speak, but who are lacking in many ordinary things, notably charity in speech—good Catholics, but poor Christians, as the saying goes. And those who are really seeking an excuse to stay away from God use these unfortunates for their reason, as if their faults were the direct result of going to church.

Yet the answer to this lies not in waiting for everybody else to become a saint before we venture a start, but in avoiding the same mistake ourselves. A true spiritual life will help us to see and remove the obstacles to the working of the sacraments.

There should be no need for greater encouragement to receive our Lord than the fact that he is there. God loves us enough to want to be with us this closely and to be our food. What more can he do to prove his love? He has given his life and now he gives us his heart. Do we demand that he die in front of us, or that he tear his heart out and show it to us? Or is it we who have hearts of stone, for it takes hardened hearts to refuse such love. Christ was looking ahead during his agony in the garden, not only at his sufferings, not only at our sins, but also at our neglect of him. Is it any wonder he sweated blood? There is no sorrow like love that is refused.

As an old man St. John tells us of his first meeting with Christ. (John 1:35 ff.) St. John the Baptist had pointed him out, and the young future apostle with St. Andrew timidly went up to him and asked where he lived. "Come and see," was our Lord's reply and invitation. His words could be addressed to any of us who hesitate outside the embrace of his love: "Would you have strength against your many enemies, against your great weakness? Come and see. Know that I am greater than all your enemies and stronger than even your weakness. Would you have peace of soul, support in all your trials, a wall against temptation, a pledge for the future? Would you have love that never fails, love stronger than you own? Then do not stand far off. I am waiting. Come and see."

Practical Reflection

The result of thinking on these and perhaps other excuses for failure in regard to Christ's gift of himself should be a confrontation with God on a personal basis. The circumstances of each life vary, and so it would be foolish for a book of this kind to set the external ideal too high by insisting on daily Mass and Communion as the norm. A woman for instance, who is in church when she should be home making breakfast for her husband and children is not serving them or God either. So each one must weigh his life and its circumstances, his time and his strength. But there is one resolution which seems possible to all, that we will go to Communion every time we go to Mass.

CHAPTER 20

Confession: The Healing of Love

If God is what we expect him to be when we think of him as uncreated love, then we should expect him to be merciful and forgiving of sins, even the greatest sins, when regretted with sincere repentance. But this is precisely how he has shown himself to us, and again the cross is our best proof of it. In the face of man's sin, all sin from Adam's to our own, God still loved enough to give his Son. How can anyone love more than that?

The Son on the cross is similarly convincing. He does not curse his enemies; he prays for them. He is not absorbed in the injustice of his own execution and in his own pain. He is ready to forgive and promise heaven to a wretch who repented only when there was little else to do except die in despair.

God's attitude toward sin is no different today from what it was then, for God never changes. His love is without measure, and thus he is compelled by his own nature always to desire repentance, and is always waiting to show mercy. He never gives up.

There is only one thing which can stop the advances of God, a stubborn will: "I'll do as I like." "No one is going to scare me." "I'll die as I lived." "My sin is too great." This is the ultimate of failure, the ultimate of evil. It is rejection of love and embracing of eternal hatred of self and of God and of all else. Compared to this, the good thief on the cross, naked, abandoned, and helpless, was a remarkable success.

Our Lord not only died for sinners, he even seeks them out. He has described himself as the good shepherd who seeks out the sheep that is lost and which will die by the teeth of the wolves. In his life on earth he did not merely tolerate sinners, forgiving them at a safe distance, we might say. He actually ate with them. No man can therefore say, "I'm too evil to become a friend of God." Christ ate even with such as you. Even if you have just finished sinning, with the filth of sin still on you, your Lord wants you, is seeking you. And the main thing is to be found.

He will not be revolted at your condition. He will take you into his arms rejoicing. Nor will your condition shock the pure angels of heaven. They too will rejoice; he has told us that too. "There will be joy in heaven over one sinner who repents, more than over ninety-nine just who have no need of repentance." (Luke 15:7)

Our Lord was so anxious to forgive our sins that he wasted no time in giving us a sure way to go about it. One of his first acts on the first Easter when, newly risen from the dead, he appeared to his apostles, was to give them the power to forgive sins: "Whose sins you shall forgive, they are forgiven them." (John 20:23) At these words the earth should have trembled on its foundations, for never before had such a thing been done by God, to give men power to forgive in his name.

But despite this unique fact, this remarkable privilege, perhaps we would want our forgiveness in a simpler way, going to God directly with our sins. But then we would lack the inner assurance that comes with being told by a man who speaks in God's name that this God has forgiven us. We would also not have the psychological release that comes from telling another about our misdeeds. And we would not be forced at least once a year by Church law to come to terms with ourselves and our guilt. God's new way of doing things also eliminates many of the subterfuges and rationalizations we put up to excuse and continue our sins. His representatives, therefore, can warn us, instruct us, correct us, and occasionally even threaten us, all in his name. This is a part of the loving providence of a God who ever seeks our souls and our love. Confession then is a sacrament of God's mercy, of God's love.

While it is still quite true that we can and should go to him immediately after any sin, whether small or great, confession adds something of assurance, not only psychologically or in our emotions, but theologically or in fact. To be forgiven without the sacrament, it is necessary to have perfect contrition. This means that we must be sorry from motives of love, and that this love for God be not so much for what he can give us, but for what he is. Perfect contrition does not mean that love must be our only motive. We may indeed be sorry also because of other good but less perfect motives: the fear of punishment, ingratitude to God, or the intrinsic evil of sin itself. It is possible to have both sets of motives, the imperfect and the perfect. But the least amount of the true love of God is sufficient to take away all the sins one could possibly commit. We should aim for the predominance of this motive as it is expressed in the act of contrition: "but *most of all* because they [my sins] have offended thee, my God, who are all good and deserving of all my love." Our act of contrition as it stands is an act of perfect contrition.

If we have sorrow based on love, we are forgiven at that moment any sins or any number of sins, providing, of course, that we have the right kind of resolution for the future. If Catholic we must intend to go to confession at least within the year if it is a case of mortal sin, although it is better to go as soon as is reasonably possible. In this last we are following the will of Christ who gave this power to men and would not want his representatives bypassed. Of course we are following the law of the Church too. And it is also necessary to note that, even though we are forgiven, we may not normally go to Holy Communion until we have gone to confession, again only if it is a case of mortal sin.

While this forgiveness is quite possible with God's grace, even to the worst of men, the sacrament provides an added reassurance that we are forgiven. We ourselves may not be capable of an adequate sorrow for love of God, or we may not be sure of it. But it is solid doctrine taught throughout the Church that the less worthy motives of imperfect contrition are sufficient for forgiveness along with the sacrament. It is then no great surprise that so intelligent a man as G. K. Chesterton used to reply when asked why he came into the Church, "To have my sins forgiven."

However, the word "perfect" sometimes frightens people. They somehow feel that any sort of perfection is only for a saint, and this they are not. These are to be reminded first of all that we have not been speaking about "a perfect act of contrition." Perhaps even a saint might fall short of that. But we say "an act of perfect contrition," and this means nothing more than we have been talking about, sorrow because of love.

Obviously, this sorrow does not have to be deeply emotional. In fact it doesn't have to be emotional at all, and it is very poor sorrow if it is only emotional and nothing else. Sorrow, like love, is essentially in the will. This means that we regret having offended God because of certain very good reasons. It means that we thus regret our sins, especially all mortal sins if there are any. All this can be done without any emotion, although, on the other hand, a healthy emotion is not to be despised or rejected. We may be certain that our sorrow is sufficient if we are determined, with God's help, not to sin again, especially by mortal sin.

Our forgiveness, whether in or out of confession, does not depend on how successful we are later in keeping our resolutions. Forgiveness comes because of our sincerity at the time, and always we depend on God's strength rather than our own. A notable failure to keep them, however, may indicate that we should examine our life more carefully, especially on the near occasions of sin. These, when they exist, must form a part of our resolution in order for us to be forgiven. We would be making a mockery of God's forgiveness if we told him we were sorry and then freely threw ourselves again and again into situations which are too compelling for our weakness.

But we do have God's forgiveness whenever we sincerely resolve to give up the sin and its near occasions. Some people become discouraged because they fall into the same sins over and over. But such falls, though they should be avoided with all our strength, are still not surprising. For, although the sin is forgiven, the bad habit remains. This force of habit inclines us to sin again and again. It can be prevented from doing this, not only by a firm resolution, but also by careful watchfulness and much prayer. The habit itself is gradually weakened by a good life and God's grace. It is effectively destroyed by the opposite good habit. Usually this takes time.

Even when it is not a case of mortal sin, frequent confession (that is, every week or two) has important spiritual advantages. In the first place, while it is true that venial sin can be forgiven in many other ways (for instance, by an act of love of God or neighbor, by an act of sorrow for this particular sin or

10. Beginnings

all sins, by the Mass or any of the sacraments including Holy Communion, or by sufferings patiently borne), this is not the same as saying that all our venial sins are actually forgiven by these or any other means. No sin is forgiven without adequate sorrow and determination to amend our life. While this does not have to occur explicitly for every venial sin, perhaps our general dispositions of love or sorrow and amendment, which are implicit in all actions by which we go to God, are not sufficient for total forgiveness. And so we can make more certain of their forgiveness by explicitly coming to terms with these sins in confession. A willingly nurtured resentment or the sins flowing from a habit of uncharitable talk may easily be examples of this. Although we may surely go to Communion as often as we wish without confessing venial sins, we are surely better prepared if our souls have been cleansed by the sacrament instituted to do it, just as our clothes may be clean enough for ordinary wear, but they will be cleaner after having been washed. The Church in the liturgy often has us pray in the words of the psalmist, "Wash me clean, cleaner yet, from my guilt." (Ps. 50:4)

Then too if we go to confession at not too prolonged intervals, we can more easily check up on our weaknesses. Thus a few small sins will not grow into many because of inattention, nor will we become so careless about them that they will weaken us for mortal sin.

We so often think of confession as a preparation for Holy Communion that we forget that it has rights of its own. It can give certain graces better than sorrow for sin without the sacrament. These graces will strengthen us against committing sin in the future, especially those we have sincerely confessed. It can do this in some cases even better than Holy Communion, just as medicine at times will do more for us than food.

Besides this, in the case of mortal sin the sacrament of penance not only restores sanctifying grace, which is the root of friendship with God, but it also can restore the same degree of friendship and the merits gained before the sin. This sacrament, like every sacrament, also increases sanctifying grace, and thus brings us closer to God by making us more like him. To make the picture complete, we must not fail to add that the sacrament also takes away all or part of the temporal punishment due to our sins, the punishment we would have to work out on earth or in purgatory. The degree of this remission depends on our dispositions in receiving the sacrament, but all things being equal, it does this better than repentance without the sacrament.

But none of these riches of God's mercy comes without a price. That price is sometimes a certain humiliation. It would be easier to tell our sins to God who knows them anyway. Yet since he wants men to have the privilege and duty of sharing in the salvation of men, we bear willingly whatever sacrifice we are required to make. We know that even small sins deserve punishment far greater than any humiliation or inconvenience, not to speak of the punishment for mortal sin.

In the face of any difficulty we might have about confession, we should hear the same words our Lord addressed to the paralytic, "Take courage, son; thy sins are forgiven thee." (Matt. 9:2) Our Lord looked deeper than the man's physical sickness and saw fear in the man's eyes, fear because of sin, fear because "it is a fearful thing to fall into the hands of the living God." (Heb. 10:31) And so he healed the soul before he healed the body. "Take courage, son; thy sins are forgiven thee."

How much suffering our Lord takes out of the world today by taking away sin. The paralytic's friends might have taken him on many roads that day. They might have taken him to a doctor, uselessly. They might have taken him to a tavern where he could get drunk, again uselessly. But they took him to Christ, the same Christ we meet in the person of the priest in confession. There is no peace in trying to forget sin, in trying to ignore it, no peace in drink, in pleasure, no peace in unbelief. Only one voice can take away our fear and thus prevent our guilt from tormenting us consciously or unconsciously, only one voice in the world, the voice of Christ through his priest, "Take courage; thy sins are forgiven thee."

Practical Reflection

How important it is for me to know that between you and me, O Lord, there is nothing for which I now deserve punishment! How good is your mercy to give this sacrament of your love so that I can have this essential assurance and thus be most deeply at peace. I will therefore see this sacrament, not as an ordeal to be endured, but as a meeting with you through your representative. May I use this gift so that I will know what the paralytic knew, that between us there is peace, so that if I die today, I will hear your words taking away my dread of judgment, telling me to take courage because my sins too are forgiven.

CHAPTER 21

Practical Suggestions on Confession

It is sadly true that everything human has unavoidable complications: marriage, commerce, eating, raising a family. When our Lord gave the power of forgiveness to men, a certain directness was lost; this involvement in the human is the price we must pay for the advantages that the sharing of his power has brought to us.

He not only gave the apostles the power to forgive sin but also the power not to forgive sin: "Whose sins you shall retain, they are retained." (John 20:23) This second part of their power brings us face to face with the human situation into which Christ placed the gift. He has made the priest, who is always a father, also a judge. In other words the priest must know what the case of the penitent is, so that he may pronounce the usual sentence of forgiveness or the rare sentence of non-forgiveness. This necessity involves more complications than simply going to God, but on the other hand there is an inestimable advantage, as we have said. God doesn't actually tell us we are forgiven, but the priest does. And we should be willing to put up with the unavoidable complications just to have that kind of assurance.

We are all aware of what these complications are. We, all of us from the Holy Father down, must kneel before another human being and in human language according to a rather formalized pattern relate the same things we should relate to God if we were to go to him directly. We might prefer to throw ourselves into God's arms and ask forgiveness "for everything." And we still ought to do this, many times. But it is greatly more beneficial to have an awareness of the precise nature of our guilt, and this comes by being more specific. "Everything" can leave an impotent vagueness about certain points upon which our sorrow and resolution should particularly rest. Disagreements between married partners provide a similarity. Many times a word or a kiss is all that is needed to restore harmony. But at other times, say an involvement in a flirtation, the issue must be settled more specifically.

Furthermore, the more specific we are the better will be our chances of future avoidance of the same sin. An obscure awareness of our sins does not produce the kind of self-knowledge that changes our lives. The more specific, up to a point, the better. And this is not only for the sin itself, but also for the near occasions of the sin. Indeed, a true sincerity with God involves being specific, despite our tendency to equate sincerity with mere emotion. We cannot divorce the rational life from the spiritual life. The overly sentimental people at best stay just where they are, in self-deluding sentimentality to the end.

This need or advisability of being specific is important first of all for our examination of conscience. Not only is a good examination of conscience a preparation to receive this sacrament, but it can many times determine the kind of reception we will get from the priest. When the priest has to do this work for us because of our carelessness, he is not so apt to mirror the kind of Christ we would like to see in him. But let us remember that a slovenly preparation is not particularly pleasing to Christ either. We have sinned and we now come into his presence asking forgiveness. Is it an attitude worthy of such a serious situation, that we do not trouble ourselves much to prepare for it?

But the seriousness of our examination of conscience should not make us become overly serious. There are people who do very little for their souls except to examine them, and this they do continually. But even when we are not afflicted by any such excess, we can spend too much time at it to the detriment of the other parts of our preparation: sorrow for these sins and resolutions for the future. The time given will vary with different people and circumstances. But a suggestion may be made for those who go to confession every week or two: the examination need not take more than four or five minutes. This is especially true if they have the habit of daily examination of conscience before retiring. If we give too much time to it, we can unconsciously hurt our relationship with God. We will give ourselves the false idea that he is some kind of narrow-minded bookkeeper, whereas he is a merciful father.

As to the manner of examining our conscience, we have freedom for any of several ways. If one is just now emerging from a life of sin or laxity, he may do well at first to use a list of questions such as can be found in any standard prayer book. After all, he must find out what is wrong besides, let us say, adultery and missing Mass. However, there are some printed examinations of conscience so detailed that they would turn all of us into scrupulous introverts. If any such effect is noticed, we would do better to abandon such a method of examination in favor of freedom from unnecessary anxiety. There are other ways to go about it.

We can, for instance, go down the list of commandments and ask ourselves how we might have sinned against them. Or we can go over the daily routine of our life. Or we can check on the sins that we usually commit. In both these last methods the presumption is that anything unusual will stand out by itself. After all, are we not the same persons with the same weaknesses living in the same circumstances? All this adds up normally to the same kind of sins. In fact, we should be grateful to God when there aren't any different ones.

A growth in the spiritual life will ordinarily bring a deeper insight into our examination of conscience, and we will discover that certain things about us are sinful that we did not know before. This should not result in discouragement but in thanksgiving for new self-knowledge—and also in a warning. We must never forget, never, that the guilt for sin is based upon how our conscience sincerely viewed it *at the time*, not how we view it now. Therefore we must judge our past actions by our past conscience, and our present actions by our present conscience.

In order for our confession to be specific, our examination should include the kind of sin and the number of times we are guilty. Such details are ordinarily necessary for forgiveness itself if there has been mortal sin. For we are obliged to tell all mortal sins, if we have any, and all are not told if we omit the distinction between one kind of sin and another, as for instance between adultery and impure desires. Yet we do not have to go into the actual details of how the sin was committed, just the kind of sin so that the confessor will know that the commandment was broken in this way and not in another.

Nor have all mortal sins been told if we fail to express, at least with approximate accuracy, the number of times each kind of sin was committed. God does not expect us to be calculating machines, and there are simple ways to meet the problems of memory. We can always say "about so many times." In other words we are not held to exactness when this cannot be done practically or would involve something as extraordinary as recording our sins on paper. To make things easier, we can tell the approximate number of times in a day, a week, or a month. This way the numbers do not become big enough to frighten us in regard to their honest telling. Often all that we need in order to tell *anything* courageously in confession is a sufficiently satisfactory formula for telling it.

In this matter of what must be confessed, it is a part of the freedom which God and the Church have given us that there need be confession only of mortal sins *of which we are certain*. Doubtful mortal sins need not be confessed, at least not by persons who sincerely want to live a good life. Our doubt may have come because of uncertainty as to the circumstances when we acted (and we may have had no reasonable way of reaching certainty). Or there may be doubt as to the degree of our consent, or as to how free our will was at the time. Doubt is usually expressed by a certain going back and forth in our mind: now we think it was mortal sin, now we think it was not.

In these cases we should at once stop thinking on the subject, tell God we are sorry, and adopt one of two courses. In following the first, we confess it as doubtful, "as it is in the sight of God." In the meantime we may go to Holy Communion, making an act of contrition beforehand. This, as we have said, will take away the possible sin if we are sorry out of love of God. This kind of confession is the course to be followed in most cases. It sets the conscience at rest and, especially in the overly optimistic penitent, gives the confessor a chance to weigh the case more objectively if he sees this to be advisable. But we must never confess a doubtfully mortal sin as if it were a fully deliberate mortal sin. This, while not making a bad confession, is still an untruth. We must call them as we see them. And we do our souls no good, but rather harm, by trying to be too safe.

The other way of dealing with doubtful mortal sin is not to confess it at all. As we have said, we are not obliged to, strictly speaking. This way of acting is especially recommended to those who have a tendency to scrupulosity, who are at the same time sincerely dedicated to spiritual advancement and, importantly, are psychologically or spiritually strong enough to live by their honest judgments. One of God's reasons of mercy in giving us confession is that all of us are not this strong, and we should not be ashamed to admit it.

It goes without saying that, even though these doubtful sins are not confessed, they are forgiven by the sacrament anyway. The sacrament of penance forgives all sins for which we are sorry at least in general. The only strict requirement is that we confess mortal sins of which we are certain, if we have any. This forgiveness also applies to the sins or alleged sins of the scrupulous when they have been forbidden by the confessor to mention them or repeat them. We shall refer to this later.

Although it is not necessary to confess venial sins at all, much less to confess them as to kind and number, there are weighty reasons for doing this. One reason is that in some cases we will not know whether a sin is mortal or venial. Confession is often the place to find out and to relieve our conscience, as we have said. Another reason is based on the hope that venial sins will be all that we have to confess. We confess them, therefore, because of the more perfect forgiveness that this sacrament brings, as well as the many other graces mentioned in the last chapter.

As for confessing the kind and number of venial sins, we will give the confessor a better picture of our souls if we do. Very often we cannot receive much help from the sacrament because we have given a poor account of ourselves. "I was angry," may mean only a slight impatience, but it can also mean a violent argument that lasted far into the night or a sulk that went on for days. Then also, confessing the number gives the penitent a chance to check up on himself. If he finds, for instance, that he has been engaged in derogatory conversation less often this week, he has cause for thanksgiving and encouragement. But if he finds more, he must then face himself with the question why.

But above all, the penitent who easily glides over his sins

without much concern for these details may be manifesting a state of soul not very much open to grace. On the contrary, a good way to give ourselves the best dispositions for grace is not only to be sorry and to resolve in general, merely "I've got to do better," but rather to be sorry and to resolve about specific sins. This, of course, should not be done for every sin—this would be too tedious—but for every kind of sin we have found in our examination of conscience. In this way we will be more apt to do something about the near occasions of sin, those persons, places, or things which may easily lead us into sin. These also must be sincerely resolved upon for our confession to be truly sincere and to be worthy of forgiveness. God expects both our sorrow and our resolution to be practical.

Our sorrow, as we have already said, need not be emotional. In fact, nothing connected with confession need be emotional. We do not have to see God in it emotionally, we do not have to be emotionally moved by what the priest says, and we do not have to feel an emotional lift as we leave. If we do have all these things, we are of course better off. But their absence has nothing to do with the basic value of our confession, just as a weepy feeling has nothing to do with our sorrow, or a desire to pound on something with our fist has nothing to do with our determination. At times these emotional states can even flatter us into believing that we have accomplished much, that once and for all we have mended our lives, whereas this may take years of determined effort in the quiet but clear light of self-knowledge and through many unfelt graces of God.

As to the manner of confessing, perhaps enough has already been said. If we have examined our conscience well, confessing will be merely putting into words what is clearly in our mind. We need, however, to be on guard against too many words. This is a duty in charity to those who may be waiting, as well as to the confessor who rightly reckons the normal hearing of confessions as one of the burdens of his priesthood. We should, therefore, not give too many details or "tell the story" of our sins unless there be some need to seek specific advice.

We are sometimes encouraged to tell the causes of our sins, but if this were extended to every sin, it would cause too prolonged a confession, and would become useless because of the very multiplicity. The causes of more important sins, however, may well be a way of opening our eyes, of strengthening our resolution, and of receiving helpful advice, especially concerning the near occasions of sin.

There must now be said a final word to the scrupulous. We have already spoken of them earlier, and we now close any further special mention with the firm admonition to be obedient to the confessor. Once they have been identified as scrupulous by a competent priest, they must abide by the advice or commands given *all their life* even if the confessor is transferred or dies. God has spoken to them through this man. He has no need to speak again; this is what he wants in regard to all these disturbing things. The command or advice must be followed regardless of what these scrupulous people might hear from others, or for others, or what their fears may bring up within them. They should, for instance, never make a general confession. This practice is sometimes advised at certain times in a person's life, but such advice is not for these people nor for anyone who has found that going over the past is a groundlessly disturbing thing. All their sins, real or imagined, are forgiven in the non-confessing to which they are usually advised, forgiven by a God who is no less merciful through the sacrament than he would be if we could enter directly into the presence of the benign Christ.

Practical Reflection

Am I determined upon a preparation for this sacrament worthy of the occasion of asking for forgiveness? Will I try to make it worthy of the God I have offended? Will I reach through the details of the sacrament and the person of the priest to the Christ who is there whether I feel it or not? Will I believe in the action of grace whether I feel anything or not? Will I afterward, instead of rushing off after a hasty penance, spend a few moments in gratitude for forgiveness and in prayer that I will use the graces received?

PART V

THE HEART OF THE TRUE LOVER: THE NATURE OF CHRISTIAN PERFECTION

CHAPTER 22

"Be Perfect"

We are about to begin a discussion which, if this book were organized in a purely logical manner, should have been written first. After all, we are not likely to move far along the road if we are not clear as to where we are going. But in our attempt to make the book practical, we have taken advantage of the fact that everyone has some general idea of human goodness. On this basis we have given some practical ideas and suggestions. Thus we have hoped to avoid what might be the tedium of generalities for anyone who clearly sees the necessity of practical action. In this way he has first been given something concrete in the spiritual life, and is now to that extent prepared to look at the ideal with more appreciation.

Similarly, by postponing the precise statement of the ideal, we have temporarily avoided certain necessary terminology which might have confused the beginner and taken his mind away from the most fundamental spiritual attitude and motive, which is the love of God. One of these necessary, but hitherto omitted, terms is that of "perfection." This book is written for those who are not perfect, and some of these might even be frightened by the word. On the other hand, there is danger that others will be misled by a natural attraction to perfection, and will concentrate on themselves too much, to the detriment of the love of God.

On many occasions our Lord was not addressing a chosen few, but the whole of a large group of people. Thus in the Sermon on the Mount our Lord commanded nothing less than perfection, and he commanded it for all. "You therefore are to be perfect, even as your heavenly Father is perfect." (Matt. 5:48) Since this is a command given to all, we are not really free as to whether we will perfect our spiritual nature or not. We are in some manner to become perfect in our way as God is in his.

The desire for perfection is anything but alien to human nature. It is this desire that turns children into mature adults, and has pushed mankind out of the stone age into the light of civilization. But man would be uselessly impelled to perfection if he did not seek most of all to perfect that part of him which rules him, that is, his soul. We know, for instance, that his perfected technology will destroy him if he does not control himself by perfecting his own spirit.

Man must perfect himself spiritually for even a greater reason, his eternal salvation. The farther he is from perfection, the harder it will be to save his soul. Most of us achieve less than we strive for. Unless we strive for more than the minimum, we greatly risk losing even that. To give God no more than the minimum, and to avoid everything that costs us difficulty or pain, is not a likely way to heaven but perhaps an easy way to hell. The idea of perfection, then, is involved in the questions each man must ask himself again and again: What am I working for, living for anyway? For success? security? money? pleasure? —all of which pass away—or am I working for eternal life?

Besides this, there are some people, built on larger spiritual lines, who will hardly save their souls in an ordinary, mediocre atmosphere where nothing more than the average is proposed to them. They will exert themselves only if they are inspired by the possibility of the highest. If there are no stars to reach for from the mountaintop, they will more easily become like animals or devils than those of us who are not built that way. For these most especially, the ideal of spiritual perfection is a necessary thing.

Perfection is so close to our nature that we instinctively admire it in many forms, as in physical beauty or in an exceptional performance at an athletic event or at the theater. But despite the fact that perfection is natural as well as necessary, enough of us fear it in the form of spiritual perfection, and fear it so much that sometimes we claim not even to admire it.

Such fear is with us for two reasons: one, that we do not understand what spiritual perfection is; and two, that we are afraid of the price we must pay for it. As to the first reason, we shall, during much of the remainder of this book, clarify the meaning of spiritual perfection, both in general and in its more practical aspects. As to the second reason, that is, the fear of what it might cost to become perfect, we have spelled out much already. The price, let us hope, now no longer seems as formidable as it once might have. It is well, however, to repeat here that the spiritual life is a growth, and growth is usually a gradual process. We are not asked to suffer all things or to give up all things, much less all things at once. We must only be willing to take the next step with God, to pay the price if there is a price, and know that there is no price too great to pay for heaven and for love.

Now as to what perfection is, it is not really a different thing from what we have been talking about all along. It is not, for instance, the distorted exaggeration of perfection known as perfectionism. Nor if it a sterile, self-admiring perfection, perfection for its own sake. It is really not a different thing from close union of friendship with God. It is really, basically, great and true love of God.

Similarly, when perfection is understood to be the pursuit of greater love of God, it follows that it does not consist in the number of prayers we say, nor in the number of devotions we have acquired, nor in the number of indulgences we gain. It also has nothing to do with great penances. And although knowledge is never to be despised, spiritual perfection is not necessarily connected with great theoretical knowledge of the spiritual life. So true is all this, that any overemphasis on any one of these can become an impediment to spiritual perfection.

Opposed to all overemphasis on any one detail, our Lord indicates that our perfection consists primarily in love. In teaching us the two great commandments, love of God and love of neighbor, he tells us that all other commands, all other counsels are only aspects of these. But although both are necessary, one of them is first and must be kept first. In fact, if we have the first, the second is, by a necessary consequence, a part of us also. The first is, "Thou shalt love the Lord thy God with thy whole heart, and with thy whole soul, and with thy whole mind, and with thy whole strength." (Mark 12:30) If we love God with this wholeness, we will love what he loves and in the way he wants us to love.

Yet the second commandment is given so that we may never forget, and so become selfish by what we think is true love of God: "Thou shalt love thy neighbor as thyself." (v. 31) In other parts of the book we shall discuss love of neighbor in detail. Here we shall explain more about the essential element of spiritual perfection which is true and great love of God.

Although this wholeness of love is our essential perfection, and although it is a command for all, it is this very wholeness for God that discourages some of us. How can we love God, someone we don't see, with that kind of love: "whole heart . . . whole soul . . . whole mind . . . whole strength"? A partial clue to our Lord's meaning is found in what apparently is most opposed to wholeness in loving God, and that is the love of our neighbor. The solution is found not so much in examining the way we must love God but in looking at the way we must love our neighbor.

We must love others, and other things, only in a manner in which they fit into love for God. Since God wants us to love others, we must see to it that we love them rightly, that they lead us to him at least in general, and that they do not lead away from him. In this way we fulfill the wholeness of dedication indicated by the commandment.

As we grow in love of God, this wholeness of dedication becomes more clearly understood and deeply lived. But then as now it is a supreme ideal toward which we must work rather than the kind of command which will bring punishment if it is not observed perfectly here and now. Yet, as St. Augustine tells us, God leaves no part of our life unclaimed.

Basically we are loving God with this wholeness, or in other words, loving him above all things, when we avoid mortal sin. Here the choice has been laid out before us; in venial sin this one-or-the-other situation is not present. Our love is basically a matter of our choices. And of course, greater love tries to make all the choices which would please the Other. Thus as we grow in love, we will find ourselves choosing against venial sin with perhaps even more vigor than some of us once avoided mortal sin. Later on, any voluntary imperfection is rejected, out of greater love. And more positively, we fill in the gaps of the commandments, not only by rejecting what is contrary, but by choosing all that is good, according to our light and our ability to choose it. True love never operates only in negatives.

This grasp of what love essentially is, that it is deeply involved in our choices, makes it possible to see how we can love God above all things in comparison to apparently stronger loves. We are so used to thinking of love in terms of emotion that we are uncertain many times as to whether or not we are loving him as we ought. We experience a different kind of love for our loved ones than we do with him. For them it is a love usually tinged with emotion and sometimes overwhelmingly filled with it. On the other hand our relationship with God may give us nothing or very little of what we otherwise experience as love. Therefore many of us may think that we are not doing a very good job of loving God, and thus we offer love only halfheartedly. This discouragement is all the more probable if we have read about the saints' being carried away into ecstasy over God. Something like this, we think, we must be able to do if it be true that we love him above all things.

Such a conclusion is far from the truth. It would, of course, be an indescribable experience if the whole of our nature would respond to God, as he deserves by being what he is. In the first place, however, we do not see him as he is, but only in an obscure manner. Therefore, we should not expect that our emotional nature will respond to him as it does to someone we can see, hear, and touch.

Furthermore, granted that we have acquired some clear idea of what God is, that he is a being who is most perfect and most worthy of love, we must still not expect our emotional nature to follow our reason. One of the effects of the Fall has been to break the harmony that should exist between our rational and our emotional natures. As a result, we often do not feel, humanly speaking, as we ought. A husband at times *feels* no love for his wife, and at times neither does a mother for her children. But there is an immediate reversal of this lack of feeling if an emergency arises when a loved one is in danger.

All this has a meaning in regard to our love for God. A woman, for instance, may love her husband with a great emotional love, and find that this is quite absent in her love for God. Yet she could easily be loving God more than her husband, and this would be apparent if she were to refuse his urging to sin in some serious manner. Our love for God is essentially measured by our choices.

In order to love God above all things, we need not expect that we will feel a love for him with those pleasing, tender emotions that are a part of our experience of love. We may indeed be fortunate enough to feel that way about God too. But if we do not, we are not inferior because of that lack. What is required of us is that we love him first with a love of the mind or soul or will, that we prefer his friendship to anything else in the world, that we make him the highest of our values as we love him for what he is. Put negatively again, this means basically a non-consent to mortal sin. Put positively, it is a choice of him and his will whenever it involves the loss of his friendship. For it would be a serious insult to put any creature above him who is God, infinite in all goodness and perfection, and from whom all creation has its existence.

This placing of God first in our lives, and its progressive increase, is spiritual perfection in its most basic concept. By making love the central theme of our spiritual perfection, we are in deep harmony with our essential human perfection. Like nothing else, love gives a sense of worth to our lives, an appreciation of the value of living. It gives us something to live for with a certain healthy wholeheartedness which distinguishes the truly human from the narrow-minded fanatic. Thus, spiritual perfection does not do violence to our human life since it consists essentially in fulfilling the commandment: "Thou shalt love."

Practical Reflection

Have I become so blinded by the merely human that, although I look for perfection and admire it in many ways, I fail to see the pre-eminence of spiritual perfection? In regard to myself, have I become too self-satisfied, too discouraged, or too cynical to desire or hope for any kind of perfection? Can I see now that spiritual perfection, achieved in progressive stages, is not impossible to me despite the distance that separates me from any ideal? Do I see that spiritual perfection is possible for me simply because it is possible for me to love and to love deeply? Am I resolved always to give God the love I am capable of giving here and now, love based on what he is?

CHAPTER 23

"If Anyone Love Me, He Will Keep My Word"
(John 14:23)

To say that spiritual perfection consists essentially in the love of God, and to say nothing further, would not adequately describe perfection. Perfection always refers to some standard of comparison. A perfect musical performance, for instance, would have to conform to the notes and mood of the composer. In spiritual perfection the same need for a standard of comparison is also present, and this we ultimately find in the mind and will of God. The better we measure up to this standard, the more perfect we will be in the sight of him who made us. Love, of course, fits into the picture because it is the way in which we consistently, and for the most part gradually, bring about this oneness with the divine idea.

The idea in God's mind by which we are to measure our perfection has a twofold aspect. One is general and for all. The other, while not contradicting the first, is personal and concerns the individual alone. Our agreement with the general standard or ideal is reached by observing the commandments. But since these are for the most part negative ("Thou shalt not"), God also has a more positive pattern for us to follow. This pattern is made up of the various virtues, and we shall see the most important of these presently. We have also been given a living model of all these commandments and virtues. This model, this perfect model, is Christ our Lord. He will be before us in our detailed discussion of the virtues.

About the particular idea or personal vocation which God has for each individual, not much will be said in this book. One reason for this is the necessity that the beginner clearly see what God fundamentally requires of him. To ask such a man also to grasp the finer details of his life is to invite confusion and discouragement. So it is enough to mention now that one man's way to God will not be exactly like that of another. No man is intended to be an exact copy of another, even of a saint. God has made each of us differently and wants us to remain different, although within reason. Each of us, therefore, has a personal vocation, not only to a state in life, but a vocation to be what we really are, what God made us to be in our personality. Often this personal pattern is not what we imagine it to be when we are beginners. Nor is this fulfillment always what we would have liked in the beginning. But it is the way God has designed us, and our peace can come only when we find that real person or our true self. The general norm is quite easy to find and understand; the commandments and virtues are readily discovered. But the more particular way is not always so apparent. It takes reflection, prayer, some experience, and often guidance before we are able to discern our personal pattern or vocation.

However, the achieving of the general standard and the finding of the individual pattern are not two separate roads to travel. Our perfection as an individual will not be found in a way diverse from our perfection as a man, as a Christian, and as a Catholic. Both aspects of perfection will come about by our conformity to a heavenly norm, to the mind and will of God as we find it in each moment. Our spiritual perfection is quite simply making our choices according to what Christ has told us: "If anyone love me, he will keep my word." (John 14:23)

But we would narrow the completeness of God's action in our lives if we were to restrict the meaning of his "word" only to what is written down in the Scriptures or what comes to us from the Church or from her many wise teachers. Quite surely, as we have said, our perfection will not be diverse from the general way for all, but many times the means God uses will not be general but individual, suited particularly to us. God thus speaks his word through the circumstances and events of our lives, and his will is to be seen in these as much as it is in the sacred pages. A certain abandonment to his will is the path our love must take if we are to grow both in the general way of the virtues and in the way of our spiritual development as an individual.

The spiritual life often has a temptation which is experienced in almost every kind of life: we wish we were in some other circumstances where things would be easier or more to our liking. We long for some peaceful refuge where, for instance, we could pray better, or where there wouldn't be great problems. In a limited number of cases some change of circumstance may be the will of God, especially for those still free to choose their state in life. But for the great majority of us it is not. Nor do these deep roots into the circumstances of our lives come about by chance or accident. God has put us where he wants us, or in other cases he wants us where he finds us. He usually means to bring about our salvation and our spiritual perfection where we are. He wants the love we can give him where we are.

One of the most stabilizing things God has told us about his love for us is his universal providence. Nothing escapes his watchfulness; everything is used for our good. "Now we know that for those who love God all things work together unto good." (Rom. 8:28) We must see his will in all things, either actively bringing about or carefully permitting the events and circumstances which shape our lives. These shape us by his grace into what he wants us to be, into our full spiritual perfection.

The degree of our love should be the degree of our giving of our lives into his hands. And with the giving, our love increases. He is then able to give us the full benefit of his wisdom. Instead of being led by our own shortsightedness, or instead of putting limits to the degree which we allow his wisdom to operate, we open our lives to his action by abandonment to his mind and will. Our joys and our sorrows, our successes and our failures will all be a part of building us up to the full stature of Christ.

We really ought to do even more about the will of God than to conform ourselves to it as perfectly as we can. At present each of us loves God with a certain degree of love, just as he in turn now loves us with that same degree of actual love. (It is in potentiality, as we have said, a potentiality based on what we can become, that God loves each of us immeasurably.) For all of us there is some reason which prevents him from actually loving us more, since it prevents us from loving him more. What is it? Despite all the obvious impediments we may see, there will be at bottom a real fear, a fear to spread our wings and fly off the ledge. It is a fear of what God might ask, a fear of not measuring up to what he wants of us, a fear of failure.

Let us ask God to remove this obstacle, as well as all others in due time, that we might be perfectly conformed to his will. But even now we can tell him that all obstacles are removed already, as far as we can will it. Our will is already conformed to his, as far as we can will it. But the full result is beyond our power. Will he then bring it about, at no matter what cost to us?

This basic prayer we must pray, and not perfunctorily. We must pour ourselves out in this prayer. We must pray and pray and pray. We must beseech and beseech and beseech. Such a gift of God, his total intervention in our lives, is not something we earn by our merits but something we gain by our ceaseless asking.

By following the will of God, we come into contact with God. In fact, we *are* in contact with him. The will of God is not really separated from the whole of God. He cannot be chopped up into parts. He is inseparably a simple being. And so when we are in contact with the will of God, when we see that this or that circumstance, whether good or bad, is the will of God, we are in contact with God himself. And that is a great privilege.

Practical Reflection

Mother of God, in this crucial work of my life, my growing more like your Son, do not forget that my arms are too weak to be held aloft for any long time, that my heart is too inconstant to beat for long with any great desire. This, Mother of God, is where I need you most. Take away my fears, you who know the security of what I shrink from, his overpowering love. Give me your protection and your love that I may have all of his. Give me your faithfulness so that I may not stop until all of God is my own.

PART VI

THE CHARACTERISTICS OF THE TRUE LOVER: THE VIRTUES IN GENERAL

CHAPTER 24

Love and the Virtues

In reading a book, the reader is compelled to go step by step, especially in this kind of book where reflection is the companion of the reading. In such piece-by-piece absorption we may sometimes acquire a temporary misunderstanding, especially if one theme is emphasized, such as the love of God. Certain possible misunderstandings have been opposed at several points in the book and now we are at another of these necessary qualifications. These are best made only after the primary lesson has been well taught. The present qualification has to do with the relation of the love of God to the other virtues.

In the previous pages it may have seemed that the love of God is the only virtue: love God with your whole heart and everything else will fall into place. Things may indeed turn out that way. But love has to know what kind of man to build up. Only a man who is built correctly can love fully and be loved by God in that same measure. This building up of spiritual perfection involves certain required good habits. These good habits go by a special name and are called virtues.

The word virtue does not apply only to one kind of morality, sexual morality, but rather there are as many virtues as there are good moral habits, ranging from cheerfulness to profound humility and total love. The sum of all these good habits is what we call character. Bad habits, on the other hand, are called vices. They are not in themselves sins—sins are always actions—but they are predispositions to sin. A drunkard who has just confessed his sin and is forgiven still has the vice to contend with.

Good habits or virtues are necessary in the spiritual life, just as they are in any good life. A habit is usually a way in which we operate without much effort, and often a way in which we operate with a certain amount of pleasure. Our lives are necessarily filled with habits of all kinds. Just as it would be an impossible situation if we had to begin each day to learn all over again to walk or to eat, so it would be an enormous burden in the spiritual life to have to fight each battle over again each time we came upon a situation involving the commandments. God has made our nature along lines of economy and efficiency by fashioning us so that we form habits which enable us to operate readily and with ease. It is just as difficult for some people to tell a lie as it is for others to tell the truth. Our love, then, has the security implied in these strong habits and can move on to greater love and greater victories.

Love profits by the virtues, but this is not all. In the mutual interaction which is true in so much of human existence, love also is the way in which these good habits are best acquired. Love is not a substitute for the virtues; it is rather their motive power. For instance, love does not lead to the neglect of discipline. It moves and gives meaning to discipline. Discipline by itself can produce an empty spirit, cold and morose. But love never.

Perhaps an example will show how love operates as the best motive for the other virtues. If you had to cook a soup over one flame, you could conceivably go about it in two ways. On the one hand, you could cook the meat separately, then the onions and each of the other ingredients, all separately. But while you were cooking the one, the others would get cool. When you put all the ingredients together, you would have a lukewarm and relatively tasteless soup.

But on the other hand, if you were to cook all the ingredients in the same pot, perhaps giving one more time than another, but still all kept hot over the same one flame, you would in the end have a hot soup and one which would have the characteristic taste of the soup you were planning.

The first way is the way of a man who concentrates on self-perfection; the second is the way of love. By the first way we get a man who is cold or lukewarm, with a certain artificiality about him. By the second we have a oneness of being, and we are warm or hot with the fire of God's love. Love is the best way to acquire and strengthen the virtues.

One of the advantages of having a clear picture of the various virtues is that self-deception is prevented. It is not inconceivable that a man may think that he loves God very much, and still glory in many attitudes and habits that are not acquired by imitation of Christ. We often carry our world with us into the spiritual life. We put on the spiritual life only as a thin, transparent coat through which show the false ideals of our world. Thus a man may proclaim that he loves God, is a loyal layman in the Church, or whatever else spiritual he fancies himself to be, and yet be a caricature of the Christ he should want to mirror.

For instance, such a man may live the world's ideas on masculinity or a woman its ideas on femininity. According to the opinions of the world these ideas are variously synonymous with ruthlessness, physical strength or physical beauty, with sexual power or attraction. But on the contrary we are principally men and women by what makes us human beings at all, our souls. Only to the extent that our souls are ennobled by the virtues are we removed from the animals of the jungle.

We somehow tend to suspect the virtues of being something that they are not, and that they will make us less manly or womanly. The virtues all imply strength, not only the strength of self-control, but often the kind of strength that is easily recognized as such. Our Lord, for instance, was a real man in the sense of masculinity. If he were not, we would find it hard to account for, not only his ability to suffer manfully, but other things such as his courage and presence of mind when he was before Caiphas and Pilate, or when confronted by his enemies in debate. Anyone with less than a strong personality would not have been a leader to a man like Peter, and speaking in all reverence, his humanity would hardly have been a channel of grace to a woman like Magdalene. Truly in Christ, our great example, we see that manliness has everything to do with the virtues.

This tendency to consider the virtues as less than humanly admirable arises because we have various ideas of goodness, and not all of them are correct. For instance, we tend to confuse virtue with temperament. This latter we are born with and it helps to make each of us different from all others. Some have been given a very tranquil temperament by nature, and this is a distinct advantage. These are the "naturally good" people. There have been saints like this; St. Thomas Aquinas seems to have been one of them. But it is equally true that there have been many wishy-washy people like this also. Nothing bothers them very much, provided they are comfortable; neither are they very much concerned about others. They commit no great sins, have no great struggles with temptation, and likewise have no great impulse to anything good except the ordinary. Such persons would be considered by most people as virtuous, simply because they are easy to get along with. But someone who struggles with a nature of fire would not be considered virtuous because he is uncomfortable to us in his failures and also difficult in his success. Our Lord once made a comparison in favor of a certain strong man, John the Baptist, and against the reeds shaken in the wind.

It is another evidence of the manliness of Christ that he recognized and praised the manliness of this other man. John the Baptist, though a young man in his thirties, was not afraid of crowds, nor of politicians nor of kings. He seems to have been liked by soldiers, to have been understanding of sinners, but intolerant of hypocrisy. This admiration by Christ of his precursor is the flat contradiction to those who would make virtue equal to the effete, to a pale weakness, to a comfortable gentility or to a respectable mediocrity.

The virtues are the parts that make up maturity. Immaturity is often shown by a servile conformity to the group. Or an opposite kind of immaturity is shown in the professional rebel. Both of these are like children, and in one way or another most of us have gone through such periods in our lives. But some stay there. Most of us who seek the spiritual life have developed to a point where we act maturely; we act because of the right rather than what the crowd thinks. At the same time we do not become intellectual or spiritual snobs in relation to the group, because we know that the group has many praiseworthy qualities too. But maturity means good habits based not only on something as indefinite as the love of God, nor, surely, on a conscience too ready to follow emotions. Maturity must include a humble desire for the objective truth implied in the virtues as standards of conduct.

In acquiring maturity, we again have the example of Christ, as so many pages of the gospels tell us. He has told us quite clearly that he is the way: "I am the way." (John 14:6) But in our attempt to beome more like him, we must not neglect the example of others who have been successful in this imitation. These are the saints. Now it is true that no man can be a perfect pattern for another, and that in many things the saint is a pattern for no one but himself. But on the other hand their holiness is guaranteed by the Church, and within the limits of our personal vocation they are proposed in general for our imitation. So, allowing always for the differences as to our spiritual condition as beginners, as well as to other innumerable differences, we can see in these men and women how the virtues can be practiced. And this is better than only being told how to practice them, just as we can more easily construct a piece of furniture if we have a picture of it than if we merely had printed directions alone.

John the Baptist was sent to the chosen people to make straight the paths for the Lord. In a true sense this is also our principal work in our own souls. We principally work to remove the obstacles to grace. If these obstacles remain, all our prayers, all our sacrifices, all the sacraments will not bring us to God. Selfishness, bitterness, pride, lukewarmness, injustice, hardness and coldness of heart to our neighbor—these are not admirable qualities, and these are what the virtues are meant to root out and supplant. Only by the virtues do we prepare the way for the Lord in our souls and do it well.

Practical Reflection

Do I now see that the love of God brings order and true maturity into my life only when it operates through all the other virtues? Do I see that Christ is the principal model or the ideal upon which these virtues must be based in my own life, since he is the way? Do I see here how my love and friendship for him will bring about a oneness of myself with the ideal, since one friend tends to become like the other? Not Christ to become like me, but I to become like Christ? And since he is God as well as friend and ideal, will I not now ask him for grace to prepare his way into my heart?

CHAPTER 25

Love Means Peace Means Change

Love and peace are threads interwoven in the fabric that makes up our lives as we would like to have them. Our human nature is so constructed that we cannot help wanting peace, just as we always will want love. Indeed, the only true peace occurs when we are in secure possession of what we love.

The spiritual life is a way to peace principally because it is a way to find love. When we are in possession of God, our hearts and minds are in deepest harmony with our own nature and with the eternal law which says that all things cannot help being made for God. The spiritual life also brings peace by eliminating so many things which disturb our peace. These are the influences both within and without which are not in harmony with our deepest nature, and which we eliminate principally because they are incapable of harmony with deep love of God.

Finally now, the spiritual life brings peace by means of the virtues. It is not enough merely to put off the old man. We must become secure in our possession of God. Strong virtues, by which we put on the new man, are the way to this security. And the stronger and deeper are these good habits, the more ease and even pleasure we generally find in acting according to God's will. How else but by the virtues can we, like Christ, be at peace from excessive inner disturbance caused by things around us? How can we be at peace in misfortunes like illness, financial insecurity, injustice and enmities, and from the pull of the endless number of things we want but never get? Worry, discontent, discouragement, the disturbance at times from an almost irresistible call of evil—all such things are the inevitable consequence of living, and they warn us that only the man of strong and deep virtues can really be at peace.

But here we encounter a mystery: since so many of us know in our hearts that peace can come only by a good life, why do all of us not take the way of the virtues to find peace instead of the ways of unrestrained ambition, greed, or pleasure, which at best give only a temporary illusion of peace? Or why do we live year after year the same fearful, vacillating, or hopeless lives when over the horizon we can live at peace if we will only make the journey?

In looking for a reason for this failure, we can honestly have little argument with the means put at our disposal for the journey. While our situation may not be the best in every detail, we can look around and see others with less who have made a success in the spiritual life. Besides, some of our means have been of the very best—the Mass and the sacraments, for instance. Quite clearly, then, the principal reason for lack of success is not something outside of us, but rather something within.

We often avoid coming to grips with the real issue by laying the blame on something relatively superficial, on some sin or fault, for instance on laziness or lack of patience. But this does not tell us why we keep the sin or fault, or why we neglect to form the opposite good habit.

Undoubtedly there are many answers to this question, but here we shall consider one which is rather basic. It is basic because it involves an attitude of mind rather than any external action. This reason for moral and spiritual failure is the attitude of mind that resists God because it resists change.

It is not so much the tongue that can't stop, the muscles that are lazy, the flesh that is rebellious. It is the attitude of mind and will underneath. For men have had stronger passions, more self-will, have been leading softer lives, and yet have turned to God and become saints. It is the stubborn human will which in the sinner says, "I will not serve," but in the sinner and lukewarm alike says, "I will not change."

When we speak of change, we must hasten to make certain that we are understood: not all change, not just any kind of change. In fact we ought always to question the attitude which lives only for change. The wise man sees that he must have a basic permanence in his life; the tree will not grow unless it has deep roots in good soil. But on the other hand, the tree will not grow if it resists all change. Growth itself implies change.

12. Beginnings

And if the tree is growing poorly, it must be made to grow well. This often implies even great changes.

A certain stagnation of the spirit is the tragedy of many good men and has caused them to stop growing both as human personalities and as spiritual beings whose destiny is God's friendship. They have put limits upon the degree in which he can love them, or they love him. They return only a part of love to him who would give all. Or to put it another way, they have weighed the blood of Christ against the stubbornness or selfishness of a human will.

When we ask who doesn't change, we first think of those who are older in years. We often speak of these people as being set in their ways. Youth is by nature more impressionable. By instinct it realizes the duty to change into responsible adulthood. So when we observe the change from sinner to saint, it is usually a younger person, a Francis of Assisi or an Augustine. The great change often implied in a religious vocation is almost exclusively a phenomenon of youth.

Yet in many cases the old have not lost this ability to change. The prodding of God, the questioning of life, or even failure in life has often brought about a great change of direction and a turning to God. One old man, confined to a bed in a large public institution, had now for some time come back to God after a life of many sins. One evening the chaplain came to his bedside and told him he would bring Holy Communion the next morning. The man's reply was one we would expect only in the life of some saint: "Father," he said quietly, "I can hardly wait."

But we meet others, both young and old, some perhaps who have never known serious sin, who have built a wall resisting the changes that God's love would work. Some are this way from early childhood. Others build the wall slowly during middle age. In fact, the second fall of Christ under the cross is sometimes invoked against this hardening of middle life, which can come by such diverse ways as self-satisfaction or frustration, contentment or deep hurt.

Although unwillingness to change is a basic barrier to God's action in the soul, it is built on still deeper foundations. Some of these foundations can go very deep, and may not be fully known until after many years of the spiritual life. But it will be helpful to look at some of these reasons for resistance to change.

One such reason is fear. This is not the reasonable fear of an imminent danger, such as an angry dog, nor even the openly unreasonable fear, as fear of all dogs. It is the fear born of deep insecurity whereby men do not change because they unconsciously fear that any change will cause an acute uncertainty and a deep, unbearable pain. It is a fear of the unknown which in their insecure state they have no courage to face. This fear will not allow them any deep insight into themselves or their lives because change would disturb the props upon which such an uncertain life is built.

Although such fear is difficult to detect, sometimes effects of it come to the surface. These are the apprehensions and even panic over what one might lose if he gave himself more to God. Instead of pressing on to freedom, this shriveled-up soul tends to suppress the desire for God by an impulsive reaction, often seizing upon some superficial excuse. Or he holds off the decision by too much calculation of the possible loss. The spiritual life, like all true manhood and womanhood, sometimes requires a bit of daring.

Similar to these fearful souls are those who will not change because they have given up the spiritual life out of a certain despair. They have tried, so they tell us, and have gotten nowhere. When the first fervor was on them, they saw the spiritual life as a blaze of glorious light. But darkness always follows day, and so after a while they concluded that the rut must not be such a bad place after all because there are so many in it.

Another reason for resistance to change, and an important one, is pride. A proud man is so in love with his own excellence that he cannot see any reason for change. Although pride seems to be the opposite of fear, many are proud only because they fear. They refuse to look at themselves accurately because of what they may see. So they *demand* an unreal superiority in their opinion of themselves. Quite necessarily then, this kind of person resists real, inner change.

Finally in our limited consideration, there are many who resist change because of pleasure and comfort. Life is filled with so many good things, not always evil, but so many and so much loved that the idea of change is uncomfortable and is quickly brushed into oblivion. There is usually added an element of fear: "What will my friends say if I dare to change the pattern or the code we live by?" And there is always the comforting thought that, even if these things are not so good spiritually, at least they keep boredom away—for the present.

There are undoubtedly many other foundations for resistance to change, but perhaps this much analysis will alert the individual to other causes underlying the barrier to God's invitation to greater love. The spiritual work of a lifetime can easily be the recognition and the full removal of these hidden foundations.

It would perhaps be well, now that we have shown some of the causes of spiritual stagnation, to proceed at once with some counsel for its removal. But there are several reasons against this. In the first place we have already spoken enough about the last cause of resistance to change, that of the love of pleasure and comfort. As to the others, any treatment would encroach upon the next portion of the book, and would try to do in one chapter what must be done in several. In any case, these deep-seated difficulties rarely have a quick, sure remedy, outside of a very special grace from God. But this is not to say that there is no sure remedy. There is one which can transform anybody no matter what kind of resistance, no matter how deep.

Is it too simple a solution to suggest that all the foundation of our resistance to change can best be dissolved by love of God? Although we must employ other considerations, as we will in discussing each virtue, is not love the most effective way to supplant the bad by the good? In the case of fear, is it not true that "perfect love casts out fear" (I John 4:18), even, eventually, the fears we do not know of or understand? We come to love enough to look at God and not at the uncertainties. And for the despairing, will not despair disappear in the hope that true love always brings? The proud man, is he not moved by love when no other force can move him? And to those who are so much with the world, is not love the treasure that can make all else in this world seem worthless?

Any change in the moral and spiritual life means the substitution of bad habits by good ones, that is, by the virtues. Again it is love of God which will be our greatest motive power to increase these virtues. From one point of view they increase along with our love of God, and this is the same as saying that they increase along with our closeness to God as measured by our degree of sanctifying grace. From another point of view, however, the virtues become stronger by repetition just as any habit becomes stronger by repetition. We make the proper choices, and we make them with the right intention and with what determination is available. We learn to select one virtue at a time for special emphasis. Thus over the years the deep and complete transformation into Christ takes place. We then find that the path of the virtues is in the long run the easier way, and at many times in life we will pause to thank God because it is also the happier way.

All who resist change must see this resistance for the evil which it is. It isn't just some law or rule we aren't obeying or some spiritual counsel we aren't following. It is a real rejection of real love. We are rejecting in whole or in part the love of God, who loves us enough to have died for us. God somehow yearns for our love, yearns to love us. These are human words, words inadequate to express the intensity of God's desires. He yearns to possess us, poor as we are, and therefore he yearns to change us.

What does changing mean? Quite simply it means letting God have his way. God has a plan for each of us personally, a plan which involves our perfection and our happiness. Only he knows all the changes he must make in order to bring us to that perfection and that happiness. But he doesn't want all changes all at once. Only the next one, the one he has been waiting for. Paradoxically, this change is often not the one we fear it might be. But what he wants most of all is in the end the most practical thing of all, a change of attitude. For we tend to be as we think. We must believe deeply that we must change, that there is much need for change. If we don't believe this deeply, we should ask for the belief. And we can ask to see and carry out the next change he wants of us. Such prayers are always answered.

Readiness to change is something of what it means to be like children, children as our Lord referred to them in the gospels. Children are impressionable; they are subject to change. When we are always open to God's action, we are the closest we can get to eternal youth. Even more than that: "He who humbles himself as this little child, he is the greater in the kingdom of heaven." (Matt. 18:4)

Practical Reflection

Since I cannot ever love you enough, I must never think that I have changed enough. Shall I continue to waste my life, just because I always have? Shall I leave praying to the priests and sisters, and be satisfied with the minimum, just because I always have? Why should I only half-live, in fear or despair, when the way of change is the way to life? Instead of crying out in some disappointment or sorrow, "Why does God do this to *me?*" I will try to see that you are trying to change me because you want me.

CHAPTER 26

The Second Chances

How well God does things if we only let him! We say this either by the conviction of faith or in the enthusiasm over some evident favor. Nevertheless our lives are a constant battle against the doubt of this evident principle. We find it difficult to accept wholeheartedly the simple truth that God's way is best. Perhaps our blindness can be cured by looking at God's masterpiece among humans, where his will and his plan had no interior obstacle. This was the case with her who is the most perfect of the merely human beings, Mary, the Mother of the God-man.

We have come to accept her so much as the fulfillment of all that is best in human nature that we forget easily that she had a human nature. Even a sinless human nature is still a human nature; there were limitations upon her nature just as there were upon the nature she gave to her Son who knew human sadness and human fear in the Garden. We look at her in the glorification of her assumption into heaven and we murmur: "How well God does things!" But we must see also that the triumphant end of God's plan for her came only at the price of constant assent to his plan all along the way, and that many times the price came hard for human nature.

We are so familiar with her standing at the foot of the cross that we forget that this was only a part of the assent she had to make to God's plan. It was a culmination, if you wish. But no such culmination is successfully arrived at without the discipline of much previous assent. We get so used to thinking of her in terms of her statue that we forget that she was never a statue. She sometimes found it hard to do God's will, just as we do, just as her Son did when he prayed, "Father, if it is possible, let this cup pass away from me." (Matt. 26:39) She could have rebelled against God's will many times, and at other times her courage might have left her.

For instance, as a girl she knew by some way that God intended her to remain a virgin. Yet she was also expected by Jewish custom to be married. It takes little insight to see that here was a source of deep conflict. Yet later in her conversation with the angel she showed no vacillation or uneasiness.

Then when she was carrying the child within her, she saw the growing suspicion in the eyes of her husband. No one but Joseph knew that the child was not his. Even in her anguish Mary saw the foolishness of telling him that the child was by the Holy Spirit. She had the quiet balance to wait for God to deliver her from a situation for which he was responsible. But her reasonable conduct in no way minimizes what it must have cost. In Nazareth, Mary probably had many agonies in the Garden.

There are other times when she could have rebelled or lost courage: the journey into a hostile land to begin a life among strangers, the fear of a repetition at any time of the slaughter of the Holy Innocents, the death of Joseph, the final departure of her Son for the life of a wandering and misunderstood teacher, her fears for him, and then the final disgrace and death on the cross—not to mention his ultimate departure at the ascension. Mary's own triumph is made up of all these. Her glory is that she kept on saying yes to God all her life. That was the way she could have her triumph, because she allowed God to have his way. The plan was his plan from beginning to end.

The truth is that, being human, she might have spoiled it. She might have said, "Virginity is too hard for me under these circumstances." "The trip is too dangerous." "Why doesn't God work a miracle to protect us instead?" "My son is too dear to me to see him suffer." "Too young to die."

Then there is the ordinariness of her life which again we forget. Just as the human nature of Christ was fatigued physically and emotionally by the enthusiasm of crowds whose interest was in material things, so with Mary, who lived in a human situation which must have known similar frustrations. This was a remarkable and talented woman doing nothing but housework in a small town. God had made her with a vocation for the whole world; people like that usually know it. When we say that her love for Jesus and Joseph made her content, we are uttering a truism. But contentment and even at times joy does not rule out the agonies of a forced impotence when there were wider areas with needs which she was made to help.

This trial of forced limitation may easily have been the same as the trial of every talented person whose world is blocked out by four walls. If we translate this situation to our own times, we can more easily imagine the words of complaint which might have arisen if she had been another kind of woman: "God's law is too hard. This is a modern world. I must have my freedom. I won't be tied down to a small house in a small town. Just a carpenter's wife? I want a career. I need a social career. After all, there was royalty in my background, you know. And besides, what will people think if I try to follow God's plan to the full? Think of the names they will call me: fanatic, killjoy, prudish, old-fashioned."—as she probably was called in ancient equivalent when she would refuse to waste time in gossip at the town well.

But Mary never uttered such words. She was obedient, kept on saying yes to God, and is now radiantly joyful in her glory. Whatever were her trials, both the obvious ones and the hidden ones, the pages of the New Testament do not give us the impression that she was nervous, fearful, or restless (despite the volatility of Middle Eastern women). Rather she was calmly, trustingly at peace.

God has his plan for each one of us. The beginning of the plan was from all eternity. His design for the universe had our particular place in it. The end of that plan is in endless happiness. We like that; we hope for it. But it is in the details of the plan that we find things hard and disagreeable. We want always to enjoy life, to have our own way. Yet for the perfect plan God must have his way. Mary's life should therefore be an encouragement. We sometimes hear people talking as if her life were an impossible ideal. But what is impossible about a life that was monotonous in its ordinariness and was more than acquainted with suffering? Mary knew God's love and wisdom; he asked, and that was enough. She did essentially only what we have to do, to keep on saying yes to God.

When we speak of God's plan, however, we often feel a deep, though hidden despair which eats at the roots of the spiritual life and blocks God's way with us. Many of us, perhaps all of us, have made a failure of God's plan in numerous small ways, if not in great ways. As a result, any words about God's plan are understood with the mind but not with the heart. Such people will go on; they will say their prayers, do their duty. But it is too late to hope for more than final perseverance, a peaceful death, then purgatory and—with a sigh of relief at having got there at all—some obscure place in heaven.

The tragedy of such people is that they have forgotten a great truth about God. He is an all-powerful God. His power is not limited even by our failures. Therefore he is able to make a great success of our lives, no matter what we have done with his plan up to now. And he is still able to put us into that place in heaven which he intended from all eternity.

In his unlimited resourcefulness he is different from his creatures. For instance, there are great generals who can devise a remarkable plan of battle but fail because of some unforeseen difficulty on the battlefield. The errors of the great generals on both sides at Waterloo bear this out. But God is not limited either by his knowledge or by his power to command effectively. If we fail him, he can still start us all over again at any time. And remarkably, he can still always produce a plan in many ways better than the first one he had for us. This is the answer to the mystery of God's permitting evil: he can always draw a greater good from it.

There is an old proverb: "God writes straight with crooked lines." He takes our failures, our rebellions, our sins, and he writes a more beautiful page because of them. It is indeed a beautiful thing not to have sinned. But who will say that it is not a harder thing, and in some sense a more glorious thing, that, having tasted the forbidden delights, a man should make his way back to God—and more than merely make his way back?

Although it is never too late to start on God's revised plan, some refuse these second chances out of a certain false pride. Because they cannot give God a perfect gift, so they say, they will give him none. And yet God sees the second gift also as a perfect gift; it is a perfect gift honoring his merciful fatherhood. And it is the kind of gift that gives most meaning to the Son's gift on the cross. As a matter of fact, such proud people can see God or themselves clearly only through the failures or sins involved in the second gift. Instead of the "masterpiece" of a life stunted by arid self-admiration, their renewed souls are now humbled enough to find the true God for the first time.

There are others who will not take the steps back into God's plan because of a certain sense of futility. They feel that they could never become the giants whom we are accustomed to use as examples to encourage them: St. Mary Magdalene, St. Teresa of Avila, St. Paul, or St. Augustine—all of whom spoiled God's original plan for them. Yet God loves and wants the little people also. And as for examples, there is probably not a parish in the world which does not have respected members who are very close to God now, but once had been greatly otherwise.

There is an outstanding example of what God can do to an ordinary person. The good thief on the cross does not seem to have been cast in the heroic mold. He was not a popular hero like Barabbas. Even if he had led a good life, he might never have been more than a good husband and father, and perhaps a successful merchant. Instead he became a thief and probably not a very effective one at that. But at the last moment he again caught hold of God's plan: he did a kind thing and he had faith. And God made more from that moment than if he had never sinned. As a result of this one man, all humanity, even the most abandoned of humanity, now knows that God never gives up.

God loves and wants ordinary people very much. They are dear to him, as even are the giants, principally because of the Son who died for all. They are dear to him also because of the great good he sees in them, good even where they themselves see no good. And, as with the good thief they are dear to him because of the work he can accomplish through them. Ordinary people can reach many souls which the giants will never notice.

But we must be careful even of examples like the good thief. We must never give the impression that the renewal of God's plan in our lives is principally to help others. God's first consideration is usually the love for each soul. This is true despite the fact that, for most of us, our lives will be outwardly ordinary as Mary's was. Inwardly they will be changed and inwardly is the way God sees them. Another example will help.

In this country there is a motherhouse of sisters who found it necessary to move the graves in the sisters' cemetery to make room for new construction. Among the bodies moved, two were found to be incorrupt. The community, surely by insight into God's purposes, has made no attempt to initiate a cult to these two sisters. God's miraculous and extraordinary approval of two unknown lives is an encouragement for us who will also be forgotten by the pages of history. They are a powerful example of the eternal regard which God has for lives whose worth is hidden in the depths of his heart.

The way to turn to God, to his renewed plan, is principally by love. This is the most important part of any of his plans. It was love that made Mary say her everlasting yes to God's asking. If we love and continue to love, if we ask and continue asking, we will see by experience that for us there is always a second chance, and if need be, many second chances. We can begin over again as many times as we will begin saying yes to God.

Practical Reflection

Have I not been living under the false assumption that my sins have condemned me to live on the borders of God's love instead of deep in his heart? or perhaps my many wasted graces? or the lack of anything extraordinary in my life? Do I not see now that such an attitude is derogatory to certain infinities of God, such as his endless mercy, his power, his endless ability to plan anew? Will I not now start over with a renewed hope, and set myself to the serious examination of the virtues which will change my life and make it successful because of God's ever-available second chances?

PART VII

THE COMPANIONS OF LOVE: SOME VIRTUES IN PARTICULAR

CHAPTER 27

Loving One Another

Our Lord does not specify uselessly that the great commandments are two in number. For it is neither sufficient to love neighbor without loving God nor sufficient to love God without loving neighbor. In the first category we find those who do well to men but neglect what is owed to God. Wisely, then, does our Lord insist that love of God "is the greatest and the first commandment." (Matt. 22:38) Similarly, in the Ten Commandments the duties to God are enumerated first. And he expects us to observe all ten, not any lesser number at our choice.

While these people of the first category are outsiders to the spiritual life, those of the second claim not to be. Yet in claiming to love God, they forget or neglect to love their neighbor, and thus they do a great disservice to the cause of God. With these it is not usually so much a hatred of neighbor as an obliviousness of him and his rights or needs. But of course this is a contradiction: "For how can he who does not love his brother, whom he sees, love God, whom he does not see?" (I John 4:20) St. John is intimating that their love is self-deception, self-love masquerading under a disguise that is often apparent to all except themselves.

Our usually gentle Lord is even more stern. In his parable-description of the last judgment, he speaks terrifying words to those on his left hand: "Depart from me, accursed ones, into the everlasting fire." (Matt. 25:41) And the reason for this eternal rejection is a lack of practical love: "As long as you did not do it for one of these least ones, you did not do it for me." (v. 45) Truly then, love of neighbor is not merely a praiseworthy thing to have, but a serious command to be obeyed.

However, there is something about love which makes it seem alien to obligation; we do not like to think of ourselves as being *obliged* to love. We would rather think of it as a free act of a generous heart, and this is the way God would have it too. But God has the problem of what to do with those who refuse to love. The employer in another parable could not be unresponsive when one servant refused to forgive the small debt of another servant, when just previously the employer had forgiven this first one a much larger debt. (Matt. 18:21–35) To be unresponsive would be irresponsible, and God cannot be that kind of God, nor could we love that kind of God.

Because our ordinary language is not as precise as that of a theologian, we often speak of love of neighbor in a broader sense than he would. Whereas we would with good reason accuse both a miser and a swindler of lack of love of neighbor, the theologian would distinguish between violations of two separate virtues. He would agree that the miser would probably be guilty of a lack of love, or in precise terms, guilty of many sins against the virtue of charity. But he would accuse the swindler of a violation of the virtue of justice. These two virtues are often confused, and it will help our understanding of a true spiritual life if we see the fundamental place of the virtue of justice.

In relation of one virtue to another, justice is more basic than charity. No amount of charity can compensate for a real deficiency in treating a man justly. Justice means that we must respect another man's rights to what is his—for instance, to his life, reputation, and property. The virtue of charity, on the other hand, means that I must give to another what is mine, even though he has no strict right to it. For instance, I must give him of my time and effort by throwing him a rope when he is drowning. In a violation of either virtue we can have sin, serious or not depending on the circumstances. But when it is a question of justice, there is an obligation of restitution whenever possible. In charity, strictly speaking, there is not.

In our discussion of love of neighbor, we shall usually not make the distinction between these two virtues because our first impression is true: a man who sins against justice isn't showing love for his neighbor. Besides, in this book we are not trying to assess precise guilt, but rather to persuade to every manner of right conduct. Nor, incidentally, shall we attempt to describe all the situations in which we ought to observe love for our neighbor. Rather we will explain why and how in enough detail so that anyone can apply these ideas to the situations of his own life.

But the question must now arise: what kind of love? or what is this love? Obviously a man is not expected to feel the same thing toward a stranger on the other side of the world as he would for his wife, son, or daughter. So, just as our love of God does not need to be an emotional love, true love of neighbor need not be emotional either.

On the other hand, some try to water down this love into something that isn't love at all. We often hear that this love is nothing more than good will toward all men: we wish others well. But St. Thomas sees this as an inadequate minimum of response to the command to love our neighbor. Good will is indeed a part of this love, but God would have us give a love that is really love. "It means a certain union of the heart between the one loving and the one loved, inasmuch as the one loving considers the one loved to be in a certain way one with him, or belonging to him, and thus he goes out toward him. But good will . . . does not presuppose this union of the heart with him." (II, II; 27; 2)

We may then ask what we can find in every person in this world which makes us one with him so that we can truly love him and thus fulfill the great commandment. The most obvious oneness is human nature. We are all, in this natural sense, brothers. But such a love would be most difficult to sustain in practice, especially since the nature we share is a fallen nature and brings in enormous impediments between the love of man for man. Many have distorted this beautiful human nature into something alien if not monstrous. On the other hand, God wants us to love more people than those we just happen to find attractive or agreeable, as he told us in the Sermon on the Mount: "If you love those who love you, what merit have you?" (Luke 6:32) Even sinners, he tells us, do this. It would seem, then, that we are asked to do something which is very difficult, something above our nature, and therefore we should seek this oneness with mankind also in something above our nature.

We find this oneness which is the basis of our love for all

13. Beginnings

men in something above the natural, though not excluding it. We are to love both God and neighbor, but not with two separate kinds of love. God is loved because of himself. Our neighbor is loved in some manner because of God.

This loving another because of God can be seen under various aspects. One of these is the fatherhood of God. Just as we feel close to the children of a friend, if only because they are the children of a friend, so we have a oneness with all men because all men are his children, although not always good ones. Yet even these can still become good, even very good, and we must love them as long as they are capable of becoming so, that is, as long as they have not put themselves outside the love of God forever.

All the more should we love those who more fully mirror what this Father is like. And this is another acceptable aspect our love may take. What we see in those who are truthful, loving, helpful, and courageous are qualities which make them like God and thus, objectively speaking, deserve from us more of this divine kind of love.

But God has devised our human nature with ties that bind some people to us more than others; our relations by blood and marriage, our friends and acquaintances, our fellow countrymen are prominent examples. These relationships are facts produced by the providence of God, and they demand that, all things being equal, we love men in special relationships to us with more love than we love others.

But there is no one who is outside our love. If these reasons are not enough for us to love the most repulsive or undeserving of men, surely the blood of Christ should plead for us to love all his brothers. It was shed for all without exception. Besides, if we face the truth, we see that any goodness we have has come from God more than from ourselves. The help he has given us does not give us the right to despise other men. In sober gratitude we should want his mercy for all men.

There is one person whom we must love who is apt to be forgotten in spiritual books, and that is ourself. Our Lord commanded us to love our neighbor *as ourself*. Obviously then, he wants us to love ourselves. It is true that self-love is the cause of most of our sins, and ultimately of all the real evil in the world. But by this we must always understand immoderate self-love, the love that chooses itself more or less exclusively instead of being one with the love of God and neighbor. Self-love is so often spoken of as evil that we shall rather use here the expressions, love of self or love of the self.

But a true love of the self is not only a commanded thing; it is something put into our nature by God the creator. This natural love takes on an even more noble note when we love ourselves for what God has made us: in his image, adopted as his children, worthy to have been paid for by the blood of his Son. If we are to love others because we must love all that God loves, then surely we ourselves must love ourselves deeply for that same reason.

Just as God loves us as he has made us, so we are to love ourselves both as to soul and body—the soul obviously more than the body, but never love of soul and hatred of body. As with all other things our love of the body must be in accord with the greater love of God and not in ways that take us away from God, as we have said in earlier chapters.

Love of neighbor is sometimes made unrealistic by those who would demand too much, in this case demand that we love our neighbor more than ourselves. This is contrary to our nature, and in extreme cases these "selfless" people turn out to be people without a self. God did not tell us to love our neighbor more than ourselves, but *as* ourselves, using the love of ourselves as an image of the love we must have toward our neighbor. But just as an image in a mirror never has the same brightness as the reality, so we should love ourselves with a stronger love than that with which we love others.

But this fact should not produce selfish people who make all the choices in their own favor. A true love of self means that we will love ourselves according to the higher things, the thing of the spirit rather than those of the body, although we usually ought not neglect the body either. Therefore, for instance, if there are two unequal pieces of meat on a platter and two equally important appetites to be filled, we ought to choose for ourselves the poorer piece, thus preferring the higher and nobler thing for ourselves. In rare cases we may be asked by God, or sometimes by God and country, to make such a choice in something that pertains to the perfection of love: "Greater love than this no one has, that one lay down his life for his friends," (John 15:13) after the example of Christ who gave his life for our freedom.

Practical Reflection

What I have perhaps avoided all along, must now become a foundation for my life, that my love for others cannot be wholly determined by my likes or attractions, much less by my dislikes or prejudices. To be perfect as my heavenly Father is perfect I must love all men in some manner as he does, with some kind of love. My oneness with Christ, my elder brother, must gradually transform my heart into his kind of heart, whose love knows no boundaries or limits, even that of death. Although I recognize the force and consequences of a command to love, I will try to love, not by being constrained to love, but freely, from a heart grateful and hopeful for the love God has for me.

CHAPTER 28

Love in Thought

One of the recurring problems of the spiritual life is to keep the various parts of spiritual perfection in perspective. Certain elements of the spiritual life will be more attractive to one man than to another, or one part may be earnestly urged on him more than another part. So it is important to keep first what the word of God puts first: "The greatest of these is charity," (I Cor. 13:13) by which is meant, of course, the love of God and neighbor. All other parts of the spiritual life, no matter how appealing, are secondary to this.

Enough has been said about love of God to make some people want to express this love humanly, that is, to want to give it some external reality. We want to do for God what we want to do for anyone we love deeply—and here we meet a disappointing impossibility. God is the only one who doesn't need anything. Even his happiness is complete in the oneness of the three Divine Persons.

But our search for a human fulfillment of our love has not escaped the planning of God, who knows this need in our nature. He has given us a way to do for him by doing for others. Our Lord's words are familiar: "As long as you did it for one of these, the least of my brethren, you did it for me." (Matt. 25:40) In God's making his Son to be our brother, and in the brother's willingness to identify himself with even the worst of us, we find that God counts what we do for others as if we were doing it for him. We should therefore almost tremble with reverence in the face of the needs of our neighbor.

When we think of doing something for God through our

neighbor, we most often think of deeds. This is so true that the name of the virtue of love of God and neighbor, which is charity, has come to mean in common language little more than deeds. But deeds, though extremely important, are not enough. In fact one of the popes, Innocent XI, proscribed two theological opinions which tried to change the clear teaching of the gospel. These wrongly said that we could satisfy the command of loving our neighbor by external acts alone, and that we were not held to love our neighbor by a real, internal love. On the contrary, the command to love our neighbor must be fulfilled not only with our deeds or words, but also with our hearts.

Our love, as we have said, must be more than just wishing well to another. On the other hand, we must not demand too much of this love; we must not require that it be the same in degree or the same emotionally as it is for those who are close to us. The solution seems to be found in going back to God's command, that we love our neighbor as ourselves. Now few of us love ourselves with any great emotional love, except perhaps on rare occasions of insight. But we do have an abiding, inseparable care and interest in ourselves, in our point of view, and in our own welfare. What God is asking of us is that we apply some degree of this same concern to others. This, of course, is most easily done in the matter of external actions, but it is true of our thoughts and desires also. And if it is not deeply true of our thoughts and desires, we are not likely to do much external good to our neighbor either.

It is necessary to enter somehow into the spiritual person of our neighbor. We must in some way feel things in the way he is feeling them. God tells us this in the words of St. Paul: "Rejoice with those who rejoice; weep with those who weep. Be of one mind toward one another." (Rom. 12:15, 16)

This oneness of mind with our neighbor does not mean that we become less ourselves, as if we were to adopt all the opinions and feelings of another, or give them an equality with deeply held opinions and feelings of our own. This would become an anarchy of relativism, by which we would agree that the opinion of one man is no better than that of the next. A true love of another means that we will appreciate why he feels this way, even when we cannot agree with him, even when we cannot help him.

We become one with the spirit of another by a feeling for his happiness. We are glad because he is happy; we sincerely tell him so, and we allow him to tell us about it. Sometimes, let it be said here, the greatest gift we can bestow on another is the moments of our time which we give in listening.

This same understanding of how things feel in another person must be true of love in the face of suffering. The painful suffering of some old woman in a hospital does not hurt me physically. But in some manner I must appreciate the fact that pain means just as much to this unfortunate as it would to me. And if I love her as I do myself, I should try to do something about it, even if I can do no more than say a kind word, just as I would want someone to do at least that much for me— and as we all should want to do that much for Christ in any similar situation.

This spiritual entering into the mind of another by seeing things affect him as if they were affecting ourselves is one of the most difficult of Christian disciplines. We can do this readily enough for those who are close to us in affection or in some family relationship. But it does not usually come readily for strangers, much less for those who do not appeal to us or for whom we have an aversion. Yet if we consider that we are not asked to do this with spontaneous feeling or emotion, but rather as something willed with love for the Christ who has made himself one with this neighbor, the impossible can sometimes become an ordinary fact.

How much better to make this effort and to ask for this grace than to embitter our lives and to narrow all happiness out of them by hatred, envy, and jealousy. Our Lord found it more difficult to reach such people than he did those who committed more shameful sins. Hatred shuts out love by its very definition. Envy and jealousy are so far from love that they are a sadness or resentment because of another's good fortune. And yet, provided no clear rights have been violated in acquiring this good fortune, should we not rejoice with our neighbor as we would surely rejoice over ourselves if we received similar good fortune, even if not entirely deserved? God has many gifts and he gives according to his wisdom, love, and mercy. We cannot expect all good gifts, and neither can our neighbor. But when God gives to him at a time he does not give to me, must I be like a spoiled child who has to be placated with a gift on the birthday of another child in the family? Love means loving our neighbor even in his good fortune.

A particular difficulty in loving in thought has to do with our judgments. In the Sermon on the Mount our Lord warned us, even threatened us about these: "Do not judge, that you may not be judged." (Matt. 7:1) In seeking his true meaning here, we must be careful to avoid any extreme interpretation. He does not condemn those whose duty it is to judge; in fact he even affirmed the judging power in Pilate: "Thou wouldst have no power at all over me were it not given thee from above." (John 19:11) We can easily see the consequences to family and society if we were unrealistic about our Lord's command not to judge.

It is equally true that our Lord does not want us to do away with our intelligence in order to obey this command. If, for instance, we heard screams and angry voices in the house next door, we would not have to assume that the occupants were merely practicing for a play. In this matter there is also a middle ground between an adverse judgment and the presumption of good, and this is suspicion. Whereas judgment means that I affirm something of another with some certitude, suspicion means that I have a prudent doubt. A woman, therefore, may not *judge* evil in a man who seems to be following her on the street at night, but she may have a reasonable suspicion, and may act on this. In short, a certain caution in our dealings with others is a part of a love of self which God expects us to follow. St. Paul surely gives us no example of accepting everybody on face value, as a reading of the epistles will readily show.

It is well also to note that it is primarily *rash* judgments which are sinful. These are judgments of some moral defect which are made without sufficient reason. Of course, in order for these to be sinful, we must be aware that our reasons are insufficient for a judgment, and yet we assent to the judgment none the less. While such awareness almost never takes place in practice, we should learn to control thoughts which, contrary to the love God would see in us, are too ready to condemn. Our love for our neighbor should dispose us to see good rather than to see evil, as we indeed want him to think toward us.

If we are not to do violence to our intelligence and also if we are to live with a certain necessary caution, we will find ourselves forced to assent to certain judgments or suspicions. But still we ought never attempt to assess the guilt of the person before God. Only God knows by what lights, or lack of them, this person is operating. Our judgments and suspicions, when necessary, should always go hand in hand with a prayer for this person who may need graces which only our prayers can bring him. It is not rare in the lives of the saints that we see such prayers thus rewarded. Indeed, God may even be permitting some evil to be done to us so that a greater good can come about through a heroic love of neighbor. "Pray for those who persecute and calumniate you," thus did our Lord teach us on the Mount. (Matt. 5:44)

Our Lord specifically warned us of his displeasure with this sin against love of neighbor. He has even implied an equivalent penalty: "For with what judgment you judge, you shall be judged." (Matt. 7:2) Although the worst penalty of all is, of course, the consequences of sin in our souls, he is not limited to the unseen and to the next world in his chastisements. One of the most frequent penalties is to allow us to find ourselves guilty of the same thing we judge in another. St. Paul long ago noted this: "Wherein thou judgest another, thou dost condemn thyself. For thou who judgest dost the same things thyself." (Rom. 2:1) Such self-revelation is given, not for our confusion, but for our correction. It is a warning that our love must be real love, and that we must judge others with the same understanding and tolerance with which we want them to judge us.

Our relationship to God is determined greatly by our relationship to our neighbor. "With what measure you measure, it will be measured to you" (Matt. 7:2)—not only as to our measuring in word and deed, but also in thought. And from this also we can see that no one is excluded from closeness to God. For, love of God and closeness to God are measured by no better measure than our love for our neighbor.

Practical Reflection

Can I now look into my heart honestly, O my God, to see how much I love my neighbor for your sake instead of merely being moved by my likes and dislikes, my repugnances and my prejudices? If I learn to see his person affected in the same way by pain and joy as is my own, will I then not feel compassion for his pain, sorrow, and misery, and be pleased over his good fortune, as I would my own? Will I not now try to give him the benefit of every reasonable doubt, at least in judging him as he must appear before you, his judge and mine, who alone reads men's hearts? Can I not, because of my love for others, then expect more mercy, protection, and love from you?

CHAPTER 29

Love in Word

Only one of the Ten Commandments has to do with our speech and our neighbor, the prohibition of false testimony against him. But this by no means exhausts the desires of God in regard to our speech. The Ten Commandments are focal points for other parts of human conduct which are right or wrong for the same reason as the specific commandment. If God did not reduce these to ten, there would have to be thousands of commandments. Ten is easier to remember.

It is also obvious that in specifying the worse sin, God does not mean to excuse the lesser. Yet people who would never knowingly tell a lie about another will excuse their derogatory talk with the protestation: "But it's true."

But is it? Often enough we aren't very sure, not sure at all. All we know is that we've heard it from someone else, and that here and now it somehow makes us feel very big and important to be passing on this rotten and stinking morsel. And just as long as we feel important, or we have a chance to even up our resentments or our jealousies or our secret envy, we eagerly accept as truth what may at best be a distortion of the truth, as distorted as the minds and tongues that have brought it to us. This lack of love we show to someone whom Christ loved enough to shed his blood.

We often describe this kind of talk as uncharitable speech. Many times it is something deeper than that. It can also be a matter of justice, not only when it is a lie, but even when it is clearly the truth. Justice is violated whenever something that belongs to our neighbor is taken away from him, and here we take something very precious, his good name or reputation.

But we try to excuse ourselves; since the matter is true, we are not taking anything away from our neighbor. In many cases the contrary is true. As long as he does not publicly do wrong in such a manner as to destroy his good name, this inestimable treasure is still intact. We may not destroy it *without a sufficiently grave reason*. A mere desire to tell someone is not a sufficient reason.

An example will help us to understand this. If you lived next door to a very respectable judge, and you happened to discover that he often became privately drunk on weekends, you are not allowed to make this fact a matter of conversation. (We are presuming that the judge is able to conduct himself in court with dignity and fairness despite his drinking.) It would be a different situation, however, if he were proposing marriage to one of your friends. Then you would be allowed, even be obliged, to tell about the excessive drinking.

Now of course, good people know all this. So in order to speak against their neighbor, they have to use subterfuges. Here are a few of them. The first is shock or moral indignation: "Do you know what I saw (heard) (received in a letter)?" Another is: "We must pray very hard for so-and-so." And then there is the double-edged dagger: "You're a friend of so-and-so, aren't you? Is what I heard really true?" Then, of course, there are those people who somehow are public property. Everybody talks about them, and so it can't be wrong to add our bit to the avalanche.

It is sometimes thought that anything to do with gossiping must apply much more to women than to men. The truth is that women do talk more than men, but what they talk about in respect to their neighbor is often trivialities—though by no means always. On the other hand, when men are guilty of the sin of detraction, it is often more serious. The recounting of acts of sexual immorality, for instance, related by a man who must prove his masculinity by bragging about his conquests, are sometimes taken lightly by all—except God and the unfortunate woman whose private indiscretions have resulted in an irreparable loss of reputation.

We must never think that losing our good name is a small thing. We might ask how we would feel to be despised in our neighborhood or place of employment, to know that others were talking behind our back, making conversation over our alleged sins. If we can acquire this insight, we will see that there are many things we would give up rather than the respect of other people.

If our sin of speech has concerned a matter of justice, then of course we must restore what we have stolen. This fact should make us pause even if love does not. In a sense, the duty of restitution is more difficult when ours is a sin of detraction (when we have taken away the good name by telling the truth but without sufficient reason) than it is for calumny (when it is a lie). If it were a lie, our admission of it, damaging though it may be to us, has a chance of restoring the lost treasure. But if it is the truth, we cannot deny it, so how then can we give back what we have destroyed without need? The best we may be able to do is to pray for the person and to be on our guard to speak well of him, thus to atone for our impoverishment of him.

Besides situations in which there is a sufficient reason for revealing the sin of another, it is generally said that we may speak without sin about such things when they are already public property. Thus to say that Stalin or Hitler were butchers of men would not be sinful, although it must be pointed out that men in public life have a right to our careful judgment. Often our judgments are based on hearsay, prejudice, or party factionalism.

Yet even when something is public property, we do not fully escape the requirement to control our tongue. If we do not, we may go from safe territory to forbidden territory before we know it. Besides, our Lord has told us that we will be accountable to him for every idle word. (Matt. 12:36, 37) And it is not befitting to the children of God to make the known faults of another the occasion for idle talk.

This kind of talk is properly called uncharitable (although there are other kinds also, such as speaking rudely to a person). Sometimes, however, even uncharitable talk can have a deadly effect on our neighbor. There are some unfortunate people who have sunk lower in life than they want but who stay there because the way back is made so very difficult. The weight of the talk which continually goes on is so heavy that they find it impossible to rise even when they want to. It seems to be expected of them to remain what they are. Added to this is the knowledge that it is the "good" people who are doing the talking. May God himself have mercy on such unfortunates upon whom his friends have none.

But are such good people his friends? Surely not as much as they think. St. James is a very outspoken man on the subject: "If anyone thinks himself to be religious, not restraining his tongue but deceiving his own heart, that man's religion is vain." (James 1:26) "One who thinks himself to be religious," who goes to church every Sunday, perhaps every day, who says many prayers, reads many spiritual books, but still, note, only *thinks* himself to be religious.

But hear God's judgment on such a man as spoken by the Holy Spirit through the apostle: "That man's religion is vain." The significance of this is incalculable: the hours spent on his knees, the long list of Masses attended and Communions received, the sermons listened to, the books read—all, God tells him, in vain because, "deceiving his own heart," he thought he could love God without really loving his neighbor.

God in some way loves everyone. This should change our thinking about others. The same personal relationship which we take for granted between God and ourselves, every other human being has a right to take for granted between God and himself. Everyone is important to God. Now, a certain quality of motherhood is in God, since all things came from him. Would you then hurt what is dear to this kind of God? Would you, for instance, hurt someone else's child, especially if the parent were strong enough to punish you for it? God takes the part of those whom we offend by thought, word, deed, or omission against charity and justice. These are God's own children you are treating that way. Even in this life he avenges them, avenges them at least by the denial of many graces we would otherwise have from him.

Thus far we have been speaking negatively, and of course necessarily so. But love of others is not so much expressed by avoiding what is offensive as by positively showing our love. Looking at our neighbor as we look at ourselves, we would want others not only to avoid what is harmful to us, but to think well of us and speak well of us. We would want them, for instance, to excuse what seem to be our faults, to accept the fact that we probably had an inner justification according to our lights at the time, or at least to presume our repentance and determination of amendment. With this kind of insight we can extend ourselves to speak well of others and, as skillfully and unobtrusively as we can, to turn dangerous conversation into other channels. The control of the tongue is admittedly a difficult thing, but some people do manage it.

There is also another positive way of showing love in word, and this concerns our duty to be our brother's keeper. Our Lord himself puts the obligation upon us. (Matt. 18:15-17) If we find someone in a sin or fault, there are situations in which we may be obliged to speak about it to the person himself. This is a duty out of love and it the same as the duty out of justice which obliges parents and other lawful superiors. But it is a duty to be fulfilled with great care and not with the intemperate zeal which is a spiritual disguise for the busybody which, if we are not careful, we can all become.

The point is that it be done out of love; therefore it is not done out of a sense of superiority or condescension, or because the fault annoys or offends *us*. Much prayer ought ordinarily to precede it and follow it. St. Paul, as we shall see in a moment, tells us that such counseling should be done in a spirit of gentleness or mildness. Love also demands that there be some reasonable hope of success. Otherwise we may change what is only a dim realization of sin into a stubborn will directly turned against God. In general our admonitions should be directed to sins committed out of ignorance or negligence rather than those which proceed from malice or bad will. Yet sometimes even then we must speak, as when grave scandal or bad example is given. It can then become our duty to protest because of the love for others who might be influenced. Again the likelihood of success measures our obligation.

But there are crucial occasions when we may be obliged to speak even when there is only a minimum chance of success. One of these occurs when someone, especially a sinful person, may die unrepentant or without the last sacraments. Our love for our neighbor can give him no greater gift than eternal life.

Although many times our admonitions will be accomplished by word, sometimes they can be effectively brought about by our manner, by a glance, by our changing the subject of conversation, by withdrawing our support, by refusing to contribute, or by a noticeable diminution of our friendliness or conviviality—that is, by so managing our silence that it does the opposite of giving consent. Some of these means can be more conveniently used when it is a matter of lesser consequence. As a matter of fact, however, we must be careful that our corrections are not given often or over trifles. Our love then is interpreted as nagging, and in some cases it is a misguided love which tries to play the part of God. But like him, many times we must allow people to go to him at their own pace, slow and uncertain though that may be. We will do better here and in many other situations if we talk to God about our neighbor, and less to our neighbor about God. The speech of love for neighbor is also the speech of prayer.

But love for our neighbor can be in conflict with love for ourselves. If considerable personal detriment were to be the consequence of our admonitions or corrections, as when an employee would speak to his employer about his immoral life, we are not ordinarily obliged to such advice. There are situations in which we may and sometimes ought to choose the legitimate love for ourselves rather than the love for another.

This choice is especially important when there is real danger of spiritual loss for ourselves. This loss is especially probable in beginners. St. Paul gives this same warning to the beginning Christians of Asia Minor: "If a person is overtaken in some sin, you who are spiritual should set him right in a spirit of mildness, looking to yourself to avoid also falling into temptation."(Gal. 6:1) Therefore it would be unwise to seek out former acquaintances, who were once partners in sin, to try to bring them to God. Some situations are best solved by prayer and trust in God rather than by action.

Again, it is always a great personal detriment for a scrupulous person to feel that he is obliged to speak to his neighbor about his conduct. Therefore he is not obliged either.

In general, for all the rest of us this fraternal correction is a question of treating others as we would want to be treated ourselves. And surely we should want to be warned and persuaded to avoid spiritual injury and danger just as we would want to be warned about physical danger—and even more so here because spiritual death has greater consequences. Christ has told us that he will reward even a cup of water given in his name. How much more will he honor us if we give to others the cup of saving grace?

Love in speech need not be shown only in such crucial matters as these, which will not occur very often in a normal lifetime. There are other situations which occur every day, and in these we can also meet Christ in our neighbor as we would if we knew he were actually coming to us disguised as our neighbor. We thus should be courteous, not with the professional courtesy of those who are paid to be courteous—yet surely not with less than these—but with the courtesy that is respectful of the dignity of every human being. We should be courteous to those who try our patience; our Lord spoke of helping the least of his brethren, and he might also have spoken of the most troublesome.

We should not save all our kindness of speech for those outside the house, but should be especially careful of those who have little choice but to put up with our worst manners if we callously wish to show them.

Finally, love in word is often the same as truth in word. We owe this to our fellow man because harmony and justice cannot come about except by mutual trust based on truth. As I need truth from my neighbor, so I must give it to him. Here in the truth we can see the important distinction between the true compliment given our neighbor because of appreciation and love, and the flattery showered on him for selfish ends.

But there is another sense in which truth is love of another. A man who lives the truth will have all the virtues. For instance, to live by the truth requires him to be courageous. He will, of course, be honest in business. He will keep his promises. Since so many sins require deception, he will not become a drunkard, an adulterer, nor an irresponsible spender. The truth will free him from all these things and many others. Truth is the direct road to true love of others, of self, and of God.

Practical Reflection

Before you, my God, who know the secrets of my life, I ask myself: Do I spend time, even long periods of time, in conversations which result in harm to my neighbor? Do I let my-

14. Beginnings

self just chatter on, never thinking? Or am I so anxious to hear evil of others that I allow others to find a willing hearer in me? Have I betrayed a trust or violated confidences? Do I lack the courage to speak out for right and justice when I see that a definite good will result? Do I talk so much that I give no chance to others? Do I give my attention to a person speaking to me? Am I overly aggressive in my discussions or arguments? Do I say hurtful or insulting things to others? Do I betray the truth, and therefore myself and you, for advancement, for money, or for the opinion of others?

CHAPTER 30

Love in Deed

God wants love from us more than he wants anything else. He wants love, not only for himself, but for all who are his children, for all whom Christ recognizes as his brothers. This love, we have seen, must be more than merely wishing well to another. Humanity would lapse into unassuaged misery and our love of God would become a mockery if we were to sit around wishing others well and doing nothing. Our love must be shown in external ways; that is to say, it must become practical.

Now this is such an obvious conclusion that it should not need to be mentioned. But God has found it necessary to express it many times. For instance, the Holy Spirit speaks to us through St. John: "He who has the goods of this world and sees his brother in need and closes his heart to him, how does the love of God abide in him?" (I John 3:17) His question, however, does not apply only to the giving of money or material assistance. There are good people—a casual observer might even say, spiritual people—of whom you never dare to ask a favor or the gift of their time. How does any great love of God abide in them?

In pursuing the noble purpose of loving God and neighbor, certain people are afflicted with a blindness, not so much to those things which they do out of the virtue of charity, but to those they must do out of the virtue of justice. They are seen at Mass even frequently; they respond generously to all appeals for contributions. But on the other hand, they defraud their employers by wasting time for which they are paid (not to speak of the injustices of employers, which are usually greater); they do not pay bills or pay them promptly; and they fail in other real duties. Of course they have excuses acceptable to themselves and perhaps to their associates, but quite truly not acceptable to God, who loves justice and demands it because he is justice as well as love. And we on our part cannot truly say that we love our neighbor if we fail to give him what is his.

In regard to the virtue of justice, even more than with the virtue of charity, we can see how we ought to act by putting ourselves in the place of our neighbor and asking ourselves the obvious questions. This is not, of course, a newly discovered device to change the world. It is admittedly even trite. But if we try it, it will change our own personal world, and it will be the surest way to begin to bring God close.

The Golden Rule is valid for the spiritual life even more than for the life in which it is applied out of enlightened self-interest. In fact, it is a part of the Sermon on the Mount: "Even as you wish men to do to you, so also do you to them." (Luke 6:31) In the spiritual life we do this out of an understanding and a compassion for others. We love others because we are caught up in the torrent of love which God has for them.

In this chapter we shall discuss some of the details of the law of external love, but only in the framework of the immediate relationships of our lives, the relationships a man is likely to encounter every day. In a later section we will discuss the things more readily understood by the word "charity." Obviously there will be much overlapping, and many things said here will apply later. But our immediate surroundings are the stage upon which we live most of our lives. Here we meet our primary vocation, and here we basically succeed or fail in the eyes of God, no matter how good may be our actions in the larger world.

Much selfishness has been excused by the comfort of repeating that "charity begins at home." But if it is wrong to limit charity to the home, it is even more wrong not to have it there. If we are required to love those on the other side of the world, or those in the jungles of the Amazon and in the mountains of Tibet, how much more must we show love to those of our own household? What would it profit a man if he were to be extolled for his good works and his piety, if his wife and children knew him only as a drill sergeant without a heart? Or what good for a wife to be praised for her activity in the many events of church and school, if she nagged her husband and children into sullenness? If we wonder at times what God may be asking of us in order to come closer to him, we may not have to look farther than the walls of our home.

In fact, the most basic way of showing love for neighbor is by fulfilling generously the duties of our state in life. Many times we look upon these only in relation to God, as the fulfilling of his will. But we will surround our life with love if we see them also as large and small ways of showing love for others.

These duties of our state in life are as various as they are apparently endless. They embrace such diverse things as providing adequate security to being willing to take time to talk and listen. They mean such things as a clean house, good meals, a neat appearance, or something as personal as generosity and consideration in the marriage relationship. In marriage they mean a whole list of things that were never thought of in the glow of courtship. For those who are not married, they mean a generous use of the greater time at one's disposal. But at the beginning and end of all the long list of these duties we find God.

It is by our fidelity to this daily routine that we can even become saints, rather than by dreams of great things which we will never accomplish. Indeed, we cannot hope to please God in the performance of more appealing works outside if we neglect his works inside our circle. For these duties are usually a matter of justice, and thus generally take precedence over all that obliges us in charity. If the individual details seem to lack the glamor of what we read in the lives of the saints, it is well to remember, as we have said before, that God does not judge our deeds by their appearances. He weighs them. And what counts most in the scale is the love with which we do them—love of himself, and love of neighbor.

But of course any true love will not be confined to the four walls of our home, but will shine through the windows and burst out of the door. It is as true for us that our neighbor is anyone we associate with or even anyone we meet, as it was true of the Samaritan who came upon a stricken member of an unloved Jewish people. Loving another as ourselves means seeing the needs of the person, really to see them. We do not become so narrowly involved in our own life, our own interests, our own troubles that we don't see them. ("I have my own troubles.") Thinking of others and helping others is one of God's ways of helping us to lose our troubles.

When we are reminded of our duty in regard to the misfortunes of others, we most likely think in terms of money. But money is often the least of our obligations. More often, within our ordinary circle at least, the gift God wants for our neighbor is a more precious commodity, the gift of our time. It takes our time to do a favor for someone; it takes time to listen patiently. We can give this time grudgingly so that is not a gift but an accusation. Or we can give it as if it were given by God only to be given to others. Thus we give it with generosity and courtesy, with a vivid awareness of the dignity of the human being to whom we are giving it, and with a vivid awareness of the Christ who is there to receive it also.

If we want to live in an atmosphere of love and peace, we can in most cases bring that atmosphere with us through the kindness that flows out from us in our words, actions, and demeanor. We learn what a good thing it is to smile at people, even those who do not mean much to us naturally speaking. And while we cannot always avoid giving pain to others, we never give unnecessary pain.

Our doing for our neighbor must never become so autonomous that we forget that ultimately we are doing these things for God. We nurture this remembrance, not only because God must be loved first—all things must have reference to him—but also because we are not likely to persevere in loving our neighbor if we depend on loving neighbor alone. Love of neighbor receives many rebuffs from the neighbor; even our Lord found ingratitude in nine out of ten cleansed lepers. In all of us the early enthusiasms die away; we tend to become case-hardened—hands without a heart. But the love of God will keep the fire alive and burning. For from the face of the neighbor, the perhaps undeserving, ungrateful, importunate neighbor, always shines out the face of the suffering Christ.

Practical Reflection

Have I, like those whose religion was a matter of externals only, passed by my suffering or needy brethren? . . . your suffering and needy brethren, O Christ? Or has it been because I have been too involved only in the affairs and troubles of my own narrow world? Have I allowed myself to drift into an indifference to the rights of others? If I were in their place, would I have their grievances against the way I am treating them? Have I allowed my heart to become hardened by the constant repetition of the needs of others? Do I forget, O Christ, that it is not emotional thrill, but the privilege of pleasing you that I seek in caring for these needs? Am I willing to renew my spirit by the knowledge that it is you who are served in my neighbor, even if I get no return from him, even if I feel no immediate return from you?

CHAPTER 31

Some Problems with Love

One of the reasons that many of us do not extend ourselves to help others is fear of being carried out too far. In some people this is an unreal excuse, but in others it is a valid fear of an extreme. Since there is so much need, so much suffering in the world, we fear that to step into the water is to be carried away by the flood. We fear we should have no time for anything else, no money for ourselves, no soul to call our own. We are not sure we would know where to stop.

The answer is found in a certain balance, and this is the same as seeing what is God's will in practice. Other things, such as the duties of our state in life, our already assumed obligations, our spiritual, emotional, and physical needs, and the time we have at our disposal, must be weighed to find the will of Christ when we confront him in our neighbor. The will of this Christ is neither in giving too little of ourselves nor in giving too much. And although our fears cry out to us that there will be no limits, it is possible to give too much, too much for our own peace of mind, too much even for the good of our neighbor.

There are no set rules to determine what Christ wants, but the law of love requires a balanced judgment as well as a heart sincerely willing to please him. Our choices are a delicate application of the art of the possible. And in this we have his example. Although he gave himself to the healing of the sick, he did not do this to the exclusion of the instruction and companionship of his own spiritual family, the apostles, and to his own need of solitude and prayer. His choice of the limited good is a lesson telling us that we are not called to do all possible good.

To refuse to accept the challenges imposed by love of neighbor is to sin, not by action, but by omission. We do no positive evil to him; we merely refuse to help or even to see that he needs our help. We allow ourselves to become involved in our own lives, our own interests, or our own troubles to the degree that we become insensible or blind to other lives and their interests and troubles. Or even worse, we become sinfully selfish so that, even when we do become hazily aware of the needs of our neighbor, we shut ourselves off from him with some irritation and then grasp some excuse in order to quiet a not yet dead conscience.

In the meantime, whether the cause be inattention or a more culpable selfishness, our neighbor must go on being in need: without help, without understanding, without practical love. Will it not be an uncomfortable enlightenment if we find out too late that it was Christ whom we left in need, without sympathetic understanding, without practical help, without practical love? It is well not to forget that the sins for which Christ, in his parable-prediction of the last judgment, found some of mankind guilty of hell were sins of omission: "For I was hungry, and you did not give me to eat. . . ." (Matt. 25:42 ff.)

The barrier between ourselves and this practical love of Christ is often made up of excuses: "I'm too busy now; maybe later." "He probably had it coming to him anyway." "He probably wouldn't help me if I were lying there." We can easily suppose that the two men who passed by their half-dead countryman had such reasons too, the reasons of the good people. But our Lord praised not them, but the Samaritan, the foreigner, who proved that he loved his neighbor as he loved himself. No matter how otherwise good we are, we too have to prove to God exactly that.

Another problem sometimes arises from the fact that much of the care of the needs of our neighbor is assumed by various public health agencies. But a visit to the various offices and institutions, or a bit of serious thought, will show us that they are unequal to an adequate fulfillment of the law of love. Although a private person is often no longer able, and no longer obliged, the full care of the needy, even of his own needy relatives or friends, there are many ways in which he is still obliged to show practical love. These do not need to be listed after all that has been said previously; most often they are things which are not valued by money.

But we may not, like the two men who passed by, take advantage of the legalities in our favor and likewise pass by. These two men, like many good people, may have had excuses in law which made them feel less uncomfortable as they rode on. In modern terms they could say: "Where are the public health people? They should take care of such things." "I pay my taxes; that satisfies my obligations." We ought not forget, if we use these comforting legalisms, that our Lord was sent to death by men who used legalisms to condemn him: "We have a Law." (John 19:7) They had blinded themselves to reality, as we will also if we do not hold fast to Christ not only in the tabernacle, not only in our hearts, but also in our neighbor.

The next problem has to do with the undeserving. While it is relatively easy and emotionally satisfying to help those who are in unfortunate circumstances through no fault of their own, the heart does not reach out so readily to those who have wasted opportunities and now find themselves in one kind of need or another through their own fault. And the matter is worse when it takes no imagination to see that the same situation will probably occur again.

Is it too repetitious to suggest that these people are easily some whom Christ would call "the least of my brethren"? Can we imagine him to want us to go about with the smugness that helps only "the deserving poor" as if the children of the undeserving should be left to starve? Yet we must again be careful of such examples lest they blind us to the frequent situations in our lives which require, not monetary assistance, but help of a more human kind. And this to the real failures, to the undeserving.

The truth is that, just as there are people with weak physical powers who are forced to become someone's charge, so also there are people with weak judgment, weak energy of will, or weak character, who likewise will not survive without the repeated help of others. While the deserving do have a special call upon our help, on the other hand we must not forget the meaning of mercy. We ourselves often ask God for assistance for the undeserving, that is, for our own selves; and any time we may have been in mortal sin, mercy has been as crucial as heaven or hell. This same mercy we must extend to others, not imprudently or unreasonably, lest we hurt them or ourselves. But our hearts cannot remain shut because a man is by some standard undeserving. Our Lord said, "Freely you have received, freely give." (Matt. 10:8)

Our last problems are really not problems. They concern sins which everyone sees as evil. Our problem will be to see them for what they are, not merely as sins, but as sins against love of neighbor. In seeing this, we will realize their greater evil, and of course will avoid them because of this.

The first of these is the co-operation in the sin of another. This co-operation can take innumerable forms so diverse that any selection of examples would tend to limit the wider field. Similarly the guilt attached to this co-operation varies from none at all to mortal sin, depending on many circumstances which must be weighed in each case. It is not the intention of this book to affix guilt, and so the solution to these problems must be sought elsewhere. But here it is sufficient to point out that it is not love for our neighbor to make it possible for him to sin when he would not be able to sin, or sin so readily, unless we provided the material, the opportunity, or the occasion for the sin. If we must have an example for clarification, there is the stupidity of good people who will force drink after drink upon others, some of whom should not drink at all.

Similar to sinful co-operation is the advice which is sometimes given to others. Many people are very free in giving advice, and unfortunately the more incapable they are in giving advice, the freer they are in giving it. Now, advice is often a serious thing, requiring much experience, sufficient thought and, above all, solid principles. Many of the problems of others involve the moral life, in other words, right and wrong, and therefore the salvation of the soul. But it is not an unusual thing to hear of advice given or encouragement given which will result in years of mortal sin, as when an invalid marriage is being considered. And yet these givers of advice blithely go on to Mass and Holy Communion as if they had opened the gate to heaven instead of the door to hell. One wonders how they could show greater hatred to the neighbor whom the Lord says we must love.

Another sin contrary to love of neighbor is bad example. Surely we are not showing love for him any time we place an obstacle on his way to God. Our Lord left no doubt about his mind on this matter. He mentions the harm done to children, but surely does not intend to limit his words only to this. "It is impossible that scandals should not come; but woe to him through whom they come! It were better for him if a millstone were hung about his neck and he were thrown into the sea, than that he should cause one of these little ones to sin." (Luke 17:1, 2) In this sense we are our brother's keeper. The man who first denied this was a murderer. By the sin of bad example we may be murdering souls or seriously wounding them.

Now everyone will see the evil of bad example when it comes from sins which lead to sins of others. But not all see it when the bad example comes from something not really evil but having only the appearance of evil, or not evil at all but unfitting or improper under the circumstances. Thus because of the appearance of evil, a man could sin if he had a dispensation to eat meat at a forbidden time, but ate it in front of certain acquaintances without giving an explanation. As St. Paul said in a similar situation, "Do not let your food destroy him for whom Christ died." (Rom. 14:15) An example of something lawful but unfitting would be married people who showed physical love to each other too freely in public.

You will hear it objected that other people should not take the bad example, that they should piously presume the best or avert the eyes from the unseemly. Those who can do this would be the strong, but love of neighbor is not limited by the strong; it is necessary even more for the weak. In all situations when the good resulting from our action or from our freedom does not outweigh the probable harm to our weak neighbor, we must choose love of neighbor.

We must therefore not only look to the right and wrong of our actions, much less to whether our sin is only venial and not mortal, but must also consider whether another will find our action a real obstacle on his way to God. It is not enough to dismiss this obligation of love by the fact that our neighbor has free will. God looks at the result, and our conscious part in it.

All of us, and especially parents, should see good example as one of the most important duties of our state in life, and this not only by our actions. Our attitudes are absorbed by others, especially the young, and what may be a small thing to us can be a bad seed we have sown for an evil harvest.

Contrary to all this, we show love for our neighbor by good example. Because of us, he is encouraged to continue the battle, knowing that he is not alone. Yet we should beware of a kind of good example which flaunts itself before others in smug self-righteousness. Those whom such people would influence or encourage are not as deceived as the actors are, and the small spark of willingness can be smothered by the dripping honey. A certain simplicity of heart will put God first in our actions, and rarely seek to edify by setting ourselves up as a model.

But on the other hand, we should not shrink from the good example which our deeds often bring, even though we know ourselves to be in many ways deficient. Deficient indeed are all of us before God, but love of our neighbor should impel us to show what is best in us while we continue our battle against what we want known only to a merciful God.

Practical Reflection

Am I aware, O Lord, that when you told us that even the least of men are your brethren, you gave heaven to those who served them, but condemned those who failed by mere omission? Have I used excuses like those which must have been in the minds of those who passed by the man dying on the road to Jericho? too busy? make me late? someone else's responsibility? not my kind of people? Do I in this and in other things become an obstacle between my neighbor and you by the contradiction between the way I live and the principles I profess to hold? Do I call myself a Christian without trying very much to follow you? Will I now try, not only to see you in your brethren, but in all things try to have your brethren, even the least of your brethren, see you in me?

CHAPTER 32

Immodesty and Our Love of Neighbor

It may be somewhat surprising to find immodesty in dress considered under love of neighbor. We would perhaps expect it to have been discussed under sexual sin. In discussing it here, however, we not only see its precise evil, but also we can clear up some misunderstandings about it.

The evil of immodest dress does not come from the human body as such. This body, in many ways almost divine in its more perfect specimens, has been created by God in all its details. Its marvel and beauty, despite its essential impermanence, are surely one of his highest visible glories. Nor does the evil come merely because the human body, especially the female in respect to the male, can arouse sexual feelings and desires. This, under the proper circumstances of married love, was the intent of the creator. Rather, the evil of immodest dress consists in providing a visual occasion by which unlawful sexual pleasure or desire will be easily aroused. And it is a sin against love to provide an occasion of sin for another.

There are, of course, many excuses by which people deceive themselves about immodesty. A favorite is the half-truth that "To the pure all things are pure." This overly optimistic principle is in the main a confession of ignorance. It has only a very limited value even for those who are at the same time morally strong and aesthetically mature. Human nature, sadly, does not react as these idealists would like to imagine.

Their presumption is that only those who are evil-minded anyway will be sinfully affected. This, however, leaves out the many who are well-intentioned but not impregnably strong—and even are weak. A true love of neighbor must take this weakness into account, just as we would physical or mental weakness. Contrary to those who flaunt their bodies in the face of weak humanity, our Lord is a realist: "If thy eye is an occasion of sin to thee, pluck it out and fling it from thee." (Matt. 18:9) He is telling us that even good people can come to a moral crisis that requires strong action. But it is not love for our neighbor to push him to the limits of his endurance, and beyond.

It is true that our Lord is not saying that every eye finds sin in everything, or that all eyes find sin in the same thing. But the world cannot be designed to fit only the strong; the strong must be willing to sacrifice some of their freedom for the sake of the weak. Even further, love will not only urge the avoidance of evil but also a climate favorable for the good.

Another reason given to excuse immodesty is the appeal to fashion. Thus and thus is decreed by the handful of people who make fashions, and humanity is expected so to abdicate its free will that we normally, and perhaps cynically, expect compliance to almost anything. Here on this issue of fashion the spirit of God and the spirit of the world often involve people in choices which are really present but not always recognized. As a result, we sometimes see good women wearing clothes that are for their neighbor a serious obstacle to love of God.

Of course the retort to all this is that we are now suggesting that women make themselves an object of ridicule by wearing clothes of a more restrained decade or century. The truth, however, is not to be so easily disposed of. As a matter of fact, such anachronism in dress can be immodesty of another kind, a drawing of undue attention to oneself, and therefore, suspiciously, a sin of pride. And it is not necessarily love for neighbor either. In general, we have a duty to others and to ourselves to give reasonable amounts of time to the care of our appearance. The beauty of women, the modest beauty of women, is intended by God to be a delight and consolation to the other half of humanity who must look at them. Besides, this care of appearance is often a condition of the self-respect of the women themselves. Now all this involves an attempt to keep reasonably in style, and yet it is very different from obeisance to every fashion regardless of its impact on others. The fashion designers do not often even pretend to be concerned with morality, but rather with what will attract and sell. Therefore, certain styles should be greeted with resistance, especially when openly advertised as attractive to men's sexual nature.

While this matter of modesty in dress applies more to women than to men, men also have the same basic responsibility as to extremes in apparel, their manner of wearing it, and their demeanor, as do women. Furthermore, they also have a responsibility in regard to women's dress. Although women sometimes dress to attract the envy or attention of other women, most often they dress to please or attract men. Thus women's apparel, at least in particular cases, depends on the man. A man must therefore avoid giving approval or showing attention to what is immodest, even though he is strong enough to withstand temptation himself. Furthermore, a man has a responsibility to see that his wife is modestly dressed in public, and also that she not unwisely allow their daughter a display which may signify beauty to the parents but will be like a lighted match in a dried forest to her male contemporaries.

Perhaps all such counsels seem unnecessary to those who are attempting the spiritual life. But the pressures of advertising and the example of others sometimes make us forget that there must be a wholeness in our turning to God, instead of a thoughtless compromise, half-Christian, half-pagan.

Discussing modesty in dress under the aspect of love of neighbor also makes it easy to correct certain misconceptions about it, and in the process to see more clearly the true nature of this virtue. We can, for instance, see how our judgment upon what is modest may change with varying times, places, and circumstances, but that the norms of purity do not change. Impurity, as we have said earlier, is unlawful sexual pleasure or desire. God's enclosing of the sexual within the embrace of matrimony is unchangeable. But immodesty is something else.

There is a fortunate quality in human nature, that it tends to get used to those impressions that come by means of the senses. The dulling effect of frequent repetition of the same kind of food or the same piece of music are examples. This is also true of much that excites the sexual appetite—not everything that excites the sexual appetite, but enough in the matter of dress to make some things that were once dangerous now a matter of course. For instance, in the late nineteenth century to see a woman's ankle was considered by some to be an event of great importance.

In the twentieth century almost no one gives attention to an ankle. Also, what could not be worn in the cheapest public show in one age has become acceptable and modest for the beaches in another.

The reason is not a change in morals, but a change in the ability of one type of garment or a certain amount of exposure to arouse the passions of the opposite sex—at least beyond the point where danger becomes great for the normal person. Yet once more, lest we be misunderstood, there are limits to what in dress and conduct our sexual nature can safely absorb. This is especially true since it is often not just exposure, but exposure so accomplished that the arousing of sexual attraction is basic to the design.

This brings up another misconception about modesty, that it is to be judged solely on the amount of exposure. On the contrary, many times a woman is quite completely covered, but is still immodest because the pattern of the design, the contours, or the tightness of the garment do more to arouse sexual attention than would another woman wearing less.

Modesty must also be judged according to time, place, and other circumstances. For instance, what can be worn modestly on the beach ought not be worn where it will attract undue attention. What can be worn at a social gathering where many women are similarly attired with some moderate exposure will not always have a purely aesthetic effect in dimly lighted privacy.

In seeing modesty as a part of love of neighbor, we can also see how a deliberate venial sin of immodesty is possible but not a deliberate venial sin of impure pleasure or desire. A deliberate sin of impurity always involves the full acceptance of some form of the unlawfully sexual, and thus is always a mortal sin, as we have said earlier. But immodesty in dress is judged as to its probabilities in arousing unlawful sexual pleasure or desire in another. To the extent that it is likely to result in at least internal sin, it can become mortal sin for the wearer. In cases where the likelihood is not great, but still concerns a garment somewhat less than praiseworthy, the sin may be venial.

As for a practical norm for modesty, only a broad principle can be given here. A woman may usually wear what is generally worn in good taste under the same circumstances. In matters of reasonable doubt, she will do well to choose the more modest

15. *Beginnings*

attire because, as we have said, the presumption is against the fashion's being designed with much regard for modesty.

Unfortunately, many good women do not know the full effect of their bodies on men. If they did, they would not let considerations such as style, glamor, and desire for attention induce them to dress so as to endanger souls. And this danger to souls include their own souls, danger to their own friendship with Christ who thought enough of these same souls to give his life for them in great suffering of his own body.

Women, because of the beautiful creation that is feminine nature, will always have more than a bit of motherhood in their attitude toward men. This quality fits them to be the guardians of men's virtue, even when a man is not disposed to guard it himself. Surely this quality is at least as deep in her nature as her desire for attention, especially sexual attention, from a man who is not hers in marriage.

We must all answer some day for our care of the souls of our weaker brethren. Few things can raise a man higher in true manhood than Christian womanhood, and few things can send him lower than womanhood which fails in its responsibilities. Have we not forgotten a truth which was trite in an earlier age, but is now smothered by the cult of the physical and the sensual, that true beauty is in the soul? and that this is reflected clearly in the face and the eyes? Should not a woman try to be attractive principally by the beauty of the soul, which does not grow old or become wrinkled, which does not lead men away from God, but shows the highest love by leading them to him?

Practical Reflection

Have I distorted my attitude on modesty by seeing the teaching and recommendations of the Church as merely the work of some narrow old men? Instead of forming my mind on the solid principles of love of neighbor, have I not allowed it to be molded by fads, styles, and fashions which work the destruction of my neighbor? Have I given up adulthood to the extent that I fear to be different, especially in the face of criticism as prudish or old-fashioned? Do I now see that there can be no full love of God if I leave a whole area of my life without his deep influence?

CHAPTER 33

Loving the Unloved and the Unloving

Most of us will accept, at least in principle, all that has been said so far about love of neighbor. But a few of us will hesitate because of an aversion or revulsion against some person or group. This hesitation to accept the whole of love may come about either because we do not understand the nature of the love required in these cases, or because we do not deeply understand certain relevant motives for loving.

As to the nature of the love required, we are not obliged to love others together with the things we dislike in them. These people may be deceitful, unreliable, unjust, or they may be uncouth, vulgar, or oppositely, too refined. We may see them as a threat to us, real or imagined, or we may bear deep resentments for causes real or imagined. In none of these and similar cases are we obliged to love what stands between us and the person; we do not have to love what makes him undesirable or repulsive. We must love the man, the human being. We love him despite what bothers us about him.

When we thus distinguish between the man and his defects, we are, of course, applying an old, but ever-useful counsel that we hate the sin but love the sinner. In this we are being perfect in our own way as our heavenly Father is in his. He loves all men despite their sins and deficiencies, and most important of all he loves *us* despite our sins and deficiences. If we protest that we are not divine enough to love with the same forbearance and forgiveness that God does, then let us consider someone in whom we continually see undesirable things and yet still love deeply. God is not asking the impossible of us; this somewhat undesirable person whom we love deeply is ourselves.

If we are honest with ourselves, we will recognize that we do many things, even every day, which are wrong, unfitting, or thoughtless. These often bring us deep shame or embarrassment, sometimes even real difficulty. Yet, although we certainly do not love these defects, we continue to do our duty toward ourselves by loving ourselves all the same.

A brief look at how we act under the burden of our faults will give an insight how we may act toward others in their faults. In the first place we do not go about telling everybody about the shameful thing we did. We hide our deficiencies when we are able. When we are not able, we usually have an excuse— except that we understand ourselves so well that we no longer have excuses; we have *reasons*. When we have no reason, or such a poor one that it is better simply to acknowledge our fault, we expect others not to hold it against us afterward. We are now no longer the same person who committed the fault; we are a new creature, and should be so accepted by everyone immediately without any remembrance or resentment—a bit unrealistic, but how reasonable to us. Along with this instinct of an understandable love of self the suggestion should be whispered that this also is the way we should love our neighbor.

Many of the things which disturb us about groups of people are essentially inconsequential as regards our basic relations with them; social level, color of skin, nationality, and religion are only a partial list. Our reactions to them are usually the result of the indoctrination of our world and are often contrary to the love of Christ which knows no such distinctions. "There is neither Jew nor Greek; there is neither slave nor freeman; there is neither male nor female. For you are all one in Christ Jesus." (Gal. 3:28) On the contrary, the code of the world would often have us seek out the company of recognized but acceptable sinners, sophisticated scoffers, or the rich who have made their money unjustly. Yet this code has only toleration at best for good men who are barred by prejudice of one kind or another. A mere mental switch of positions, that is, putting ourselves in the place of those we unreasonably object to and then seeing ourselves treated as we treat them, is one way of getting the point of view necessary for us to love our neighbors.

In loving these unloved, a true Christian will not make the opposite mistake of an exaggerated attention, which is the worst kind of condescension. This is usually recognized for what it is, and to sensitive people it is more difficult to bear than the neglect or the insult to which they are accustomed. We must treat these people as we do everyone else, that is with a sense of their dignity as human beings, as God's children, as brothers of Christ, as brothers in Christ. We must have an understanding of their problems, just as God wants us to have a sympathy and understanding for everyone's problems. We are obliged to help them as far as we are reasonably able, just as we are everyone who comes into our knowledge and within our ability.

The other side of the coin, however, is equally authentic. Every unloved group has members who are patently unreliable, dangerous, disagreeable, or basically incompatible, just as every "acceptable" group also contains such kinds of individuals. While we must always love these undesirables, and must help them in real difficulties as the outcast Samaritan helped the Jew, we are not obliged to make them our special friends, invite them into our houses, or give them opportunities which we would not give to similar undesirables of "acceptable" groups. The law of love does not oblige us to throw caution or common sense out the door just because a man happens to belong to an unloved group. We may sometimes understand with deep sympathy why he is what he is, but our sympathy does not change the fact that as a person he has become what he is. If we have the opportunity, the means, and the hope of helping him, as we would help an undesirable of a more "acceptable" group, our understanding and sympathy may reasonably incline us more to help this member of the unloved group. But when there is no such reasonable opportunity, means, or hope, our love may be restricted to the help of prayer, as it is in all similar circumstances.

Except for the truly undesirables, or those individuals whom we prudently fear may be truly undesirable, we must treat the unloved group with that equality to which they have a right as human beings under their present circumstances. This does not always mean an absolute equality; men are only equal in their basic humanity. Neither love nor justice means that all men must be given here and now all possible rights, civil, social, and economic. Many other factors of sound judgment must complete the picture; the common good and the good of the unequal individuals must be considered. Love means that we should want and work for that equality of which they are now capable, and to desire and work for the increase of their capabilities to the extent that they are now not capable.

In many cases the members of the unloved group are equal or superior to those of the "acceptable" groups, and we should not deny their rights because of prejudice. In those groups where not all, or perhaps not many, are qualified to assume equality, we must still not impede but rather help the individuals who are qualified. Both love and justice demand this of us, but love demands it especially because in this way is raised the level of the sub-equal group.

As to our personal associates, while in justice we have a right to choose them as we will, it is surely against love to limit them only to the socially acceptable people, no matter how well the others are qualified. Such genteel snobbery is not fully Christian, is not following the Christ who was taunted with being the associate of the socially unacceptable.

Love demands that we never hurt anyone unnecessarily in choosing our acquaintances and familiars, much less that we hurt the cause of God's love by our lack of it. Prejudice is difficult to root out of the heart since it is deeper than reason, and an individual may never be entirely free from its pull. Even a man like St. Peter had difficulty in eating with the new non-Jewish Christians and had to be reminded of his duty by a more universally minded Jew, St. Paul. Like St. Peter, we must then compel our conduct to follow reason when we are not moved by higher instinct like St. Paul.

For the rest of this discussion we shall consider only those who are conveniently lumped together by the admonition to "love our enemies." Now, few of us have enemies in any real sense, someone who is plotting to take our life, our fortune, our job, our friends. But we all do have people in our lives who have done us what at least appears to be an injustice; we have people who talk about us, who treat us poorly. And then there are those against whom we feel a deep resentment because of the harm they have done to others. Since the word "enemy" fits the worst of all these people, what our Lord said of the worst will also apply to those who are not so bad. Here, in the Sermon on the Mount, is what he said: "Love your enemies. Do good to them that hate you, and pray for them that persecute and calumniate you." (Matt. 5:44)

What does our Lord mean by love under such circumstances? Perhaps part of our difficulty comes from expecting that he means a more intense and emotional love than that with which we love all men. If so, we make the problem harder than it is. Love in the sense we have been using it does not mean that we must embrace our enemies, that we must invite them to dinner and introduce them to our friends. In some limited number of cases this may indeed be considered to be the perfection of love of neighbor. But as in so much else in the spiritual life we must here draw the line between what a man is required to do and what may be desirable, between what is possible here and now and what must be grown into gradually.

In general then, we must love our enemies with the same kind of love with which we love all men. There are a few practical points, however, which may be overlooked. Love will put out of our hearts all hatred of the person, and it will do the same with all thoughts of revenge. If on occasion we are obliged to act against him, we still are somehow to act out of love, out of love for ourselves and other men who might be injured by this person, or out of love for the man himself, that just punishment will bring about his correction. But we may not do it just to get even. "Vengeance is mine; I will repay, says the Lord," and it is so important that it was said in both the Old and New Testaments, (Deut. 32:35; Rom. 12:19) just as the law of love is repeated in both Testaments. (Deut. 6:5; Matt. 22:37)

Another way in which we show dislike or hatred to others is by silence; we just don't speak to certain people. In some few cases such silence may be justified, usually cases where one fears harm to himself. In a few other cases, such as a parent to a child, a rare temporary silence is a way to teach a lesson; too easy a forgiveness makes the fault seem less. Then silence is really love for one's neighbor and should be accompanied by prayer before God. The sin of silence occurs when it is an outward sign of enmity or hatred. But God's command is to love. So we must help our enemy as we would anyone, greet him as we would anyone, answer his questions, treat him courteously. Somehow in meeting this person, we are meeting Christ, even as Christ courteously met the betraying Judas.

One of the advantages in keeping open the lines of communication is the possibility of reconciliation. If hatred and enmity are not to draw us away from God, there must come the eventual peace, and usually the sooner the better. Only in exceptional cases, as when a reconciliation would renew an association which is harmful to us, can we maintain the separation, and even then it must be clear that there is no lack of forgiveness.

Although in justice the one who has committed the offense should be the first to ask pardon, in love it may be the offended one who has to make the first overtures. Very seldom is the exact guilt clear to both people. Consequently, if the dark clouds are not to remain overhead for weeks and months, the injured party makes the first move. To do this he can usually find some defect in his conduct too, and so apologize for having (let us say) spoken sharply. Love of neighbor sometimes requires pious subterfuge.

A further requirement, however, is that we really forgive, that we don't deceive ourselves with the half-forgiveness by which we tell ourselves and others that we "forgive but can't forget." Of course, it is quite true that the rupture may have taught us lessons which we should not forget. It may also be that the hurt is so deep that it will take much time before it can be forgotten, no matter how much we wish to forget. But what puts a curtain of darkness between the soul and God is the mockery we make of our words of forgiveness by nursing the resentment, by recalling the incident over and over or by allowing it in our minds for long periods without any attempt to distract ourselves. Something like this can do more harm to our souls, shut out more grace than many other sins. Our sins are acts, and, except for mortal sin, they do not shut out grace, especially when repented promptly. But here is the *state* of a soul, perhaps still in God's grace, but which cannot respond to his love. We often wonder why we don't inherit all the promises of the spiritual life, especially love and peace. We wonder why our prayers aren't answered. We protest that we don't commit this or that sin as others do. We point to our good works. But underneath we have kept God out because we have not loved, because we have not fully forgiven.

The fear of pushing God away is one of the motives we may need in order to forgive. On the other hand the love of God may enable us to do the impossible. The love we have for God will impel us to love his children. In the words of St. Thomas: "Thus if we loved a certain man very much, we would love his children, though they were unfriendly toward us." (II, II; 25; 8)

God does not leave our good intentions unsupported. In the background is the simple fact, mentioned many times in the Scriptures, that if we do not forgive others, he will not forgive us. Our sins, our unfaithfulness to his love, our refusals and waste of grace, our squandered talents, the many second chances, God's many inspirations and corrections, the blood itself of Christ, also wasted—for all this we need forgiveness. God must show love where there is little or none. But he will not, if we will not show the same kind of love to others.

In learning how to forgive, we will do well to recall our ways of overcoming other temptations. Unforgiving thoughts are truly temptations, and yet they are sometimes neglected by those who would not live with an impure thought for a moment. Sometimes we can get rid of them by an opposite action; we do a kindness for the person. We can also turn our resentful thoughts into prayers for him and thus do much good for him as well as for ourselves. But we must not become discouraged by the difficulty. Even the saints had to use strong methods. One of them, Teresa of Avila, tells us that sometimes the sense of injustice weighed so heavily on her that there was no other course but to pray that God would reward those who caused the suffering just because they caused it.

Practical Reflection

Have I not, in making my own life, O God, forgotten that all men are your children? Do I draw lines of sinful prejudice instead of becoming a living fulfillment of the prayer of your Son, "that all may be one"? (John 17:21) Am I willing now to accept as brothers those who have never hurt me, as well as all those who have? Does not my own need for continual forgiveness make me determine to forgive from my heart?

CHAPTER 34

The Love of Friends

The subject of friendship is a crucial one, not only for our salvation, but also for the spiritual life. Our choice of God will often mean a severance or a curtailment of certain relationships with those whose ideas, urgings, or example will draw us from our hold on him, from the vital meaning and inner peace which our life with him will bring us. On the other hand we will see that we cannot live in a vacuum devoid of all close human relationships. So we will watch for and carefully cultivate those people who can encourage and help us by what is human in true friendship and who will be at the same time watchful companions in our journey toward God.

We have spoken sufficiently of love of neighbor to understand that love of God does not mean a love so exclusive that it cannot tolerate any other love whatsoever. We are even commanded to love our neighbor, and we will find it easier to love some more than others. When our attraction is for the right reasons, we will be following the example of him who *is* the way, Christ who chose twelve and of these loved three more than the others, who was friend to both the penitent Magdalene and to Martha, and who loved Lazarus so much that he wept at his tomb.

Nevertheless, friendship in the spiritual life is never an entirely simple thing. We can never naïvely expect that it will be brought about and preserved without experiencing opposition, real or merely fearful, between our friendship and the love belonging to God. Indeed, we should expect this conflict. We may sometimes find that we love a friend far more emotionally than we love God emotionally. This should not surprise or discourage us. With our minds and wills we are obliged to love God first with a love of preference; we choose him as the highest and first object of our love and try to make all our thoughts, words, and actions fit into complete harmony with this love. By this love of preference God must be preferred before all things; all our other loves must be able to be included in this first love. This is the meaning of the command to love God with our whole heart, our whole soul, and our whole mind.

The opposition, or at least apparent opposition, arises when our emotions do not follow our reason in this love of preference. They go out toward someone humanly lovable in a way they do not go out to God. Yet this is not necessarily in opposition to true love of God. The emotions are drawn out by what is pleasing to them, by sight, voice, mannerisms, and other characteristics, not to leave out the attraction rooted in our sexual nature. They really should follow reason and be on fire with love of God in an overflow of love from the soul. But in our fallen state they do not always react as they should, and we cannot force them very much either. We must be content with using their help when they are on the side of God, and be watchful for tendencies that lead away from him.

Despite this unavoidable divergence of the emotions, we are still loving God first if we are determined to do his will rather than that of a friend if the two are in opposition. Yet here we must beware of stating the case too simply. For it is possible that the very strength of the emotions may dim our clear insight into God's will so that we don't see the opposition. At times also, this pull can so fill and delight us that we are not likely to seek God with the intensity with which we should—and would, if it were not for so emotionally all-absorbing a love. It should not surprise us that even a saint found these difficulties. In her personal account of the making of a saint, St. Thérèse of Lisieux tells us that in her earlier spiritual life she was obliged to put restraints upon her love for her sister. Later on, when she became strong, such restraint was not necessary.

The answer to such a dilemma is not necessarily to cut off the friend or to try to shut off all emotion. First of all we must examine our situation and see if we are actually less ready to do the will of God. Despite our emotion, or even because of it, we may not be less ready, but rather more ready to follow and accept the will of God even in the slightest matters. If our friendship does this for us and does it consistently, it has survived the best and most practical of all tests of its goodness.

Then as to whether our emotions are blotting out the desire for the presence of God, we must again be sure that it is doing so. Most of us, and not only beginners, if left emotionally dry of human love, will find ourselves dry of all love, especially love of God. Rather we find God in and with the love of a friend. We will turn to God many times in thanksgiving for our friend, in asking his blessing on the friend and on the friendship, and in pleading that this relationship lead us to him. In this way the spiritual life is greatly advanced.

But if we still perceive that the fine edge of personal relationship to God has been blunted by too much contact or too much thought of the friend, the necessary course of action is still not elimination of the friend or all thought of him. We should rather take the matter to God in solitude in order to reorganize our thinking, make some practical resolution, and ask for God's help in so important a matter. Sometimes an excessive attraction to the human is really an invitation from God to pursue prayer more intensely. If this results, the difficulties themselves of the friendship have become a help to our spiritual life.

On the other hand, a reasonable attitude toward emotion should not deceive us into thinking that every emotional situation is a true friendship. While some emotion ought to be a part of all friendship, a true friendship is never predominantly emotional, at least not consistently. Predominantly it must be based on qualities such as the virtues, and on aims which are basically spiritual. Besides this, it must have the effect of bringing about the spiritual good of the friends: "By their fruits you will know them." (Matt. 7:16)

It sometimes happens in the spiritually immature that what is thought to be a friendship based on spiritual qualities is really only an emotional attraction in spiritual disguise. It is quite true in these cases that God is professedly loved, that a great deal of help is professedly given, and much time is spent listening to problems and giving advice. Yet the results in the long run do not show. Instead the dependence upon the friend becomes greater, in opposition to a growth of true dependence upon God, and the emotional attachment becomes the underlying reason for the discussion of problems and spiritual things.

The error here is in a misunderstanding of the sharing which is an essential part of all friendship. A true friend, it is said, is one to whom we can tell anything. But this is not the same as telling him everything. There are some things which should not be shared; for instance, what are often called "the secrets of the King." If we tell the friend everything that goes on in our soul, we will never grow spiritually; the seed is not kept in the ground long enough to grow roots. This is even true of the friendship that often comes with spiritual direction, as we will enlarge upon later. In any case, instead of using the friend to go to God, we risk using God to go to the friend.

The same error of sharing too much is also found in the discussion of the trials of life. Now a friend is surely one to whom we may turn in time of distress to seek encouragement, understanding, and counsel on problems or situations which are too big for us. But these incidents are rather rare as the weeks and months of a lifetime go by, allowing always for periods when difficulties may arise with more frequency or intensity. Yet when contact is made too easy either by proximity or by letter, there are usually not enough things which *need* sharing, so the small things become the media of prolonged discussions. One wants contact with the other, and even emotional contact; so the small disappointments, and the small difficulties and trials are shared with the hope of an emotional response from the friend.

This is, however, a false notion of friendship. We are to be strengthened by the friend and not weakened. If we look to another for comfort, understanding, and advice in those things we can endure or decide for ourselves without too much difficulty, we are weakening ourselves. Going to God with these things will not weaken us.

As a matter of fact, in this excess of sharing we can easily have the sin of detraction or any of the other sins that set man against man. Detraction, for example, is the revealing of the true faults of another without a sufficiently grave reason. Now surely when some real crisis occurs in our lives, we may have sufficient reason to speak our feelings and seek counsel even though it involves the sins, faults, or policies of another. We may need encouragement, advice, or even an emotional outlet where we can relieve feelings which may injure us if we do not talk about them freely. God in such cases relinquishes a part of his comforting love into the careful hands of a wise friend.

But again, these crises are rather rare over the months and years, and even if repeated frequently during some particular period, the knowledge of the friend's understanding and the recollection of his words should carry us some distance along the way. Decidedly, however, such occasions are not the trivia of disappointments, rebukes, or frustrations that fill our days. Therefore, if the difficulties coming from our neighbor can be borne by ourselves with God's personal help and comfort, we do wrong to make the sins, faults, personality, or policies of another the subject of frequent communication.

Because of the incalculable good that can come from friendship, several obligations become apparent. The first is the care in choosing the friend. The transition from acquaintance to friendship should be a gradual one, despite feelings of emotional or intellectual compatibility. It takes more than strong attraction to make a friend, and it takes more than an enormous amount of common ground to make the kind of friend we are talking about. Before we let anyone into the sanctuary of our soul, we must have first lived some time, longer than we may want, in watching and praying. And even then, we give of our inner selves only as we are sure that the other is worthy and capable of receiving it.

Another obligation imposed by the value of good friendship is to see that it becomes and remains a relatively unselfish thing. Although it is intended to give us much personal joy and help, we must consider the good of the other more than we consider our own if we are to love truly. From this it can be seen that friendship does not have the exclusiveness of the love of courtship and marriage. For instance, a man ought to love his wife or his intended in such a way as he loves no one else. But friendship is not that exclusive; we can have many friends. Indeed, our love for the friend will want to see him happy in other helpful relationships besides the one we share with him.

Friendship has this quality that the love we show one friend does not take away from the love we show to another, unless this amounts to neglect of the one or an overly emotional attachment to the other, both of which are foreign to spiritual friendship. In this possibility of the love of many people, friendship is like the relationship of all of us to God. The fact that God loves many does not take away from his love for me. The actual love between us is determined by my fitness to love him. So it is with spiritual friendship. The fitness of friend to friend determines the amount of love between them. This fitness principally arises from their closeness to God, but there are other considerations in the attraction of one human to another. And so we may well love one more who is less close to God than another. The heart, as Pascal has told us, has reason the mind knows not of.

Another obligation of friends is the carefulness needed to preserve this divine treasure. At the heart of every friendship must be respect and its externalization, which is courtesy. When we are unlearned in these matters, we think that our friendship can survive anything we can possibly do to it. And so we become careless, not knowing that a sudden storm can end it forever. Special care must be shown in the communication needed to keep this closeness alive. It is possible for friendship to survive all difficulties and storms, and yet to starve to death because of lack of feeding.

A final obligation concerns loyalty and constancy. There is really no need to expand on these since the mere mention of the words carried the full lesson to our hearts. But in a higher sense the friend must be basically disloyal. He owes his first loyalty to God. Insofar as the other person is in harmony with this loyalty, he is to be cherished as another self. But on the other hand if after repeated attempts and much prayer, the path is not toward God but away from him, only one course is open, even if it means a martyrdom of the spirit, the opening up of a lonely and aching soul to be filled, at least for the present, only by God.

Our friends, if they are the right kind, are in many ways reflections of the goodness of God. We love many of the other reflections of God without scruple: the white purity of clouds on a blue sky, the majesty of mountain ranges, the family talk of sparrows, the loyalty of a dog, the grace and dignity of a cat. Yet we should see him so much more in the love of something that mirrors him best, another human being. But just as we love him in the sky and in the clouds and in the birds, so we love him in the human being, and never forget that it is he whom we must thank for what we love in the friend, and to whom is due praise and glory from this friendship.

Practical Reflection

Will I now see friendship as one of the greatest gifts which you, my eternal friend, can give me? a gift reflecting your love and care for me? Will I not select my friends with the care required for any of the other great decisions of my life? Will I not be guided by the deeper qualities which I should expect in a great gift from you, rather than only attraction and superficial compatibility? Will I always judge my friendships principally by the greatest of all tests, the growth of all the virtues? If I have found such a friendship, will I then not cherish the friend as a treasure, and without becoming overly attentive or protective make the preservation of this friendship a major responsibility of my life?

CHAPTER 35

Doves as Serpents

In speaking of love of neighbor and our obligations toward him, we have already come up against the problem of how much. This problem will also arise in many other practical situations of the spiritual life, the problem of excess in good, the obligation sometimes to say no. We know well that God is not found in extremes; the difficulty is largely in finding out what is an extreme. An extreme for one person may not be so for another, and an extreme at one period of a man's life may not be so in another. But on the other hand, it may always be an extreme.

Practical solutions to this problem often involve a delicate judgment. For this we must not expect that God has left us without adequate help. The ultimate sources of guidance are twofold. One is a part of human nature, and this is our reason. The other is close to us, and this is God. This, of course, is a simplified picture and we shall have to fill it in.

When we say that reason is a means of guidance in our spiritual life, we are really saying that truth is this guidance. Reason is God's gift to enable us to get at the truth for ourselves. Reason is our light. But again this is too simplified; God has also given us two other and better ways to get the fullness of truth. One is his revelation, his own speaking to us, and this is found especially in the Bible. The other, not diverse from the first but applying his word to our minds, is the Church. But even though these are superior to reason in finding certain truths, they are insufficient for practical spiritual life. For the most part both the Bible and the Church give us principles and laws; to see how to apply these laws and principles to the details of our life, and to bring our whole being to the perfection that God and the

Church want of us, something else is needed. This again is the light of reason.

Despite the fact that reason is our personal light, we must honestly recognize that it is often a poor one. It is subject to many unreasonable influences such as our mutinous emotions, our prejudices, and the rationalizations brought on by our desires or by the enormous forces buried deep in our unconscious which we rarely even see. Our light is an uncertain light, and knowing God's care for us, we expect that he will not leave us to certain shipwreck. He perfects this light; he strengthens it; he makes it shine more clearly by his own personal care in another of the virtues, this one, holy prudence.

The word "prudence" makes us hesitate; it has become so clouded with undesirable connotations that it is hard to see it as bestowing the maturity as well as the boldness and decisiveness of judgment which, for instance, we associate with manliness in the reasonable man. On one hand it often signifies a timorous, overly careful person who is unappealing either as a Christian or as a human being. On the other hand certain spiritual literature has made some of us suspicious of all prudence because of denunciations of the false prudence of the world. And yet prudence is a good word. If we tried to get a better one, we would be cutting ourselves off from a tradition going back to the wisdom of the ancient philosophers and through two thousand years of Christian history.

This virtue which strengthens and rectifies our practical reason is what makes man the truly admirable man. Because of our romanticists we all have somewhat absorbed the idea that the boldly rash, the impossibly idealistic, or even the quixotic man is admirable. But life and history are full of partial successes, total tragedies, or once-alive hopes now dead, not always because of bad men, but sometimes because of unwise good ones.[1] And while we would not praise a lack of true prudence in our doctors, our architects and builders or in our cooks, we often take it for granted that the spiritual man is to be identified by a pious sort of foolhardiness. We at least expect him to be impractical. Of course, there have been some few saints like this, just as there have been some impractical scientists, but they are not the ideal.

---

[1] The reader may have a full and excellent explanation of this misfortune in the history of religion by reading Ronald Knox's *Enthusiasm*.

Our love of God and neighbor will induce us to use the best means at hand; to use less wisdom is to show less love. Our Lord would have us follow a practical ideal: "I am sending you forth like sheep in the midst of wolves. Be therefore *wise as serpents,* and guileless as doves." (Matt. 10:16)

The virtue of prudence is not a negative, timorous thing; it is positive and dynamic. It is man's power to assimilate certain truth, not as a lesson in a textbook, but as a means for practical, creative use in the governing of himself and others. It does not tell us what is our goal in life; it does not supply principles. These we must acquire elsewhere: from revelation, from the Church, and from our own study and reflection. But it tells us what means to take to our goal, what road to travel, what by-paths to avoid. It is, in short, our way to concrete reality, to the personal truth of our lives. This way of practical truth is then the highway to inner peace.

We have already considered this virtue without naming it, especially when we discussed the near occasions of sin. In these as in many other situations in life, God does not do everything for us. Asking him for help, without using our own powers of reason or common sense, explains some of our failures. Instead of only praying, the wise man will also think about his problem and think about it in practical terms. For instance, just what can be done to make this near occasion a remote one? One man who had a weakness for drinking on business trips overcame it quite simply by bringing his wife along with him.

Not only are there problems in regard to sin, whether great or small sin, but there are also, in the spiritual life, problems between the good and the better. As examples, we have already seen that the love of God is a higher law than love of neighbor; and so, we must avoid those who may not be evil but who are, none the less, not good for us. We must also give consideration to our health. We must limit the time we can give to others. But no number of examples can give us the exact answers for all the problems in our own life. The many solutions require the application of our reason (or someone else's reason, if we seek advice) to the principles and to the problems. It is the glory of man that he has been given this power of reason to do it, and it is his good fortune that God is with him to help him do it.

Some of the decisions, as we advance in the spiritual life, require a very delicate judgment. To compensate for this, the virtue itself becomes stronger, fortified as it is by the grace of God on one hand and by a growing body of experience on the other. Then too, in some cases God gives a special help by imparting the decision to us. This is not the same as revelation, and it can come about by human counsel or our own thinking and studying. The essential element is the inner assurance that a certain course of action is God's way for us. This is a manifestation of one of the gifts of the Holy Spirit, the gift of counsel. We all have these in our soul through baptism, but they are not often used by God in the lives of beginners. The gift of counsel is there both as a reserve light in emergencies and as an instinct to enable us to select from the many paths and ways of the spiritual life the one for which God made us, our personal vocation as we called it earlier.

We will want to increase the virtue of holy prudence because no one will wish to suffer the dangers, the delays, the pain, and the regrets that come from a lack of wisdom. But how to increase this virtue and the help of God which comes with it? We shall discuss several ways now.

The first way is profoundly and terrifyingly simple. In general we increase the efficacy of this virtue by a good life. Conversely, we do the most harm to it by a bad life. Our minds are influenced by our lives, by what we find appealing or pleasurable. We rationalize our conduct, that is, we make our reason subservient to our conduct so that we can live with some sort of enforced peace. But in doing this, we abandon the guidance of reason; we fail to reach the truth; we are strangers to reality. For instance, it is the considered judgment of the broad, sweeping mind of St. Thomas that sins of the flesh can distort our reason more than other sins. Those who willingly immerse themselves in them are unable to see the way to God clearly because of the blinding nature of this impelling pleasure. He also observes that too great a desire for material goods can result in a counterfeit of prudence which is mere craftiness.

Another way to increase in the virtue of prudence is a willingness to learn from mistakes. Of course, this means, first of all, that we have enough true humility to admit to ourselves that we actually make mistakes. Some of us avoid this truth by a grand gesture to the proposition that "we all make mistakes," but fail to admit concrete mistakes here and now or even after the passage of time. Just as mankind must learn lessons from history, each man has his own history and must read often in it if he will be wise. As we grow in insight through the spiritual life, we will continually be reviewing and perhaps revising our past decisions, always into a higher and broader synthesis. As to our mistakes, we will be better for them because we will profit by them, and thus is God's goodness at work. He cannot tolerate evil without eventually drawing out of it some greater good.

Another way of increasing holy prudence is to use its conclusions promptly. This is not the same as acting thoughtlessly. Very few of our major decisions must be made on the instant, and for these we must trust divine guidance and the well-developed habit of choosing the best path to get to our goal. But for most important things we can and must take time for deliberation. Once the decision has been made, we nurture the virtue and open ourselves to the further guidance of God by acting promptly when this is possible or advisable. We sin against our minds by remaining in indecision, especially over trifles. In one way or another we must make ourselves decide and then hold to our decisions. St. Francis de Sales counsels something like tossing a coin to solve minor dilemmas. Even if an occasional mistake is made in this manner, it is infinitely less a mistake than the danger of remaining in chronic indecision.

Thus true prudence is the opposite of what it is often pictured as being, overly cautious. The irresolute man is not the prudent man; he is apt to be the fearful man or a man beaten by life or chained by laziness or some other vice. The prudent man does not try to get more certainty than the situation can give him. He is supported by trust in God and by courage, both strong virtues. The whole goodness of his character makes his decisions. In the end we cannot have one virtue perfectly without all the others.

The virtue of prudence, even in its perfection, does not make a man proudly independent of others. True wisdom is manfully humble. It knows that our thoughts tend to be egocentric, and that this is a barrier to objective reality. A truly wise man will take counsel of others; the virtue of prudence will then enable him to know when to take it, of whom to take it, and whether or not he has received good advice. A man's best counselor will usually be his friend, because a friend can penetrate to the inner situation of the soul and yet see the external reality better than the one so involved in his inner impressions. In certain matters we are led to contact with reality only by the love of a friend. But this love is not the same as sentimentality which impedes the objectivity of vision.

The need of wise human counsel only emphasizes the greater dependence we must have upon God. He is able, not only to guide us in ways direct and indirect, but even to guide us despite faulty reasoning and poor advice. We should include him in all our plans, not as an interested onlooker, but as a friend deeply involved. Our prayer should be always before him for light, for decision, and ultimately for the secure accomplishment of what he knows to be the truth in our lives.

Practical Reflection

A little reflection should make it clear to me that the virtue of holy prudence must rule all the other virtues in order for them to be truly virtues . . . all except the love of God because I cannot love God too much (although imprudence is possible in the manner of showing him love and in the time I might want to give to it). I should also see sin as the greatest imprudence of all. I must be careful not to confuse prudence with timorousness or mediocrity lest I be moved to think that rashness and caprice are admirable qualities. I must make my memory serve me by recalling the reasons for past decisions and the mistakes which perhaps have caused them. I must constantly keep God in my plans so that they will have the ultimate success of being the same as his plans.

CHAPTER 36

Love and the Humble Heart

No one has ever reached closeness to God merely by following the rule book, just as no one ever learned to play baseball by its book of rules. To a great extent we must learn by doing, and we do this best by having someone show us how. Our heavenly Father has given us someone to show us, to be our model for the life of the spirit. This is, of course, his Son, Christ our Lord. This divine teacher has proposed a path which our love must take if it would follow his steps: "Learn from me," he tells us, "for I am meek and humble of heart." (Matt. 11:29)

In learning from him, we must note not only what he says, but also what he does not say. For instance, he does not say: "Learn from me, for I am wise and prudent." Wisdom and prudence need something deeper; humility makes us wise and prudent. He also does not say: "Learn from me, for I am strong and powerful," as he surely could say in all truth. He knows that if he proposed strength and power as the great ideal, he would be tempting us into the root vice of all the evil in the world, the weakness which is pride.

Often we really do not know what pride is, and so find it hard to escape it. What knowledge we have of it is a mixture of accuracy and inaccuracy. For instance, we recognize pride in an arrogant man or a vain woman. But on the other hand we often admire a truly proud man, someone who is ready to fight at the least insult, or some Catholic intellectual who seems in rather complete doubt about the wisdom of the Church of God, but who has no doubt at all about his own. We even sometimes make such men our heroes and leaders, but we should rather pray for these unfortunates.

The confusion about the meaning of pride is increased by the use of the word in a good sense, as when we say that a man takes pride in his work or a woman in her cooking. Quite truly there may be some vainglory involved here, but we usually mean that such people are careful workers. And this care is in itself a virtue.

St. Thomas says that "pride is an inordinate desire for our own excellence." (II, II; 162; 2) It is a lust for some kind of supremacy. In extreme cases it means contending even against God. This was the original sin of the devil as well as of our first parents. In fact, the devil tricked Eve, and Adam through her, by telling her that if they ate of the forbidden fruit, they would become like gods and, of course, be independent of the true God. If we look closely into ourselves, we will see that we are still sometimes fighting the same battle.

A proud person obviously cannot love God deeply, nor can he truly love his neighbor either. He is apt to be demanding of others, perhaps in subtle ways. He loves them only if they are useful, subservient, or flattering. Or he loves them so that he can do good to them and thus glory in his obvious excellence. Or he can be cruel to others, for are not all men competitors with the god he has made of himself?

We sometimes come across good people of whom we are not sure. They do everything that the Church asks of them; they are diligent in all the externals of worship; they do many praiseworthy things for others. Yet we fear that some day they will meet opposition or contradiction in such a way that they will turn from God or from the Church in what will seem to be a sudden reversal. The truth is that the background for the change has been there for a long time, not outwardly and consciously, but inwardly and unconsciously. Like the seed that fell on the shallow ground in the rock, these people never had deep roots. Their show of virtue was a performance for an audience, even if the audience was no one but themselves. In how many cases also were they not dwelling on the deficiencies of others, thus assuring themselves of their own applause for themselves?

God knows a terrifying thing about pride and he has told it to us three times: he must resist it. "God resists the proud, but gives grace to the humble." (James 4:6; I Pet. 5:5; Prov. 3:34) It is impossible for him who is truth to tolerate what, if left unopposed, would turn itself into the falsehood of being a rival, a falsehood, because every part of such a rival has come into being, and still has being, because of God's will and power alone.

What a terrifying thing that God who loves us should so have to proceed against us as to resist us. Despite all the good works, all the protestations of love, all the penances and the prayers, he must resist us if we are proud. Our talents become like plants that try to grow without sunlight. Our ambitions are constantly thwarted. Our intelligence is allowed to pilot us into stupidity. And our lower nature leads the would-be god around like an animal. But in all this, God is still loving us. He spends most of his grace trying to get us to be humble. The remorse for sin, the embarrassment for errors, the lessons from temptation, difficulties, and discouragements are, in the proud man, all principally for this purpose.

Just as some of us do not always recognize pride, it is also true that we may not understand humility. This word often gives us an image of an unpalatable, cringing sycophant, a man too self-effacing to have a personality of his own. We see this virtue in terms of weakness, whereas it is really the result of strength.

Humility has all the strength implied in self-control and self-conquest. The victory consists in controlling but not destroying the overpowering desire we have for our own excellence. Our human nature compels us to love and desire our own excellence as a basis for self-respect. God has made this an unavoidable force within us. But by original sin it has gotten out of control, and we are in the position of trying to harness a tornado. Success is an accomplishment possible only by God's grace and a growing maturity.

A part of the poor image of humility comes from its counterfeit, false humility. A false humility is always denying that it possesses any good qualities at all, and often does this with one eye hopefully upturned for more praise because of the denial. True humility, on the other hand, does not prevent us from acknowledging our good qualities, whether natural or spiritual. It is deeply rooted in the fact that all things come from God: "What hast thou that thou hast not received?" (I Cor. 4:7) God is to be praised by us for all his gifts and in all his works, even those we find in ourselves. A certain prudence may prompt us to keep a modest reticence, while humility will prevent us from concentrating on our gifts so much that things get out of proportion. True virtue, then, does not allow us to flaunt our gifts before others, but it does not prevent us from acknowledging them or using them.

To know ourselves is a necessary part of the progress of maturity, including spiritual maturity. According to St. Thomas, "It is requisite for a man's perfection that he know himself." (II, II; 132; 1 ad 3) He has to know what he has been given so that he can develop and use it. Through self-knowledge he finds his natural and spiritual personality and also the personal vocation for which God has designed him. Through self-knowledge he will also arrive at a sense of his own value as a person and thus will be able to believe more easily in God's love for him. But a false humility, which refuses to look at the self except to find fault, will not accomplish any of this.

Such a recognition of our good qualities, however, is really not the work of humility. It is rather the work of another virtue which must go hand in hand with humility to make us balanced human beings who are also capable of the highest spiritual life. This virtue is called magnanimity, and means greatness of soul. By this a man's mind is made clear so as to recognize the highest things as being within his grasp, and at the same time to give him heart against fear in order to achieve them. This virtue keeps humility from becoming something which would have us always crawl the earth, but on the other hand humility keeps us from flying too high, in an exaggerated estimation of our own powers.

To do this, humility makes us willing to face our limitations, our defects and weaknesses. Such recognition is not for the purpose of discouraging us into hopelessness, but to show us the goodness of God and our need of him. All the words in the books, even the words of the Scriptures, are not as efficacious for this as the bruises that come to us through our blindness and willfulness. By these bruises we are forced to acknowledge our need for God, and our need in turn prepares us for the unbelievable revelation that, despite the depths of our wretchedness, God still has enough goodness to love us and want us. Humility is the wholehearted acceptance of this reality.

The acquiring of this most necessary virtue must begin with the deep conviction of entire dependence. Our relationship then is not the same as a partnership of quasi-equals: "God helps me whenever I need him." Nor is our need reflected in the self-satisfaction that sometimes comes with success: "I worked thirty years on this job and never missed a day." There must be a totality about our thinking which, while it allows for our own part, must give to God even the credit that there is our part. We have received even this from him. The will and the strength to accomplish our part, the circumstances of our success, the prevention of circumstances which would bring failure, are all the gift of God. It is this kind of dependence which we should mean when we say, "Give us this day our daily bread." The humble man turns to God automatically in everything. God is at his elbow and he knows it.

Another help in acquiring humility is a certain kind of love for truth. This truth is the actual recognition of what we are here and now, in our present state of spiritual growth. This love of truth resists the adoption of pious attitudes by which we sentimentally come to think we are much better than we are. Someone may, for instance, have read of degrees of humility which are variously listed by solid authors. But instead of expecting that the perfection of this virtue will come with much added grace, he goes around saying how contemptible he is or how he longs to be treated with contempt, when the truth is that such treatment would bring forth violent resentment or plunge him into deep depression. Pride does not leave us just because we are determined on the spiritual life. The adoption of attitudes takes us away from reality, and reality is the only basis for the spiritual life. If we are not real human beings we are imitations, and the spiritual life cannot be built on imitations.

Instead we practice humility to the degree possible to us here and now, and this practice of the virtue is a way to acquire more of it. This does not mean that we must do stupid, irrational, or boorish things just to become humble, as some falsely interpret St. Paul's reference to being a fool for Christ. (I Cor. 4:10) But we turn away unostentatiously from praise; we accept reproaches when they are deserved, and we try to accept them even when they are not deserved. We accept the humiliations that come from our faults and deficiencies, and there probably will be enough of them. We accept the principle of authority in its many variations and representatives, and we accept the regulation of our lives that comes from authority, even when not ideally exercised. We accept the challenge to personal submission by obeying laws even when we are not watched. We accept the sharp word, the discourtesy, and the thoughtlessness of others in imitation of him who allowed himself to be blindfolded and ridiculed for us.

We accept humiliations, of course, but not on every occasion, as neither did our Lord. The virtue of holy prudence operates more intimately with humility than perhaps it does anywhere else. We are sometimes obliged to maintain our rights and dignity. These then become more important than the benefit to our soul in accepting humiliation. A beginner, however, and many who no longer would consider themselves beginners, will wisely be prepared to accept more than they will give back.

It will help us to acquire humility if we avoid the appearance of pride, for our outward activity can influence the interior in good ways or bad. This does not mean that we go about with head bowed and fancy ourselves to be humble. But we avoid seeking applause; we avoid the first row, the demand that we be the constant center of attention. God even seems to dislike it when we brag in fun, not to mention real bragging or the embellishments we add to the account of our exploits.

To grow in this virtue, we can hardly expect success if we do not proceed from love of God. The necessity to love is even more crucial here than with other virtues. For instance, Benjamin Franklin tells us in his *Autobiography* how he carefully set aside a definite period of time to concentrate on one virtue after another. From such careful planning one would expect success, and he did achieve it except, he tells us, in the virtue of humility. For, when he found that he had acquired a bit of it, he simultaneously found that he was proud of it.

But when we love God, and because we love God, we do not want to take away from him anything that belongs to him. We do not want to take away the glory and the credit for what he has given us. We love him enough not to want to give ourselves what is truly his. Besides this, we want him, and we see that we cannot have him as long as we are rivals with him. Humility draws this loving God close to us. Only the truly humble man can truly love.

Finally, to help ourselves acquire humility, we must pray for it. It is so important that we must pray for it every day. A habit of saying "Jesus, meek and humble of heart, make my heart like unto thine" at some time during the day will remind us to ask for it more often than once a day. Humility, as we will need it in the spiritual life, is a virtue above human nature and we will need help from above to get it.

The spiritual life is not foolproof. There is an endless number of ways to spoil God's work in our souls. But humility is the best insurance we can have that we will remain in God's love. There really is no better way. Not by good works, because some of God's best workers are far from him because of their pride. Not by detachment from material things, because the devil is, in the sense of the material, the most detached creature there is. Only by humility can we draw God down to us, as Mary did: "Because he has regarded the lowliness of his handmaid." (Luke 1:48)

The truly humble man loses much of what makes for unhappiness. Although he may have high goals even in this world and although he works diligently, he does not proudly demand unrealistic success for himself. He does not worship at the shrine of the false god he has made of himself, nor does he see himself as a shining example for all men to follow. Therefore he does not have to force himself to live up to such unreality. If ambition tries to persuade him to drive himself beyond measure and to thrust others ruthlessly aside because there is always room at the top, humility reminds him that there is always room at the bottom too. He heeds the advice of our Lord, to take the lowest place at the banquet. He trusts God and himself enough to work diligently and to wait for God to provide the opportunity for advancement without crushing others—if God so wills advancement. The truly humble man is a man at peace.

Our Lord thought so much of this virtue that he told two of his parables to illustrate the principle that "everyone who exalts himself shall be humbled, and he who humbles himself shall be exalted." (Luke 14:11; 18:14) This idea of being exalted, as we have said, is not alien to the lowly virtue of humility. St. Thomas tells us that "it is contrary to humility to aim at greater things through confiding in one's own powers; but to aim at greater things through confidence in God's help is not contrary to humility." (II, II; 161; 2 ad 2) The lowly handmaid of God tells us that too: "Because he who is mighty has done great things for me, and holy is his name." (Luke 1:49) Even the proud man can respond to this. The proud usually have one redeeming feature on which the grace of God can get a hold; they want the best, they seek the highest. Yet God has what is best and highest waiting for these tortured souls if they will see their need and be changed by his higher wisdom.

The lowly of this earth, the meek, shall possess the earth. Many victories will come to them that will be denied to the proud, and besides they will also possess the land of the promise. There our exaltation will be the exultation of possessing God in love forever, and our love and joy will have been determined in great measure on earth by our humility.

Practical Reflection

Am I willing, O Lord, to face you with the truth of what I am instead of with some comforting falsehood I have invented? Despite my failures with what you have given me, will I not still be certain of your love because my personal nature is your work according to a certain design and measure? Will I not see the same godliness of design in my neighbor, who is also the work of your hands? Will I not only be gratefully humble before you, but also before your work in my neighbor? In the development of my life will I not look for your guidance and help in every step, and learn humility in patience, in the long waits for you to show your will, in the seemingly endless days for my plans to find completion?

CHAPTER 37

"Love . . . Believes All Things"
(I Cor. 13:7)

If we love the Christ of the gospels and the Christ in the Blessed Sacrament and the Christ in our hearts, then we have no choice but to love the Christ in his Church. The Church is so close to him that it has identity with him. This identity is so close that the Church has been called in the Scriptures the Body of Christ: "Now you are the body of Christ." (I Cor. 12:27)

From this identity of Christ with the Church it follows that we must love her even as Christ loves her, and the Scriptures tell us how he loves her. St. Paul, when speaking of another kind of love, uses Christ's love as a persuasion: "Husbands, love your wives, just as Christ also loved the Church, and delivered himself up for her, that he might sanctify her . . . that she might be holy and without blemish." (Eph. 5:25 ff.)

Our love for the Church has other motives besides the excellent one of following the example of Christ. The Church has been for all of us the way to God. It was she, for instance, who preserved for us the sources of our faith, transmitting the New Testament substantially unchanged through all the perils of the early ages. It is she whom Christ put on earth, not merely as guardian of the word, but as its authentic interpreter as well. It is she who as a mother, not only teaches us, but through the sources of grace, also gives us spiritual life and nourishes it within us. Like every child to its mother, we therefore should give her love.

Our love for the Church would be a sentimental fantasy if it did not have faith for its source and obedience for its fruit. Both faith and obedience are necessary if we would reach our potential stature. We must, first of all, be ready to be taught and guided by God so that we can reach beyond the merely human, and also have greater certitude about those religious truths which are not beyond the grasp of our human powers. We must furthermore be ready to be taught and guided, not only by God directly through the Scriptures, but also by a further means he has put on earth to teach and guide us, and this is his Church. For it is his way with men that he wills them to help one another rather than to have all help come directly from himself. Men must always be a part of the salvation of men.

Since the Church has received the true faith from Christ, she has no choice but to teach it integrally and without compromise. We who are fortunate enough to be chosen by God to receive this word have no choice but acceptance of the doctrines which she teaches, which he teaches through her. "He who hears you," our Lord told the first bishops of his Church, "hears me." (Luke 10:16) Now all who are truly Catholics believe this. They clearly see the contradiction between accepting the Church as the true Church of Christ, as the voice of God, and then denying any one of her doctrines or refusing to obey her laws.

In order to teach us what God wants taught, the Church has been given a special power from God whereby she is infallible; that is, she cannot under certain conditions teach a false doctrine in matters of faith or morals. So great are the consequences of this gift that we must know when she speaks with this authority. She does not claim to be infallible on all occasions but only in three different circumstances: one, when the Holy Father, speaking as head of the Church, solemnly declares to the whole Church a doctrine of faith or morals; two, when the bishops of the Church, united with the Holy Father in an ecumenical council, do the same thing; three, when the body of bishops in union with the Holy Father, but now in their own dioceses throughout the world, agree in teaching that a doctrine of faith or morals is the truth of God. Thus, as an example of the last instance, it was infallible teaching from the time of the apostles that Christ was God, even though it was not defined until A.D. 325 by the first council of Nicaea.

Now obviously the Holy Father may choose to speak without using his power of infallibility. This is particularly true of most encyclicals and of all such communications as addresses on various occasions. He may indeed, and often does, repeat on these occasions doctrines which have been solemnly defined previously, as, for example, the real presence of Christ in the Eucharist. But there are other occasions when the subject matter of the encyclical or address is not in that category.

The fact that such teaching is not infallible does not allow us to disregard it. We must give it not only external, but internal religious assent. Here we will do well to see what the Church under the inspiration of the Holy Spirit says of the obligation of accepting her ordinary, non-infallible teaching expressed through the bishops and especially through the Holy Father.

> Bishops, teaching in union with the Roman Pontiff, are to be respected by all as witnesses to divine and Catholic truth. In matters of faith and morals, the bishops speak in the name of Christ and the faithful are to accept their teaching and adhere to it with a religious assent. This religious submission of mind and will must be shown in a special way to the authentic *magisterium* of the Roman Pontiff even when he is not speaking *ex cathedra;* that is, it must be shown in such a way that his supreme magisterium is acknowledged with reverence, the judgments made by him are sincerely adhered to, according to his manifest mind and will.—SECOND VATICAN COUNCIL: *Constitution on the Church,* No. 25.

The reason for our enlarging upon the doctrinal aspect of our assent to the faith is the conflict, and not always a small one, between the obligation to accept the authority of the Church on the one hand, and on the other the right to freedom of thought in those things which are not of obligation. The wise man will not draw that line too sharply in favor of his own opinions, however sincerely held. He has no real guarantee that even his most cherished personal opinions have the guidance of the Holy Spirit, as the history of other greatly cherished opinions will tell him. But the authority of the Church has precisely that assurance.

The man whose respect and love for God has led him to a certain intellectual humility will try not to avoid God's teaching or to minimize it, but will embrace it wherever he finds it. He will, like everyone, have difficulties with the faith, but will recognize that difficulties are not doubts. He accepts on faith what he does not see clearly, on the authority of God who speaks through the Church. And he accepts the fact that, even though on some occasions she is not teaching with the awesome power of infallibility, it is still God's Church that is teaching. Christ made no distinction between infallible and non-infallible when he told the apostles, "He who hears you hears me." (Luke 10:16) On the day of judgment Christ will judge between his Church and those who use every means to challenge her authority, short of denying it or separating themselves from it.

An intellectually proud man will seize upon the distinction between infallible and non-infallible teaching. He will parade his superior knowledge in his attempt to be considered an authority or to grasp the ever-elusive phantom of false freedom. He will find words to ridicule those who accept non-infallible teaching. He will do much harm to others—and let us not forget it, to himself most of all, for God resists the proud. He gives so much attention to avoiding all but the barest minimum of belief that he misses much of the truth that God would teach him. By his pride he is blocking God's way into his heart.

The Church must be a strict mother in preserving those things entrusted to her by her founder, but her energy is not all confined to the exclusive preservation of the past. She must also be a wise mother in not inhibiting the orderly development of her children. Therefore, within the limits of holy prudence she allows free discussion on the many points of doctrine which are debatable. Indeed, she uses the truth that emerges from these discussions to crystallize her own mind. This is how her teachings grow and develop. Her teachings do not grow by further revelation but by seeing more clearly what is contained in the original revelation of God through Christ, the apostles, the prophets, and other sacred writers. It is like seeing a drop of water, then finding out that it is made up of atoms of hydrogen and oxygen, then discovering that each atom has a nucleus, and so on. But it is the same drop of water. Similarly in the development of doctrine, none of the new conclusions contradict the previous ones. They blessedly enrich our knowledge of them.

This discussion, of course, is principally carried on by theologians. Much of it never becomes known to ordinary Catholics because it is done in professional journals in various languages. The Church, as we have said, has need of these men who have the courage to take the prudent risks of embarrassment at the hands of the better-informed or the clearer-thinking of their equals. But confusion can come to the people in the Church when this crossfire of opinion and counteropinion is carried in readable books and in the popular press. Because of this confusion, a few words on these discussions may be helpful.

Although the Church permits and encourages her trained and erudite members to discuss matters of Scripture and doctrine, we must never forget that it is the Church which ultimately must teach us, not these scholars and theologians, no matter how expert and how erudite. The point is that none of the discussion which reaches out beyond accepted doctrine is Catholic doctrine until it has been accepted by the Church in one of the ways we have mentioned. Only she has our Lord's promise of the Spirit of Truth.

An *imprimatur* on a book is by no means an infallible decision nor even outright approval by the bishop, much less by the universal Church. It is only a reasonable guarantee that the book contains nothing contrary to faith or morals. Perhaps sometimes a bishop will even approve a book of doubtful value, but he is thus concluding that error must be risked or even tolerated up to a point, so as not to put out the candle of enlightening discussion by too closely trimming the wick.

Two attitudes toward such books or articles are to be avoided; one, the fear that the Church itself is changing in those things in which it may not change and still be the Church of Christ; two, and oppositely, a rush to espouse every new opinion as if it had just come from the mouth of Christ. A certain reserve or skepticism in regard to what we read will save us from both this fear and this rashness.

On the other hand, it may seem more rash to advise the layman to appoint himself as a judge of those who have spent years in the study of things of which the layman has only a fundamental grasp. But that fundamental grasp is important; it is the "Catholic sense" which does not always come with intelligence and knowledge, even great intelligence and knowledge. Because there are varieties of gifts in the Church, as St. Paul is always telling us, a theologian may be brilliant and know enormously more than the rest of us, but he may not be blessed with a particularly good judgment in matters of the faith. Origen in the third century seems to have been such a man, easily one of the most brilliant men the Church has ever contained, and a very good man besides. Yet the early Church found it necessary to take time in an ecumenical council to condemn some of his opinions.

On the opposite pole to those who would endanger the purity of the faith by too great an attraction to their own reason, there are those who will make of the faith little more than a superstition. If there is any small rumor of some extraordinary or miraculous happening, these people tend to give it, in practice at least, a greater importance than the intrinsically greater wonders of the faith itself. Many times we hear reports, see the publicity, and even read books about these alleged occurrences, only to learn later that they have been condemned by the bishop or by the Holy See as having no evidence of supernatural intervention.

The avidity for the extraordinary brings the Church into disrepute and cannot be a solid foundation for a life close to God. A true spiritual life is based on faith, hope, and love; it is nourished by the sacraments and it grows in prayer. What authentic supernatural occurrences there are have been given to us for our encouragement or warning, but they are not the essence of a Christian life.

At the root of our relationship with God, and therefore at the heart of our love for him, is belief in him. For we cannot love or serve him if he is not somehow known to us. By our faith God has taken us into his confidence. He has told us about himself and about ourselves, that he loves us and will help us. He has told us about his plans for us, that he has an everlasting home waiting for us. And he has told us how to get there. By our faith we have a direction and a meaning for our lives; our conduct is guided and corrected; our human nature, with its inconsistencies, its infidelities, and its cruelties, is ennobled by it.

With how much care should we not guard this faith from real dangers, nourish it by careful reading, and increase it by prayer and by living it. Living our faith deeply gives more insight into it than much study of it. On the other hand, an evil life or a life lived according to the world puts enormous pressures on it, because one way to kill the voice of conscience is to kill the God behind the conscience. But with God's grace the faith is strong enough to overcome everything that opposes it. "This is the victory which overcomes the world, our faith." (I John 5:4)

Practical Reflection

Do I see that I have many reasons for loving the Church, the principal one being that it is "the body of Christ"? When I say that "I believe in the Holy Catholic Church," do I really mean that I accept her teachings as the expression in human language of your mind in heaven? Am I aware that, contrary to appearances, my submission to your Church brings me freedom, since it gives me truth I would not otherwise have, and it is truth that makes me free? Will I then not only be grateful for this faith which you have given me, but also willing to acknowledge it, prudently defend it, and, above all, live it?

CHAPTER 38

Love and Authority

Our love for Christ, as we have just said, also involves love of his Mystical Body which is the Church. This love is not only for the human beings in the Church, the people and those who rule and serve the people. We love all these with the love of neighbor for the love of God. Love for the Church is something beyond all this, beyond all that is human. It is the same love as our love for Christ.

For that we should be thankful; the human Church is not always that easy to love. In its human components, even in its human leaders, it is not always the unspotted bride of Christ, "holy and without blemish." The same Christ, who loves the Church with the intensity that a husband does his bride, as a man does his own body, has risked the care of this beloved creation into the hands of mortal men. He chose not to rule it directly, nor even with the close indirectness with which God ruled the chosen people through Moses and Samuel. He chose to rule his Church by means of men who must grope and search to find his mind and will, certain only that he will not allow doctrinal error or permit her complete destruction.

Furthermore, Christ risked his Church not only to good men, but also to the certainty that there will be evil men. "It must needs be that scandals will come." (Matt. 18:7) And they did come and they will come because of men, proudly ambitious or negligently indolent, shortsightedly safe or foolishly enthusiastic, repellingly severe or scandalously lax. Christ, who chose Peter who was to deny him and Judas who was to betray him, gave his bride no assurance of better treatment. And yet, despite the humanness of the Church at its worst, it is a thing to be loved, and not only loved but also to be obeyed.

It was partly in view of the tragedies that would eventually happen that our Lord reassured us that he would be with his Church "even unto the consummation of the world." (Matt. 28:20) We would then be sure that he is always in the boat of Peter. No matter how fierce the storms outside or how weak the men within, he is there in his Church; he is there in his representatives, be they wise or not, be they worthy or not. His power, once it is given to the Church, is not retracted, as it was not retracted even in the case of the denying Peter.

This, of course, is stating the case in terms of its lowest common denominator. In reality our respect and obedience to authority will not have to be that stark and naked. It will be clothed with the warmth of many leaders whose care, wisdom, and love do honor to the Christ who chose them. But in any case we honor Christ in his representatives; we honor Christ rather than his representatives, be they pope, bishop, or pastor. And we obey because it is Christ we are obeying.

Men are always saying that we should follow the example of Christ and that our spiritual life should be based on the word of God as revealed in the Scriptures. But there is hardly a lesson more explicitly taught by Christ and the Scriptures than that of obedience. "My food is to do the will of him who sent me." (John 4:34) "Father . . . not my will but thine be done." (Luke 22:42) It is also a fact that he made himself subject to the law of Moses and to the law of the Romans. Although he sometimes spoke with considerable force against the Pharisees, who were not in official authority, we have not one word against the high priests, who were in authority, nor one word against the Romans, who had usurped authority. And then we must finally observe that none of these leaders were admirable men. In the end they would put him to death unjustly. He knew this, and still he respected and obeyed their authority.

The matter of obedience is so important to us that Christ could take no chances with even the possibility of appearing to give bad example. Many misguided men have tragically distorted the words of Peter spoken against a clearly defined and serious misuse of authority: "We must obey God rather than men." (Acts 5:29) So our Lord in his wisdom and love could not risk showing us less than perfect obedience. Therefore he was "obedient to death, even to death on a cross." (Phil. 2:8)

Our difficulties with obedience are perhaps the most understandable of all the difficulties of fallen human nature. Personal initiative and creativity, as well as the urge to have all our desires fulfilled, make this virtue burdensome. Some of this is God-given instinct and involves human dignity and human freedom. Ideally, of course, we should see the necessity of authority, if everything is not to become chaos and anarchy. Our freedom must logically give way to the common good and sometimes to the good of our neighbor. But in practice we do not welcome interference with the personally conceived world we would like to build. We don't like to have someone tell us what we must do, especially if we can't see his reasons, or if his manner offends us (or we make it offend us in order to have an excuse), or if he is less cultured than we are. Some of the early Christians would have had the same problem with certain fishermen. And yet Christ built his Church upon a fisherman.

The Second Vatican Council has put into remarkable language the dignity of laymen. It has even mentioned their right and even at times their obligation "to express their opinion on those things which concern the good of the Church." Note, however, that this advice or protest is not to be made in any manner that one sees fit, certainly not from the housetops so as to force the decision by inciting to rebellion. But "when the occasion arises, let this be done through the agencies set up by the Church for this purpose." (*Constitution on the Church*, No. 37)

Despite this statement of rights, the council has not freed us from obedience, even when we disagree, even if our plea has not been accepted or heard. Perhaps those in authority may at times fail in their obligation of listening or fail in their wisdom to decide as we feel Christ would have decided. The principle of authority is so sacred that God wants these men obeyed unless the command *clearly* is intrinsically evil or is something *clearly* beyond their jurisdiction. Christ himself accepted misguided authority and did not call for twelve legions of angels to deliver him. Therefore, "the laity should, as should all Christians, promptly accept in Christian obedience the decisions of their pastors [pope, bishops, and their representatives], since they are representatives of Christ as well as teachers and rulers in the Church. Let them follow the example of Christ, who by his obedience even unto death, opens to all men the blessed way of the liberty of the children of God."

Is it not mere rhetoric for the council to indicate the connection between liberty or freedom and obedience? On first glance there seems to be a contradiction because obedience must, of its very nature, put limitations on liberty of action. But if we look at liberty as God wants it, we will see that we have a true freedom with obedience rather than without it.

For instance, obedience frees us from the limitations of our own shortsightedness. A wise man realizes his own limited perspective. But someone in a position of greater eminence can see the situation more broadly, just as we can get a better view of the terrain if we climb a hill. Furthermore, obedience frees us from the despotism of our desires, including unconscious desires. These last can influence and even become our reasons for acting, thus putting us under the slavery of inner compulsion. Such motives, of course, do not explain the totality of our difficulties with obedience, but they are true of enough of it. Passion, the current enthusiasm of our times, or the sympathy for a real injustice with a poor solution can cause us to demand that all authority bow to our wishes. We lack insight to see wisely, and hindsight would be too late. Sometimes it is only the powerful binding of obedience that keeps us truly free.

As an ultimate, even if there is no other benefit from obedience, it helps our souls. It frees us from pride which would make the self stand supreme and answer to no one—our shortsighted, variously be-deviled self. Obedience is the most practical exercise of humility. And as we have said before, humility draws God to us.

Obedience is also a manifestation of another important virtue, trust in God. It takes trust in him, trust in his providence, to see that he most often guides us through others. But the more we trust him the more he is obligated to guide our lives through the obedience we give to those who act in his name. Even if they make mistakes in ruling us, God has so planned our lives that we will make no mistake in obeying. This ability to believe that God will make order out of the errors of authority is a way to find peace. Such peace was surely in the soul of Christ before Annas, Caiphas, and Pilate. It is the peace which comes only to those who accept God's strange ways like children, destined to be "the greatest in the kingdom of heaven." (Matt. 18:4)

How far from the ideal of Christ, how far from Christ is the man who is constantly challenging authority: "by what right?" Far distant also is the man who flaunts authority or who obeys only in what he chooses to obey, and thinks that his distorted soul is enjoying freedom. Obedience is not the servile thing he imagines it to be. Neither Christ nor St. Paul were servile men. We do not have to agree mentally with the command as we must agree mentally in matters of faith or morals. Yet, as we have said, perhaps after years of struggle with it, we will come to see that God was in it, anonymously if you will, and through it he was working out in a human situation his plans for us.

What has been said concerning obedience in the Church applies also to all legitimate authority, particularly that of civil government. This too is God-given authority, as St. Paul told the Romans: "Let everyone be subject to the higher authorities, for there exists no authority except from God. . . . Therefore he who resists authority resists the ordinance of God. . . . Wherefore you needs must be subject . . . for conscience' sake . . . Render to all men whatever is their due; tribute to whom tribute is due; taxes to whom taxes are due; fear to whom fear is due; honor to whom honor is due." (Rom. 13:1-7) This is the same doctrine which Our Lord had previously taught, not only in telling us to render to Caesar what belongs to Caesar, but also in telling Pilate that the authority before which he was being put on trial was also from above. (John 19:11)

God could govern the world directly if he so chose. He could personally direct the various public services, provide protection, keep order, and levy taxes. But he chose to do this through men, and he ennobles them by giving them authority and responsibility. Thus their lawful commands are his own commands. Therefore we must obey even if we are not watched, even when we can avoid our responsibilities by undue pressures or influence. We must show respect for those who exercise this authority. We must give example to the young by our actions and by our speech, so that all society, civil and religious, will have strong foundations in the future.

All of us will meet situations in which we honestly believe that a certain law is unjust. But before we may disregard it, there must be no doubt that the law is unjust. In doubt the law is to be obeyed. A great presumption is in favor of the legislators, both because we must presume the guidance of God even in civil matters (especially since we pray for it), and because they have a broader view of the situation and access to better information than is given to the individual.

Sometimes, however, we may have to obey an unjust law out of prudence because of the penalty to ourselves or others if we are apprehended. Likewise we may be obliged out of charity to others, who would interpret it badly, for instance, if Catholics evaded taxes under certain circumstances. It need not be said, however, that we may not obey a law which commands us to do evil.

Our difficulties with laws are sometimes self-made—or at least the intensity of our reaction is more a matter of passion than the injustice warrants. Very often we ourselves keep the fires of rebellion burning high by supplying enormous amounts of fuel to a relatively minor situation. We can keep our peace of mind, in those matters about which we can do nothing, by avoiding inflammatory reading and conversations, and by bringing the matter to God in prayer. Bad government is usually his punishment upon a people that has forgotten him.

The sin of disobedience "is contrary to love of our neighbor, as it withdraws from the superior, who is our neighbor, the obedience which is his due." (*Summa Theologica*, II, II; 105; 1) It is also against love of neighbor in a broader sense by weakening the authority which our neighbor needs for his protection, welfare, and peace. For the law, let us not forget, is not meant principally to help the strong, but to protect the weak.

It needs not to be emphasized that disobedience is also contrary to the love of God. What our Lord said of the apostles is true of all authority which comes from God, whether religious or civil: "He who rejects you rejects me." (Luke 10:16) To reject Christ, even indirectly, is surely not to love him. Without obedience there is a proportional diminution of love. If we truly love him, we will obey. "Love is the fulfillment of the law." (Rom. 13:10)

Practical Reflection

Is my pride such that I assume that I make few or only minor mistakes, but that your representatives always make many and great ones? Am I often criticizing the pope, the bishops, and the priests, and do very little in praying for them and cooperating with them? Are my criticisms rooted in a desire to be left alone, not to be asked to do any real work? Or are my criticisms only a pretext for not obeying the law? Have I been disloyal to Christ to the extent that I have spread out before unfriendly eyes the Church's internal problems? In regard to law in general have I done as I pleased whenever I thought I could get away with it? Has my conscience been allowed to become so exclusively ecclesiastical that, while I fear you when I break a Church law, I do not see you in other laws? Am I now determined to show you love by the fulfillment of the law?

CHAPTER 39

"Love . . . Hopes All Things"
(I Cor. 13:7)

Our life, by the fact that we are children of God, is essentially different from the life of those who are not his children. Many of them are sometimes as good as we are or perhaps even better: honest, kind, generous, and so forth. But the deeper life is different. With them, for instance, seeing is believing. With us, believing is seeing; by faith we can see more clearly, more deeply, and more broadly than they. But faith is only the beginning of the ways in which our life is different. Equally basic and equally diverse from their life is our life of hope.

Now, all men live by hope through an almost ineradicable instinct. But those who do not belong to God must hope in themselves or in others or in some vague power of fate against a threatening, fearsome world. We, while not abandoning our own powers and the help of others, have the deep and enheartening assurance which comes from trust in God.

We sometimes rather admire those who seem to be impenetrably independent. They are the captains of their souls; they are masters of all they possess, and their mastery has sometimes enabled them to possess much. Sometime, but not always. The great failures of life and of history are made up principally of this kind of man. Napoleon is an example. And even with the successful ones, the public façade hides the inadequacies of the private man. Even if he were not, like the rest of us, subject to fear, shame, and personal tragedy, he must in the end come to terms with his declining powers and his ultimate dissolution.

Our dignity as human beings does not consist in becoming substitute gods but in understanding and acting according to what we are. Just as it is written in our nature that we must accept help from other human beings, so it does not make us less than noble to accept help from God. Truth compels us to see that we are not universally strong, farsighted, or provident. Faith tells us that God is.

This truth helps us find peace. Instead of trying to be foolishly, stubbornly, thoughtlessly, or fanatically self-sufficient, we live the truth that "without me you can do nothing." (John 15:5) Even if God chooses to remain hidden behind the powers he has given man, it is he who is working by means of these powers all the time. No one has but what has been given. God is the only one to whom nothing essential is given.

Sometimes our difficulties with trust come, not from an overconfidence in ourselves, but from a lack of confidence in God. We see so many troubles in the world that we lose the assurance that God is intimately concerned with every life, with every soul. Our difficulties come because we are trying to get more assurance than is possible. We would need to project ourselves into every life and see how God acts in that life, in order to be assured of his fairness. For, all suffering and tragedy are ultimately solved only in the individual. But of course we do not possess this impossible insight, so some of us despairingly trust in God only because there isn't much else to do, instead of being calmly and even joyfully assured of his goodness and his care for us.

But if we cannot know all that God knows and does in each life, we still do know God. We know him by the cross upon which he hung for us. Such a God is not a negligent God, nor an unjust God. Despite our disappointments and our sufferings, despite our resentments and our complaints, that figure hanging by nails assures us that there is love, purpose, and hope in every day of our lives. When we are able to see things honestly and clearly, we will understand his love and fairness in the one life we know, our own. To some of us our later years give this insight. For others there is a grim waiting for eternity to give understanding.

Sometimes these doubts come because we don't understand God. He has not promised the same thing to all. He has promised to take special care of those who are close to him. He does not necessarily say that he will take the same care of those who have disregarded him or those who have brushed him aside, but only those who deeply trust in him.

To understand his care for us, we must understand what he has promised. From a basic point of view he has made only one promise. He has not promised to make us rich or successful or healthy or popular. Therefore we may serve him faithfully and have difficulty in earning enough, we may not be promoted in our job, we may be sickly and we may not climb very high in the social ladder. But in none of these things can we accuse God of not keeping his promises. He has really promised us only one thing; he has promised to take us home. And having done that, he will have kept his promise.

This is what our Lord promised in the Sermon on the Mount when he told us to "Seek first the kingdom of God and his justice, and all these things will be added to you besides." (Matt. 6:33) Not all things will be given, not even all the things we want him to give, but only those things which will help us get home. He will indeed give us many things on earth, some for which we may never have dared to ask or for which we may find ourselves totally undeserving. But we must be careful not to *demand* a particular gift or a particular solution. He has promised to take care of us as he does the birds of the air and the lilies of the field, but this must be understood in the light of his wisdom and in the context of his particular vocation for us.

Although our minds and hearts grasp for more, and we cry out that we will have all there is to get or at least this one thing that God is denying us, in the part of our lives which will last forever we will see that he has done more than we could have asked for. Do we suppose that in heaven we will be able to accuse him of the least lack of fidelity to his promises, that we will have anything to hold against him? Herein is the difference between those who have God and those who do not. With them all depends on this world which someday will slip out of their dying fingers. But by God's mercy in giving us faith, we have a distant view into another world, and hope is our hold on it.

Because of our shortness of vision it is not easy to solve all problems in terms of the next life. For most of us our immediate concern is not with ultimates but with particulars, our needs and problems here and now. For these our Lord gives us the assurance of care as for the birds of the air and the lilies of the field. (Matt. 6:25-34) But we fail to be impressed by what seems to be so impractical: "They do not sow, or reap, or gather into barns. . . . they neither toil nor spin." Where would we be if we did not toil or gather into barns?

Our Lord is not trying to teach us improvidence, but trust. As a matter of fact he and the apostles did not live like the birds but kept a common purse for their expenses. Rather he is telling us that his heavenly Father takes care of the birds and the lilies even though they do not do the normal things which we must do in order to survive. How much more then should we not trust him when we have done our best?

We must always do what is in our power. The life of trust is not a life of indolence. Our Lord was condemning worry and overanxious solicitude, not work and diligence. The birds must still seek their food, and the lilies must sink roots and open up to the sunlight.

We must not mistake difficulty in trusting for a lack of trust. By its nature hope is concerned with things that aren't here or aren't here yet. On the other hand the need or the crisis is overpoweringly before us. Our hope for a solution may be barren of any emotion of confidence, but we have not failed God if we keep on looking to him and asking. Indeed, our hope is measured, not by our emotion, but by the enormity of the difficulty and the seeming impossibility of a solution.

The difficulty of trusting must not make us think less of our trust. Even the saints had the same difficulty. St. Paul surely did, and most probably did St. Joseph. St. Joseph was called upon to trust God enormously, despite the closeness of the Son of God. He may have had no different idea of the Messiah than any other Jew, and so was expecting a powerful king like his forefather David. And his expectations would have had a strong support from the miraculous origin of the child, from the appearance of the angels to the shepherds, and from the coming and the gifts of the Wise Men. But one night his warm, glowing world came to an end forever. Terror threatened him and his little family. An angel told him in a dream to flee to Egypt immediately. Joseph got up from his sleep and went immediately.

In the comfortable position of hindsight we take the successful outcome for granted. Of course they will be saved; it says so in the next line. But Joseph couldn't help but be impressed by the percentages against him: one poor man against a king, three people against an army. And then all these dreams could be illusions or even a trap to destroy him. It was a dream that made him go against the obvious in the first place, when he accepted Mary and her son. All this dreaming might have looked very uncertain in the middle of the night as he set out for an unfriendly country. His mind, like ours, could be so filled with one side of a problem that it would be difficult to see the reasonableness of the whole.

But no matter what may have been the emotional and even reasonable barriers against trust, Joseph did trust and was delivered. In our own journeys into the night, God wants us to trust for a particular solution if we see one. But in our agony of uncertainty we may only have the light or the courage to trust *him*.

It is especially by the great crises in our lives that our hope is not only tried but increased, and our love likewise. The more difficult our hope, the more love is implied in it: "Love hopes all things." Also in every successful solution we see God's love active. In this way too we get to know what he is, and our love for him increases correspondingly.

While we must trust God for our many material needs and desires, an even deeper hope must be concerned with the spiritual life. For those who may have despaired of the transformation they once glowingly hoped for, there is the consideration of a neglected attribute of God: he is all-powerful; he can do anything which in his love and wisdom he wishes to do. The disheartened man can rest on this omnipotence. If he has hitherto failed, perhaps there was too little dependence on this power which God puts at the disposal of those who trust him. With God it is never too late.

Hope, here as in any part of our lives, is a most necessary condition for the action of God. Even the loving Christ usually chose not to work miracles unless there was faith and hope. We must trust that God is able to bring about what he wants in our spiritual life, regardless of the imperfections he may see there. In fact he may even find fewer obstacles if we are not as certain as we would like to be. A mind that is too confident is not easily guided. A healthy uncertainty can open the mind to God's guidance. We plead to know the way, to be made to follow it. We can only grasp our future by our hope in him. In

18. Beginnings

trusting this all-powerful care, we are no longer under such inner tension that peace is impossible. In our trust we find a strength beyond our strength, and we find love. Through the helping and supporting hand of God we know his love. In the certainty of this love is our peace.

Practical Reflection

In seeing that life will surely have situations which can only be overcome by a strong hope, do I value this virtue as I should? value it enough to pray for it? Does this virtue also not give me an appreciation of the strength implied in the spiritual life, since only the cowardly refuse to hope? Do I see that a holy prudence must govern my hope, lest I overestimate and thus fall into a rash presumption? But will I not beg God to enlarge my soul enough to accept the fact that my defects are no barrier to hope, if I hope for the right things, since my trust is not based so much on what I am but on what God is? And knowing God for what he is, goodness, power, and love, can I not hope for the highest if I make that highest the perfect fulfillment of my personal vocation and the oneness of love with him?

CHAPTER 40

"Love Is Strong as Death"
(Cant. 8:6)

Unfortunately it is a true observation that in some ways the devil has a better public image than the angels and saints. For instance, in later art, from the Renaissance onward, he is usually portrayed as having a certain virility, whereas the angels (except for a few St. Michaels) have generally become more effeminate when they are not actually women or cherubic babies, not at all like St. Matthew's description of the angel of the resurrection. (Matt. 28:3) This emasculation is also true of many portraits and statues of the male saints, and the ultimate artistic blasphemy is that it is also done to Christ. It is no wonder, with this ineffectual image of our helpers, that we have come to be timorous in our spiritual life instead of confident and courageous.

There is a certain human limitation which is responsible for this one-sided portrayal. It is difficult for us to hold the whole truth at one time. Thus, it is so necessary for us to look upon God, and those associated with him, under the aspect of mercy and love that we tend to eliminate anything which appears to conflict with this image. But if we sometimes picture Christ as only "meek and humble," we should be grateful that our faith has shown us that God is basically gentle and loving. But we must also be aware that this is not the complete picture.

True love demands a hard core, and our Lord showed this strength, not only in enduring his sufferings and death, but also by his defiance of his enemies by bravely walking into their trap because it was his Father's will. After such an example we cannot but expect that the following of Christ in the spiritual life will also demand of us bravery and courage.

The strength that is required of the followers of Christ is a more complete strength than that which is usually accepted as strength by the world. It does not exclusively lie in feats of bravery, usually physical bravery, such as those on a battlefield, or even those on an athletic field which win the cheers and plaudits of the crowd. The strength of which we are speaking lies rather within, and embraces complete life of a man, much of it hidden from others, some of it calculated to bring anything but praise from the multitude. We would expect this of the followers of the Christ who wore no crown of the world's giving except one of thorns. His bravery, and therefore our own, basically means living the truth that is in us.

Religion has suffered much since the age of the martyrs from the timorous good people. And the spiritual life has perhaps for that reason sometimes been called a refuge of weaklings, something to give a feeling of inner prestige to those who are unable to fight the greater battles of life. However, not all of us are weaklings, and not all the weaklings are concerned with the spiritual life by any means. But still enough of this criticism is true. How many of us are cowards all our lives. We dread pain, discomfort, inconvenience. We dread the opinions of others. We are uneasy in our relationship with God: scrupulous, mistrustful, guilt-ridden. We are uneasy in our relationship with men: suspicious, narrow-minded, isolated. We cover our cowardice by a petty devotion to things, we become meticulous and fussy over details so that we will have no time for the big things that take effort and courage, so that we still can convince ourselves that we are something of worth. If the beginner has doubts about the spiritual life that it is a comfortable refuge for such weakness, this chapter is written to assure him that it is not.

It has been wisely said, "Hypocrisy is the homage that vice pays to virtue." But there is also an opposite kind of hypocrisy, the homage that virtue pays to vice. This is found among those who pretend that they are devotees of sin or the world, whereas they are not. Before others they violate their inner selves, and do this out of human respect which is fear of the wrath, judgments, or ridicule of the wicked and the thoughtless. Although this inverted hypocrisy protects them from the ostracism they fear, it brings no peace. Rather it makes them secretly hateful to themselves because it is a sin of cowardice.

Of course, if we are normal and mature, we don't like being different. The gregarious part of human nature usually finds it difficult to be in constant movement against the current. Not only do we get tired with the effort, and depressed because of the moral or spiritual unconcern around us, but we even sometimes question our principles, since it is easier to doubt them than live them under the circumstances. The weakness of the world is made to appear to be the real strength. Ruthless intimidation of one's associates or competitors, bullying those who are paid to serve and sell things, loud talk, dirty talk, or sophisticated superiority, these are the marks of the strong ones. Reckless driving, fast living, loose living—again the strong ones and the admirable ones.

But a more rational view of the situation will make us see it differently. In the first place it does not really take strength to live the way one's crowd does. It is not even the misguided strength of the lonely rebel who must be different out of the weakness of inner compulsion. In fact it is the easy way, despite all its appearances to the contrary. And if any of these strong people should doubt this, there is a simple way to prove it. If such a man were to live up to his conscience, or to the Christian conscience if he has none of his own left, and do this for one month or at least for one week, he would begin to see where the strength lies.

When we speak of the courage to be different from others, we do not mean that we must become public spectacles, to have a Bible or a prayer book under our arm, or dress in a black shroud and wear a sad face. Often these are the exaggerations of the spiritually weak who need these public props to make them feel superior to others. But courage means that we act with God's help according to God's will in the face of any opposition, that we be different if necessary in the right way of being different.

This inner strength is often given the name of fortitude. It is a virtue and comes the closest to giving us a ready picture of what a virtue is, a power or a strength. While it is not the greatest of the virtues, it is an indispensable one. St. Teresa goes so far as to say that for beginners it is even more important than humility. In the affairs of this world it is most strikingly needed and exemplified in warfare. But the spiritual life is a warfare also. For this reason those who lack this manly virtue never succeed very well. In calling it manly, however, we only intend to personify it, and not to exclude women, for the Scriptures praise the valiant woman.

We often read much in spiritual books of the other virtues, and perhaps it is a success of the Deceiver that we read almost nothing of this. But without fortitude we cannot overcome the obstacles that are in the way of the love and close friendship of God. If we lack courage, we will disobey him when he asks something difficult—or more probably, we will find excuses, or we will unconsciously blind ourselves so that we won't see what he asks. We may thus to a great extent be sinless in our failures, but they are failures all the same. We will fail to reach the heart of God.

The virtues are given us, not only to help us onward, but also to remove obstacles which would prevent us from doing what we ought. Thus, the virtue of purity keeps us from being pulled away from God by the appeal of the flesh. Fortitude removes an even more basic obstacle, and that is the undue influence upon our judgment and conduct which arises from the emotion of fear.

Now, we do not have to be told that fear is a gift of God. Its reasonable influence foresees and protects us from many dangers to our souls and bodies. Indeed, if a man never acted under the influence of fear we would not call him brave but foolhardy. For our encouragement as well as our enlightenment our Lord gave us an example of physical fear in the Garden. Inordinate fear, on the other hand, is an evil and is truly labeled cowardice if we give into it unreasonably. This can even be a sinful kind of fear because God did not create us to be under the domination of our emotions. We are not meant to be like certain timid animals whose instinct makes them preserve existence as the highest value. We are made to act according to a certain nobility which chooses the true and the good as the highest values.

The fear of death is, of course, the most basic of our natural fears. All past ages have known our fears of death from disease and accident. Some have also known other fears of our times, such as atomic warfare, but under the form of barbarians suddenly appearing at the gates or enemy galleons darkening the unsuspecting horizon. We never know when heroism may be our own narrow passageway into death. We cannot usually foresee this, but we can prepare ourselves to meet it.

We prepare ourselves for the heroic, first of all by our thinking.

We must soberly understand that, just as men in the past have given their lives for what is right and noble, so it may be our duty to give our own life or those of others, dearer to us than our own. We must see, as even the pagans saw, that there are things which a man should never allow himself to be forced into doing; he should rather die. Even without the light of faith they knew that "it is better to live a twelve month of noble life than many years of humdrum existence." (Aristotle, *Ethics*, Bk. 9, Ch. 8) Wars, as well as crises of all kinds have always found heroism, not only in professional military leaders, but in ordinary people who went to ordinary schools and worked at ordinary occupations. Most of us can take courage from that.

We acquire strength in another way, by accepting the small challenges which come to us often, perhaps every day. The fearful person thirsts for peace but he will not get it if he will not fight for it. If he sees his unenviable state clearly and if he sees that freedom from fear is what he wants, he can bring himself to endure the temporary crises for the sake of a future, more permanent peace.

But we should not demand of the fearful person, and that includes most of us, more natural courage than he need have. Surprisingly, this is not very much. When we intimated that the spiritual life is for the strong, it must be understood that we are speaking of a different kind of courage than natural courage. Spiritual courage which comes from the grace of God is not incompatible with a considerable amount of natural weakness. While it is an undeniable advantage to be naturally courageous, weakness, properly adjusted for, can have advantages too.

It is not only the fact that weakness and the resulting self-knowledge will be weapons against our greatest enemy, which is pride. In addition, the knowledge of our weakness makes us turn to God for his help. We are closer to him because of our need, and then in answer to our prayer, his strength becomes our own. A knowledge of our weakness will also have us depending on the virtue of holy prudence; much of our battle can be won by strategic maneuvering, by avoiding what is too much for our forces, when this can be done with honor.

There is one lesson which the weak do not have to learn but which the strong find hard. As the spiritual life progresses, it is necessary to learn that God must do more and we less. This is a difficult lesson for the strong. Perhaps this is why St. Paul says, "the weak things of the world has God chosen to put to shame the strong." (I Cor. 1:27) And St. Paul himself, one of the most heroic of men, was forced to his knees to learn this lesson: "Gladly will I glory in my infirmities that the strength of Christ may dwell in me." (II Cor. 12:9)

To be strong doesn't mean that we must go to martyrdom with a joke on our lips as did St. Lawrence and St. Thomas More. We can, as a matter of fact, lose our strength by a poor opinion of the strength we do have. Since we don't value it, we have no core around which our forces can gather. The virtue of fortitude is principally concerned with endurance, and this is apt to be an unglamorous thing as we exercise it. But if we look into our vacillating, complaining lives, we will probably find that we have more of it than we think.

In time we see that our strength is more God's strength than our own, for many times we will be confronted with situations which are too big for what we know to be our strength. By such situations we learn a lesson which is always hard to learn, that we must become like children. We must *expect* him to do many things for us, and to solve many problems for us, especially those which would be too much for us, and even to prevent them so they won't have to be solved. But when we do have to look forward to something beyond our strength, we ask for and confidently expect an outpouring of his strength into ours.

This we do, of course, without rash presumption on God. Growth in the virtues and growth in love mean doing the part that is put before us to do. In the virtue of fortitude this part may be hanging on by such an earthy thing as courage for the sake of courage: we dare not be cowards. This is not too unlike the advice that St. Paul gave Timothy: "Stir up the grace of God which is within thee by the laying on of my hands." (II Tim. 1:6) We have had a different kind of imposition of hands at Confirmation, but the idea of latent strength is there.

Practical Reflection

O God, do not deny me courage, this noblest of the virtues. With this I can persevere to the end in your service and your love. Give me, O Lord, not only a strong heart, but also a mind to know that not every situation is meant to be overpowered by attack, but that some must be overcome by endurance, and others avoided by retreat. With you as the one who will receive me, may I overcome my natural fear of death and any excessive fear of the things which lead to death, which are usually accident and disease. In all my difficulties may I always remember that I have your spirit within me to enable me to act as you would have me, as a strong and perfect Christian and soldier of Jesus Christ.

CHAPTER 41

"Love . . . Endures All Things"
(I Cor. 13:7)

To say that the virtue of patience is concerned with impatience would be true, but it would be a rather superfluous observation. If we accept patience only in this limited sense, we are doing an injustice to one of the most important virtues in the spiritual life. By restraining our impetuosity and tempering our fears, it brings to our souls the quiet in which they are most responsive to the more delicate operations of God's grace. In this sense patience is the mother of many other virtues. In the one single word we have an authentic picture that most people have of the spiritual life, as when we say that an exasperating situation or person would try the patience of a saint.

The vice of impatience is usually understood to arise from the passion of anger, and so we shall have to know something about anger. In the process we shall learn something surprising about the spiritual life. For anger has every right to be a part of the spiritual life. This is not a paradox, a play on words to illuminate the truth; it is the simple truth itself. Anger is not so much an enemy to be repressed, as a friend to help us in need. One of the works of patience is to bring this part of our nature under useful control.

Anger is a gift of God to help us overcome difficult situations. These are often a matter of injustice to ourselves or others. We become aroused and thus call upon certain physical and emotional reserves which prevent fear or inertia from paralyzing our reason. We act with more decision and firmness; our intentions are more readily understood; and it is one way that an impelling influence is exerted by one personality upon another. This is the way our Lord became angry at the buyers and sellers in the temple. A temper under control is an arsenal for the battles of life, including those of the spiritual life. The spiritual man has this useful passion within him like the strong heroes whom the world honors; but even more, he has it under control.

In practical life anger is a help in family affairs. Many married people consider that they have sinned when they have spoken with some anger to each other or to the children. Perhaps so, but not necessarily so. Anger can help in dealing with those we love, in situations where love may overpower our reason. Married partners need correction, not too much but some. Children need correction, some more than others. If we fail in this, we not only fail in our duty, but we also leave our frustrations and resentments underground like worms to eat at the roots of love and true harmony. It is normally difficult to bring oneself to the emotional crisis of correcting a partner whom you have told and will tell again that you love beyond the power of words. And it is also difficult to punish one's own flesh and blood in a cold, calculating manner. Anger, moderate anger, gives an added strength to do our duty; it helps us to do many difficult things. This moderate use of anger is the meaning St. Paul took from one of the psalms: "Be angry and sin not." (Eph. 4:26)

But even good anger should work its purposes quickly. For married people, and for all who live closely together, St. Paul's next words are important: "Let not the sun go down upon your wrath." (*Ibid.*) The excess of anger, that is, the sin of anger, can come by being justifiably angry too long.

Of course there are other ways for anger to become a disordered passion. We can be angry at the wrong things. If, for instance, we have been justly corrected by someone, it would be an uncontrolled anger to lash back with bitter words or to brood over sullen thoughts. We can also become sinfully angry even when at the right things, but being more angry than we ought. To lose our temper so that we say irrational things or conduct ourselves before others in an irrational manner is not using God's gift according to his will. "The wrath of man does not work the justice of God." (James 1:20) And it is not being a mature man or woman either.

Anger, even though rarely a mortal sin, is a capital sin; that is, it is often the cause of other sins, some of them more serious. Control of it has this difficulty, that we do not always know when we are going to get angry; the attacks are often sudden and unexpected. But when there is a known cause, such as a topic of conversation, this should be avoided as far as possible. If a dangerous situation cannot be avoided, then our conduct must be planned and prayed for down to practical details. We can prepare as we do when we go out in bad weather.

Since, however, we cannot always foresee the stimulus to this passion, we must learn control of the passion itself. If we are easily angered, the only solution may be to turn the mind away immediately from *any* consideration of the irritating situation, like turning a key in a lock, until enough time has elapsed for calm thinking. The same firm treatment must be given to angry thoughts which can possess us for hours and for days. Just as an obscene thought can arouse a man until he cannot control lust, so also angry thoughts can keep this passion at boiling temperature when they are encouraged or given only token opposition.

Countermeasures sometimes work better than attempts at direct control; there are many ways to guide or distract our minds into reasonableness and tranquillity. Counteremotions can be used here as in so many other cases. We make ourselves think the opposite thoughts or feel the opposite emotions; there is always a good side if we will look for it—not always a bright, happy side, but a useful side such as a warning or a pathway for action. Another helpful countermeasure can be the humiliation which comes from asking pardon in each case of unjustifiable or excessive anger. The difficulty involved in doing this will sooner or later send the message to our irascible nature that immaturity is unprofitable. This method, however, can only rarely be used by those in authority, or their authority would be weakened. These must usually ask pardon of their neighbor by asking pardon of God.

The powerful action of God, which knows no opposition when it chooses to act, will be the decisive factor in many of our victories. He can, by this power, get to our will before the emotion does; he can make us not to become angry even though we were previously helpless. More than one man has found this out. St. Francis de Sales was once a high-tempered young man, but eventually became known as "the gentle saint."

The virtue of patience has a close connection with the virtue of fortitude; it indicates a most difficult duty imposed by fortitude, the duty to endure. There are, in general, two situations in which we exercise fortitude. One is the attack, by which we set out to accomplish a difficult work, and the other is endurance. But the more difficult of the two is endurance. It is a military truism that the attack is preferred to the defensive, and the siege tests the man more than the charge. In the endurance of difficulty, pain, or harassment we do not have our natural impetuosity working for us. The glory of the martyrs is that they, more than all men, were completely on the defensive. Patience and meekness are not popular or glamorous virtues, but they imply that self-control which our Lord showed us and which the Scriptures praise: "Better is the patient man than the strong man; and he that governs his temper than he that storms cities." (Prov. 16:32)

We will have much need of the courage which storms cities, which carries us through great but superable difficulties. But such courage leaves us as only half a man if we do not endure with patience the difficulties arising from fear: fear of failure, harm, or death, fear for ourselves and others. The commonly experienced form of this fear is called worry.

All sorts of things will worry us if we will let them, some as big and as real as impending major surgery, others as small as a bit of dizziness or the delayed arrival of husband or child. We worry about health, about the family, about the job, about religion—and we may honestly believe that it is this precise situation which is disturbing our peace. But more pervadingly there is something else that has a hold on us; we are in the grasp of demoralizing fear. It is really fear that is the matter.

One advantage of self-knowledge is that, once we realize what is the root difficulty, we can bring our forces, offensive and defensive, to bear upon it. So very often we hear that worry is to be solved by trust in God, but trust is only a part of it. If we do not have courage, we will not trust. God intends to be trusted, but he also intends that we have valiant hearts to control our fears. Too great an emphasis on trust implies that God will somehow place us back in an Eden where we may never know fear. But God has placed us in this world to become strong, and our trust must grow in the midst of fears, whether real or imaginary.

Now there are ways to control worry, but it may take all our courage to use them. The first way is the advice which always seems so futile: "Stop worrying." Well, why not? Many of us can soberly look back over lives filled with anxiety and see that we need not have worried perhaps even once. Then, since this crippling torture has been so uselessly with us, why not manfully put an end to it? How? Simply by refusing to think about the problem, its possibilities or its consequences.

Now, of course, this isn't going to solve the problem itself, and it isn't going to bring absolute peace. The problem will be solved in God's time, and our peace is meant to be only relative when faced with difficulty. Fear is a part of our nature, and is meant to put us on the alert, to bring certain of our forces into action against the difficulty. But this controlled anxiety is not the same as the constant distraction from peace and the gnawing away of our vitality which we call worry.

Another way of control has to do with the fact that worry, even though it is an exaggeration of fear, is still an emotion, and thus was created to be under the power of reason and will. Therefore, most of our major worries can be settled by analyzing them; the minor ones are best brushed aside. Reasoned analysis is also unwise for those worries which imply deep-seated psychological problems, as may be the case with scruples or hypochondria. Here an analysis may only keep the paralyzing and compulsive fears in the foreground where they are uncontrollable. But for most people and for many worries, the quiet analysis of problems (often done on paper) is a way to bring peace. In certain extreme cases, however, the only way to peace is through professional help.

Often we will find that the principal cause of the disturbance is fear, and although this is real enough, it shows that the pressure is psychological, from within rather than from the outside. We then make the courageous resolution to shut out the fear because, as is so often told us, we "really have nothing to worry about."

We must, in both of these methods, prevent our minds from thinking about the forbidden subject, as we prevent them from entertaining temptations against the other virtues. We do not merely try to keep the disturbing thought out; we change the pictures in our minds by using our free will and our powers of concentration. We distract ourselves to God (perhaps only for a moment) and then to something which may have greater power to draw us from anxiety. Our peace of mind will come by determined, yet reasonable forgetting.

Of course it is not always easy for the worrier to achieve such concentration. But it can be learned and developed mainly by a determined and sustained effort to *do what we are doing.* For example, when we read, we read; when we reflect, we stop to reflect. We do not try to reflect as we hurry to finish the page. By means of self-discipline in small things, we can acquire the habits which will help us in our larger problems.

However, there is always the thin edge of the wedge which starts worry all over again: granted that the catastrophe isn't likely to happen, it *could* happen. Our Lord has told us what to do about this: "Therefore do not be anxious for the morrow." (Matt. 6:34) A great secret of inner peace is to live in the present moment. We resolutely do only what planning must be done, and close the mind to the pull of unreasonable anxiety. Even in our necessary planning, we do well not to imagine ourselves in fearful situations, possible but not probable. It is one of the deceptions of the imagination that it can make fear rise more vividly in anticipation of what will never happen than in an actual situation itself. Besides, here and now we do not have the grace which God will give in any future real situation, and therefore we are actually trying to see ourselves through without his help.

Living in the present moment must go hand in hand with trust in God. But what is to be our manner of trusting him since the fearsome evil *could happen?* One way is to trust him that it won't happen. God wants to be trusted this way; it is the basis of prayer. We are like the apostles who pleaded with Christ sleeping in the boat. Our storms too will be calmed.

But other boats have sunk and carried good and even holy people with them. What about trust here? There is a kind of trust which we come to understand by love. By love we get to know God, not what he will do, but what he is. This again is what our Lord meant, that we become like children in our trust. Christ is within us, even if not in the boat. Somehow, all the tangled threads and fears of our lives will be woven into a meaning by his hands. So we look to him; we love his will. Our love becomes our peace.

In dealing with extended worry, we should not neglect natural means involving the body. If we go to a doctor and tell him we are worried, he will tell us to take food, rest, exercise, and diversion. If we tell the same troubles to a priest, we expect him to tell us to pray and trust. But why not do both things together? Many people have failed to solve their emotional and spiritual troubles because they neglect the support of a healthy body.

There are, of course, many other things besides fear that call forth our power to endure. There are other sufferings of body, mind, and soul. The carrying of our cross in union with the cross carried by our Lord will make us grow both in patience and in love. There is also the delicate quality of being patient with ourselves, but without pampering or excusing ourselves. We accept our limitations, and our ability to make mistakes; we are patient under our mistakes. And finally, we must learn to be patient with God. Here above all, we see that patience is humility in action. There are many things we will have to settle between ourselves and him all during our lives. He has told us: "My thoughts are not your thoughts, nor your ways my ways." (Isa. 55:8) But it is these ways of God, irrevocable, often unpredictable, time-consuming, even seemingly contradictory to our best interests, which are the only way to love and peace.

Practical Reflection

Will not a little reflection enable me to see that patience is a guardian virtue of all the other virtues, indeed of all the things I hope to attain in life? I would destroy my plans, my loves, my friendships by my impetuosity, by my anger, by my unwillingness to sustain and endure what I must for success. But this virtue is advertised as the virtue of success: "Patience gain all things." I ask, O God, that you deepen within me the roots of this virtue so that I will grow with an inner strength that will make possible the victory over life, the peaceful acceptance of myself and your mysterious ways.

CHAPTER 42

"Rejoice in the Lord"
(Phil. 4:4)

We have come, in this chapter, to a point of summation. The reader has been urged to love God, to avoid the dangers to this love; he has been held to the difficult love of his neighbor; he has been counseled to be hopeful, humble, wise, strong, and patient. This is the good life, but what comes from all this? Will he be any happier? Our Lord gives the answer in the affirmative: "Come to me, all you who labor and are burdened, and I will give you rest. Take my yoke upon you . . . and you will find rest for your souls." (Matt. 11:28, 29) The issue is then resolved; the spiritual life is meant to bring happiness.

To understand what he means, we must interpret our Lord's promise intelligently. It would be unreasonable, for instance, to expect that a hundredfold of happiness will come immediately upon the completion of this book. Ordinarily it would be unwise for God to lavish his riches of conscious love and complete peace upon one who has only begun the work of conformity to Christ. Much self-knowledge, constantly increasing, is needed in order to see the hidden obstacles which are at once obstructions to the spiritual life and to peace. The constant acquiring of the inner strength of the virtues will enable him to love God more, and thus prepare him for the greater insights and greater perfection which are a condition of greater peace and love. His present degree of love is an urging to a higher degree; only when he is able to give God his whole heart will he find the whole of God's peace.

Before we can understand happiness, we must be able to distinguish it from something which is often mistaken for it, but is quite diverse, and this is pleasure. Despite some uncomplimentary things which are sometimes said about it in spiritual books, pleasure is an authentic human experience; it only becomes a counterfeit item when it tries to masquerade as happiness. There is nothing wrong with pleasure in its proper place. God made it; we all need it in various ways, and indeed it is one of the components of the complex thing called happiness. But it is of its nature a temporary thing; happiness is meant to be more permanent.

Pleasure is usually, though not exclusively, associated with the senses, and these are notoriously inconstant, easily surfeited, and restless for something different. Life is left bored and dreary in its absence. Despite the remarkable perseverance of those who would sell us sense-pleasure, we can have much of it and still be without happiness. Of a higher order are intellectual pleasure and spiritual pleasure (though we usually have other names for this), and these do not have many of the disadvantages of the pleasures of the senses. But still no one can build his life on them because again they are temporary and depend on many factors outside of a man's control. Happiness, on the other hand, is a state of being; it comes from within. Although it is not the unobscured and ecstatic experience of heaven, even on earth it can be our companion for much of our journey. It has many variations which at the peak we call joy, but even at the bottom is still peace amid difficulties.

Such a state of relative tranquillity and gladness is won at the price of fulfilling two basic conditions. The first of these is that it be happiness in the Lord. There are, of course, many other reasons for happiness; human love and human accomplishment are easily the greatest. But God has so made us that the deepest, most complete, and utterly permanent happiness must be in him. Many difficulties of life are so arranged to show us that this is true.

The other major requisite is that we find our personal vocation. This, as we have already said, is a broad complex of important details which constitute the personal way in which we are to go to God. Many times this involves external conditions which are possible of attainment. On these, then, a certain amount of happiness rests. Yet they are not essential to it, despite the urgings of our limited vision. We usually demand for happiness what we would like, but sometimes this demand is mistaken; it is not what God has designed us for. A large number of difficulties of life can come during the process of learning what God wants. Many of us are slow learners, and in the learning we cannot expect to be very happy.

What is more important, when considering happiness in the Lord, is finding our personal vocation as regards our interior life. Many times we have within us obstacles from our previous education, manner of living, from our temperament, or from our ambitions. While these are with us, even if unobserved, they are pulling against our happiness because they are incompatible with what we really want, and so our soul is a divided house. But in the maturing process of spiritual growth we sort out these characteristics, the good from the unsuitable. By instinct or by reason we keep those which bring us peace on our way to God; the others, no matter how good in themselves, we discard. Our life then becomes less and less an interior conflict. We find God and relatively great happiness in God because we have found ourselves.

For one reason or another we all carry around an emotional burden which works directly against our happiness. This is the state of discouragement. It is really one of the great psychological and spiritual evils, and might really be called an eighth capital sin when it is permitted deliberately. Like the seven capital sins, it is not always a grave thing in itself but is the cause of other often more serious deviations from God. It dries up the fountains of enthusiasm, purpose, and love, and substitutes the poisonous waters of depression, pessimism, and hopelessness. All of us have had it, and St. Paul may well head the list. Not one of us at some time has not said, "What's the use?"

Since discouragement can turn good people away from the dedicated quest for God more easily than anything else, we must use any legitimate means against it, even if not always a spiritual means. Most of these means are the same sound advice we might read in popular books on mental health and personality problems. Such books are not to be undervalued just because they do not carry an *imprimatur*. One of the underlying principles of St. Thomas is that we should accept the truth wherever we find it.

In summary, however, much of what has been said elsewhere in this book, especially when discussing temptation and worry, will also apply in the difficult fight against depression. Therefore, not only is sufficient rest an essential weapon, but also any legitimate means of distraction such as recreation. Constructive work and the helping of others have enormous usefulness here. Talking it out may help, but too frequent talking sometimes deepens the mood, as it also can with our resentments, fears, and pains. The important thing is not to let the depression get inside us, so to speak. Once it does, it sets up certain changes in the body chemistry which make it more difficult to pull out than if we kept the battle at a distance.

Besides these indirect methods, we must keep our lives balanced by a determination of the will; we simply will not give in, no matter how black the thoughts or circumstances. We remind ourselves that we have been through the darkness before, and always have seen the return of the light. "This too will pass." We encourage the thoughts and feelings that were with us before desolation set in. We do not veer from the course upon which we had determined when we had peace and light. We force ourselves to positive thinking.

Besides these natural measures, which, however, become supernatural because of our intention to use them for God, there are two even more important helps provided by the spiritual life. One of these is obvious by now and this is the strength of God obtained through prayer. We will need strength in order to take the means to crawl out of the depths. Then also, the spiritual life not only encourages us to change the pictures in our mind; it also gives us healthy pictures and the motives which will make us use them.

Instead of inducements to discouragement we have stronger ones leading ultimately to joy. Our joy is founded first of all on our faith; by this we have the reality of God and his love; we have Christ for our savior and brother, and we have Mary for our solicitous mother. We are rich through our faith, and we reach out for these riches by hope. Through God's promises we have a hold on happiness; because of his promises eternal joy is possible to us. We are not always happy now, but we are like people working at a job that is sometimes hard and distasteful, yet has a positive hope of a generous and happy retirement. Throughout all this there is love, love eventually to fill the endless thirst we have for it. And not only love in the end, but much of it on the way. We have God's word that this love will be immortal; our happiness will be immortal. This is why heaven is sometimes called the eternal nuptials. We should be as happy in anticipation of this kind of eternity as a man would be in anticipation of his wedding night.

Other advice often given for discouragement is to "count your blessings." If we are honest, we find that we have enough of them, including those just mentioned. But the spiritual life provides an added facility in using the insight into our true situation. It encourages us to be thankful at all times. Having acquired the habit of gratitude in the days of light, we will keep this insight into saving reality in the days of darkness.

Even though thanking is one of our duties, we usually fail to do as much as we ought. Perhaps this is because of forgetfulness, but it may also be more deeply rooted in an unconscious desire to be independent, even of God. Our pride or our insecurity demand that we be the author of our own good, lest our fragile self-esteem crumple under the fact that we have received from another. Ingratitude, however, can rob us of our joy because in our attempt to forget the giver, we also may forget the gift. We also forget the love and care of the giver. And so in our next depression we are without a very strong rope which can pull us out. The saving truth for us is that God will keep on giving—and this, despite our failures; we can't possibly get into a hole that God doesn't know a way out.

In thanking for the gift, we immediately bring the giver close to us. The clouds of depression then do not separate us; he is right beside us in hope and love. We mean something to him even if to no other. Our greatest gratitude must be for himself.

The problem of happiness is largely the problem of how to deal with suffering. There will never be a time when we will be able to say that we will have no more suffering. While not anticipating a particular suffering, we must adjust to this inevitable fact. We then will have solid earth under our feet and be more able to accept suffering when it comes.

The truth is that it is possible to be happy and suffering at the same time—not perhaps in the moment of pain, but happy in the fact that suffering has a deep value. We show our love for God by loving under distress. We amass much merit for ourselves, "treasures in heaven," as our Lord is not too sophisticated to remind us, "where neither moth nor rust can consume, nor thieves break in and steal." (Matt. 6:20) We gain graces for others; we atone for our sins. Our sufferings are a pledge of God's love; if we carry our cross, we are sure we are following Christ.

Our sufferings may be like Good Friday but our hearts must be like Easter. Too often suffering is preached as if it were the purpose and highest good of the Christian life. Yet St. Paul who preached "Christ and him crucified" (I Cor. 2:2) spoke much more about the resurrection, Christ's and our own. This is the way we should see the battles of this life, even many of the defeats of this life, as preludes to the final triumph. Through Christ crucified we see love, but in Christ risen we see love and hope. Ours is a triumphant God, a triumphant lover who will as surely take us to happiness as he himself in his human nature found happiness. What else in the world is as important, as consoling, as encouraging? We have an empty tomb but not empty lives or empty hearts.

Practical Reflection

Am I immature in my outlook so that I believe happiness to be the same as pleasure, so that I think I am not happy unless I am being amused, entertained, or flooded with sense enjoyments? Am I so unrealistic as to expect that happiness is always a spontaneous experience, that it is not often something to be worked for as I would work at a job to keep away need or work at the dikes to keep my house from being flooded? Will I therefore determine on specific practical measures to keep my mind free from depressing moods and thoughts? And will I not see that for sustained happiness I must open my life and my heart to the Lord?

PART VIII

LOVE AND THE WORKS OF LOVE

CHAPTER 43

Work and the Spiritual Life

The reluctance to take up what is feared as the uncomfortable spiritual life is sometimes stimulated by those for whom an active enthusiasm seems to be the only virtue. They cry out for action, for the apostolate, and have little time or patience for the steady growth implied by the spiritual life, as indeed it is implied in all healthy life. They mistake their enthusiasm almost for a revelation from God, his manifest approval of their projects and their way of doing them.

This single-minded cult of mere energy is notably found where the project is new and different. Unlike the plodding monotony connected with so much that is unnoticeably accomplished, it is an exhilarating experience to be in the forefront of some new movement. But unfortunately one can become so involved in the exhilaration as to lose sight of the purposes of God. It would be likewise exhilarating to stand in the front of a boat and toss one's head into the exhilarating breeze. Some do this to the extent that they never apply the rudder, and the breezes take them on an aimless course, even onto the rocks of shipwreck.

They tell us, of course, that we must become sanctified by our work. In this they have a hold on a great truth. Work calls forth virtues that are hard to develop in any other way. Yet it is not action alone which does this, but rather the love of God and neighbor by which we are dedicated to action. Even in activity we need more than the virtues of activity. We need self-discipline and that insight into the will of God which comes through obedience. We need holy prudence, humility, and prayer, all of which will keep us on our course. In short, to be successful in the active life, we need the heart of the virtues, God himself, and thus we need the spiritual life.

The active man who trusts to luck that his work will give him the inner virtues of self-conquest, and who does not seek God for his own soul, eventually becomes the superficial man, the man who dissipates his energies in non-essentials, and often the man who finally loses his zeal quite completely. And sadly we see that instead of building up the body of Christ, his efforts sometimes result in tearing it down. Unless purity of intention is kept alive by the intimacy with God implied by the spiritual life, a man will seek his own glory; greatly beneficial works will be prevented by factionalism, by the fear that someone else will get the credit.

The relationship between work and the spiritual life is more complex than it seems. More than one beginner has failed in a serious attempt at the inner life, with consequent failure in the active life, because he sought the spiritual life exclusively as a help in the active life rather than seeking it for God. While the help is undeniably there, we may never subordinate the relationship which the soul must have with God to the relationships we must have with men. God must be loved and served primarily for himself; this is the first law of creation; it is the first of the two great commandments. After this, as a part of the second commandment, comes service of neighbor. In any such inversion of this essential order the spiritual life will not survive the watery abyss of discouragement or the dry sands of day-after-day routine.

Similarly, we may not do the works of the active life primarily in order to advance spiritually. Instead of Christ in our neighbor, this would be making ourselves the end of our activity. Instead of being wholehearted in the service of others, we would always be calculating its effect on ourselves. As a result we would not work as well, nor even see the work to be done. Therefore we must work principally because it is God's will, because Christ in the Church and in our neighbor has pressing needs. And as a consequence, regardless of our success or failure, the good to our own souls will be incalculable.

If these words on the relationship of work and the spiritual life have been small sparks illuminating the darkness for those who have avoided the spiritual life, they should be lightning flashes for those who are enjoying a selfishly isolated spiritual life. Not only these words, but also all that has been said previously on practical love of neighbor, applies to those who are able to work for God, but who find contentment in a spiritual life surrounded by Mass, the sacraments, spiritual reading, a method of prayer, and a spiritual director. This is not to say that there is no such thing as a predominately contemplative vocation even in the world. But such a person must be sure that these inclinations are not a comfortable drama acted out for his own enjoyment.

Work is so much a part of our lives that it is important to see it for what it is, more than a penalty for original sin or punishment for other sin. We must integrate it into the whole of our lives and find its place in the spiritual life. For this reason we will interrupt our consideration of the works of God, and briefly consider human work.

Since it is true that "My Father works even until now, and I work," (John 5:17) we must not be surprised that work is a law written in human nature. Even in the Garden of Eden man was sent to work. "And the Lord God took man, and put him into the paradise of pleasure, to dress it and to keep it." (Gen. 2:15) It is only in our immature years that we thought that absolute ease meant happiness.

To be happy at work, man must have a vision of it. He does not live by bread alone, nor ought he to work as if for bread alone. This vision is a broad one: work is his co-operation with God in the further unfolding of creation.

Creation is never a completed thing. For instance, petroleum was formed under the earth during long millennia, and now man brings it up and refines it for his many needs. The corn which the Indians gave to Columbus was dwarfish compared with the magnificent improvement, now spread across the plains and steppes of the world. Not all work has the ennobling characteristic of imitation of God's work of creation and co-operation with it, but only that which helps the human race, even though indirectly. True work must perform some service which man needs for his existence of his better existence; food, shelter, transportation, the movement of money, and even recreation are only the beginning of an endless list. In this light it is easily seen, of course, that homemaking is one of the highest of human works.

Seeing work as more than a livelihood, and surely more than a means of amassing wealth, can bring peace to the many who must work at apparently unsatisfying jobs. In this view their work becomes a part of the vision of the whole of humanity co-operating, one with all the others, in the common pilgrimage through this world. This vision brings a man peace because he must feel that he is worth something in order to be truly a man. And his work can go a long way toward helping him see that.

This co-operative effort of man with God, and man with man, has a crescendo in the teaching of the Scriptures on the Mystical Body of Christ. The Mystical Body is, of course, the Church. But although the word "mystical" is necessary to distinguish this body from the real body of Christ, perhaps nowhere else is there a better example of the principle that the adjective is the enemy of the noun. St. Paul used no such adjective, and his meaning is clear at once: just as a real body has many members, all fulfilling different but necessary functions, so also the many members of the Church fulfill the pruposes for which God called them in both their general and personal vocations. All are harmoniously a part of Christ, using the metaphor of a body; all receive from Christ who is the head of the body—or as he himself put the same truth: "As the branch cannot bear fruit of itself unless it remain on the vine, so neither can you unless you abide in me. I am the vine, you are the branches." (John 15:4, 5)

We have seen this identification of Christ and ourselves before: "I was thirsty and you gave me to drink . . ." (Matt. 25:35) He did not say "your brother" or "my servant," but he said it of himself. To St. Paul at Damascus the identification was unforgettable. Christ did not rebuke him, "Saul, Saul, why dost thou persecute my Church?", but "Why dost thou persecute *me?*" (Acts 9:4) It is no wonder, then, that the apostle uses the identification implied by the metaphor of Christ's body to teach so many lessons. Some of these fit our vocation to work.

The first of these lessons involves a deep truth and more than a little of humility. Many of us waste our lives trying to be something we cannot be and ought not be. We eat ourselves up with envy and die a thousand deaths of frustration. But from the doctrine of the Mystical Body we see that we all have our place, that we all are useful in some way, perhaps mysteriously hidden from us, to the whole of God's plan. "And if the ear says, 'Because I am not an eye, I am not of the body,' is it not of the body? If the whole body were an eye, where would be the hearing?" (I Cor. 12:16, 17)

Secondly, the awareness of the Mystical Body will help us to work better even at our ordinary work, better since we can make it the work of Christ. If we do our job poorly, people will lose their respect for us and for what we stand for, and we are thus weak and unhealthy members of the body of Christ. Similarly, if we fail as Christians, we will fail to impress those whom he expects us to impress. This is all the more true if our position is one raised above the multitude. Catholics in the professions, in business, and in politics have not always made a sensation by their ethical superiority over their associates.

Realizing that all men are either actual or potential members of the same Christ as we, we will not neglect the apostolate of friendliness. Especially in our large cities it is quite possible to go to church every Sunday of the year without being greeted or smiled at even once. We will spread the feeling of oneness which all Christians, and especially all Catholics, should feel in Christ. If dark days come, a loosely loyal Church of respectable individualists will be a poor match for a united Satan. But as Christ's body, united, one helping another, all helping by prayer and sacrifice, there will be no darkness from which we cannot emerge intact.

Practical Reflection

Do I not see that I have an apostolate in all my surroundings, including that of my own home? Have I concentrated too much on good works outside my own home that I have neglected the duties of my state? On the other hand, have I concentrated too much on my own circle that I have neglected God's work for me outside? Do I understand that there is an apostolate which consists not so much of information and admonitions as an atmosphere of happiness, helpfulness, and understanding? If I am able prudently to influence others, have I used that influence to raise the ethical practices of my associates, or at least kept my own ethics higher than those of others who know God less? In my concern for others have I also seen the wholeness of the body of Christ of which I must do my part as a member? Will I see all my activity as a practical fulfillment of the love I have for God, the first love of my life?

CHAPTER 44

The Apostolate of Love

Love for Christ means that we will become more and more like him; our minds and hearts will become more like his own. This is not an extraordinary statement, but it has the possibility of changing the world. Quite certainly it is the only thing that can change the world. To see and to love as Christ sees and loves does not mean loving only our family and friends, or only our country, or only Catholics. The embrace of this love is as wide as the world: "Go into the whole world." (Mark 16:15)

An authentic spiritual life can never become confined to a narrow isolation with like-minded people and an occasional financial contribution to some worthy cause. No matter how intense might become our desire to have more and more of God, a true love will also become concerned with the interests of God. The triumphs and failures of his work in the world, the sufferings of his children, the salvation or loss of souls, all will affect us deeply. We will be impelled by the love of Christ to do what we can, even if our vocation allows no more than fervent prayer and a willingness to suffer. This willingness to embrace the world even at our cost is a conclusion drawn from the doctrine of the Mystical Body: "What is lacking of the sufferings of Christ I fill up in my body for his body which is the Church." (Col. 1:24)

It can now no longer be thought that the layman has no vocation to the whole world, that this is the exclusive province of the clergy and religious. Perhaps in centuries past, when populations were smaller and problems were simpler, these could handle most of the problems of the Church with only the indirect support of the layman. But this was never the intention of Christ, and it was not the everyday practice, although this kind of history is seldom recorded. But for the fact that St. Augustine told us his own story, we might think that he was converted by St. Ambrose, the bishop who baptized him. But a reading of the *Confessions* tells us that this most original mind of the Church was brought to a confrontation with God by two laymen. The influence of personal contact has always been a major way of spreading the knowledge and love of God, and it always will be. The layman will always be able to meet people who would run from a priest. But in our days the enormity of our problems, the growing indifference of so many people, and the great numbers themselves make it impossible for the clergy and religious to do any adequate proportion of the work that is waiting to be done. And so the layman is now being called specifically to help.

This call is given unmistakably and irrevocably by the Second Vatican Council. Although occasioned by the need of the Church and of mankind, the basis for the call is contained within the layman himself:

> The laity derive the right and duty to the apostolate from their union with Christ the head; incorporated into Christ's Mystical Body through Baptism and strengthened by the Holy Spirit through Confirmation, they are assigned to the apostolate by the Lord himself. They are consecrated for the royal priesthood and the holy people (cf. I Peter 2:4-10) not only that they may offer spiritual sacrifices in everything they do, but also that they may witness to Christ throughout the world.—*Decree on the Apostolate of the Laity*, No. 3.

This entire decree should be read by every layman when he has grown roots sufficient to supply the strength needed to work for Christ.

Although the call to the layman has come by baptism and confirmation, thus constituting the priesthood of the laity, the motive force for even the greatest works is still no other than love of God and love of neighbor. This motive force simplifies our vision when confronted with the multitude of things to be done: they are all works of love, just as both the healing and teaching of Christ were works of love. If the work is apostolic in the strictest sense, it is love sharing the faith, not as a rich man might toss a coin to a needy person, nor as an attempt to prove that "we're right and you're wrong." Rather it is to make God loved and served better, as he generally will be by those who have the faith, and to enable our neighbor to have a better chance to get to heaven. On the other hand, if the work is that of rebuilding the social and moral order, love is then desiring and working for the ideal that all men will have justice, a sufficient share of the bounty of God to keep them and their families from want, and a favorable climate for the moral health of mankind's children. And finally if the works are what are called the works of mercy, love is so much a part of them that they are given the name of an exclusively spiritual kind of love, which is charity.

When we build up the body of Christ because of love, we avoid certain defects which are like diseases upon it. We have already mentioned self-seeking and factionalism. Another is the type of organization which seems to exist solely for the purpose of running the organization. Very little good is done; yet they are called Catholic and absorb energies which could be spent more profitably elsewhere. This is not to say that there is not a place for the purely social organization or the organization whose sole purpose is to raise money, but the men or women who love God will want to see their time and effort put to more productive use.

There are two general ways in which we may exercise the apostolate of love. One is by acting alone and the other is by working with an organization. Some people and their circumstances will be suited to one way more than to the other. But even those who work with an organization must also be prepared to work alone to infiltrate their surroundings with the truth and love of Christ, even if only by prayer and good example.

An organization, however, has advantages. The group can provide encouragement, training, and direction both in the work and in the spiritual life. The loyalty and obligations imposed by the group will sometimes be a barrier against discouragement when the first fervor of the apostolic experience has worn off.

In this book there can be no attempt to single out one kind of work rather than another. God has given certain talents and inclinations to each of us and will demand a return on his investment, as our Lord has told us in the parables. But one word might be said about the duty of enlarging the kingdom of God by directly spreading the faith. Now of course, we don't have to address a group of people on a street corner, and a wise man will be careful not to argue. But we should all be willing at least to answer questions about the faith, or to find someone who can answer what we cannot. As for example, the religion of Islam is without a priesthood as such and, despite some use of the sword, it owes much of its remarkable spread to the contact of one man with another. Yet non-Catholics in their search for the truth are often rebuffed or ignored by good Catholics. Some of us excuse ourselves by a certain smugness: "I go to church, but I mind my own business." But our Lord didn't put things exactly that way. He said, "Go forth into the whole world and preach the gospel to every creature." (Mark 16:15) And after the Second Vatican Council we have no doubt that, according to our ability and vocation, he meant every one of us.

To complete this part of the picture, a word must also be mentioned about money. Napoleon is said to have declared that three things are necessary for a successful war: the first is money, the second is money, and the third is money. Now of course, he knew he was exaggerating, and we have no desire to apply these words literally to the works of God. But the sober truth is that money is so important that even our Lord couldn't do without it. And only a little thought will show us that his Mystical Body can't do without it either.

Not only is financial contribution a law of the Church, a way in which we support those who give us supernatural life, nourish it all our days, and seal it at the end, but it also enables us to participate in many of the spiritual and corporal works of mercy impossible to us because of our condition of life. While it is quite true that holy prudence is a pertinent virtue here, many people figure very closely in giving to the works of God, but spend lavishly for themselves and their way of life. In judging us, our Lord is not so apt to use an adding machine to total our contributions, as to calculate them against our assets. We are sure of one thing, that he will not be outdone in generosity. For example, a reasonably rich man gave very generously to many causes. A priest once asked him how he was still able to be prosperous. "Well, Father," he said, "as fast as I shovel money out, God shovels it in. The only difference is that he uses a bigger shovel."

But no amount of money by itself will insure success. The

human channels of God's grace will always be the more important element. These, however, like the first apostles of Christ, always need preparation. We must, of course, avoid the weakness which hides under an ever-present excuse that we are not sufficiently prepared to undertake the apostolate. Yet the value of preparation is not to be underestimated.

First of all, as the Second Vatican Council has said, this must be a spiritual preparation. The work of God can be impeded rather than helped by the undisciplined enthusiast or the man who seeks his own will with his own strength rather than God's. How else but with this kind of preparation will a man be able to submit to the difficulties of obedience which is the rock of all Catholic apostolic activity, as it was with Christ? How else avoid discouragement and disillusionment? How else acquire the long patience which alone brings many victories? How else can we always remember that the only way not to lose ourselves in becoming "all things to all men," (I Cor. 9:22) is by having it deeply impressed that we dare not lose God in the process?

Although men often look to the heart before they look to the mind, we cannot expect the heart to solve all questions and doubts; man is ever the rational animal. Therefore we cannot neglect intellectual preparation, depending, of course, on our ability and circumstances. A true intellectual preparation is hardly less arduous than the spiritual. Neither will come by contact with light, fascinating literature. Both will require thoughtful reading and much reflection. For a thorough intellectual preparation it will even be necessary to study. For the layman this can often be found in competent lectures and perhaps even better in supervised study groups. It need hardly be said that the authors studied must be solid, not given to pushing their favorite theories or trying to enlarge the frontiers of theological thought in their own chosen direction. This solid kind of book will not be spectacular, but on the other hand non-Catholics will not want to know what this or that theologian says about Catholic doctrine; they will want to know what the Church says, and why.

The lay apostolate often involves working for or with a priest. Therefore it may be well to digress here for a moment about the conduct of the laity toward their priests. God has placed on the shoulders of his priests the awesome duty of representing himself, and sometimes they are weak shoulders indeed. The duty of the people is to be friendly to the priest so as to warm his heart, not cold and suspicious so as to break it. Nor so familiar as to betray it. More than one promising priest has fallen away because of the misguided familiarity of some of his people. The goodness of priests is greatly in the hands of the people, and these hands should rather be joined together in prayer than open in social conviviality ("Father's life is so hard.") or to an initially innocent embrace which has swept away an important barrier to anything further. When priests fail, it is usually not at the hands of the wicked, but of the thoughtless.

But to return to our subject, in the Mystical Body there are many members and all must find their place. No part is without its use to the body, and if that part is not there, there is a defect in the body. But just as there are parts which do not appear on the surface, there are others which surely do. It is the sincere hope that some of those who read this book will see that they are called to be leaders.

Leaders do not necessarily have to be those on the firing line. They must direct or influence others, perhaps from an obscure desk. Even so influential a man as St. Thomas Aquinas hardly saved a soul by personal contact. For one thing, there is need for the Christian to be competent in his own field. One great scientific leader, for instance, acknowledging the existence of God makes far more impression on the people than thousands of priests, ministers, or rabbis. In some sense, however, they must not only be leaders in their field, but also must prudently be apostles. Then the possibilities are enormous. Bismarck, the Iron Chancellor, acknowledgedly the strongest man in Europe, having united the many German states and defeated France, now proposed to conquer the Church. This seemingly all-powerful man was beaten, not by priest or bishop, but by Windthorst, a small, frail man who used the force of logic and undeniable principles, along with political ability. Without leaders, and these must in great part be lay leaders, society will never be restored to Christ.

Many of our lives are unsatisfactory because we are concerned with only the essentials of living, and hope to make the unpleasantness more palatable by large doses of pleasure. No single job, no single profession in itself can fill a man completely. We instinctively want our lives to have some deeper worth than drawing a paycheck or collecting fees. In this life there is no work more an ultimate than working for God in the many ways there are to work for him.

Practical Reflection

Do I now see that the more your love enlarges my heart, the broader must become my vision? Do I see that the love you have for me, O my Redeemer, is the same love you have for all men? Is it not more than possible that there are certain people who will never put their hand in yours unless I be the one to lead them? Am I also convinced that, although I must not neglect any competence which will help your work, in the end the indispensable means of drawing men to you is love? And where love of them is not enough, and prayer is not enough, will I be willing to offer for them the sacrifices and sufferings of my life, in union with yours, in the plea that this will be enough?

PART IX

PERSEVERANCE IN LOVE

CHAPTER 45

"I Am the Mother . . . of Holy Hope"
(Ecclus. 24:24)

It is a great thing to have made a good start in the spiritual life and to be determined on running the full course to final victory. But no matter with what momentum this start is made, the laws of human psychology, like the laws of the physical world, determine that there is always a deterioration toward a zero state unless more energy is added along the way. In this final section of the book we will look into several ways by which we may be hopefully certain of perseverance.

The first of these is perhaps what we should expect when we are taking our first steps, the help of a mother—except that she is not only a help for our first steps in the spiritual life, but for all the steps, especially those last when we must venture from this familiar world into the world unknown. So little is said of Mary in the Scriptures that the Church, when it wishes to praise this greatest of women, must select passages from other parts of the Bible and apply them to Mary in a poetic sense. Thus she is called the mother of holy hope.

There is sometimes a tendency of certain people in the Church to downgrade the devotion to Mary. In part this is a reaction to the excessive devotion of others in the Church. Very little needed to be done, apparently, by Christ, our mediator, and by the Holy Spirit. But while allowing for the truth of some of the accusation, is it not possible that the downgraders have not fallen into an opposite extreme of too little of Mary? Too much is not solved by too little. For this reason a few words will be necessary, even in a practical book, to show the solid foundations of our love and confidence in Mary. These foundations are two in number.

The first basis for thus honoring Mary is her motherhood of

Christ. It was solely from her flesh that the Son of God took flesh when he first came to dwell among us. This relationship with him quite clearly involves a relationship with us. Since she is the mother of Christ's physical body, she is in some sense mother of his Mystical Body. Or another path to the same conclusion: Christ is brother even to the least of us, and brotherhood implies a common mother: his real mother, our spiritual mother. We did not take a vote and choose her for our mother; like all mothers she was given to us. Since God loved her enough to choose her for his mother, dare we reject any part of her motherhood over us?

Mary as mother embodies what we humans know to be the strongest of all the bonds that anchor one of us to another. God uses this love of mother for child to assure us of his love for us: "Can a woman forget her infant, so as not to have pity on the son of her womb? And if she should forget, yet will not I forget thee." (Isa. 49:15) It is not as if Mary were more loving, merciful, or faithful than God. But because we as humans must and do live by symbols, she personifies for us what we hesitate to believe as strongly about God. She is a gift to our insecurity, which is not always an entirely unreasonable insecurity in view of our sins and waste of grace. She brings us the assurance of being loved, no matter what we are. A father may symbolize justice, but a mother always mercy. She is a living revelation of God's message of undying love to the world.

In regard to love there are two kinds of people: those who have known real love and those who have not. Those who have known it, know the unbelievable richness it brings to life, how it fills almost the whole of life, how wholly the one lives for the other. These do not have to be told how much Mary loves us. They know her heart because they know love. It should be easy for these to love Mary. It should be easy for these to trust Mary and ask Mary.

And those who have not known real love: are they few or many? We are not seldom loved falsely. People love us for themselves, for what we can give them, for the pleasure it gives them to love us. Lovers forget, friends forget, close relatives even forget, but a mother never. Mary saw her son's blood flow out of his wounds, drop by drop, and will not want even one drop of that blood wasted. For those who search for human love, in Mary the most unloved of us can be sure of someone.

Our relationship with Mary is meant to be close: not just so many "Hail Marys" a day, but someone we can talk to, pour out our troubles to, and if necessary cry out our hearts to. We should bring her our joys as well as our sorrows, and not hesitate to bring our temptations and even our sins. For we are dealing with a mother, and nothing is too small, too troublesome, or too shameful to be understood and helped by this mother.

The second basis for turning to Mary for perseverance also is a relationship to her son, but a different kind of relationship. The New Testament clearly teaches that Christ is the new Adam: "As from the offense of the one man the result was unto condemnation to all men, so from the justice of the one the result is unto justification of life to all men." (Rom. 5:18) Thus Christ is spiritually the father of a new race.

If there was one idea about Mary, other than her divine motherhood, which impressed the early Fathers of the Church, it was the idea that she is the new Eve. St. Augustine makes the typical comparison: "Eve was the beginner of sin, Mary the beginner of merit. Eve harmed us by killing us; Mary helped us by giving life. The former wounded us, the latter healed us. Obedience is exchanged for disobedience; fidelity compensates for treachery." As Eve would have been a helpmate to Adam in the spiritual formation of perfect men and women, so Mary, the second Eve, is associated with Christ, the second Adam, in our salvation and spiritual perfection. And after Christ in his human nature, she is the highest example of the divine principle that humans are to help other humans to get to God.

Christ and Mary differ in the way they help us. Only Christ has effectively redeemed us; by his death God owes us something. "There is one Mediator between God and men, himself man, Christ Jesus." (I Tim. 2:5) Mary, on the other hand, pleads for us to Christ, and to the Father through Christ, just as we do but with greater effect. God does as she wishes, not because he owes her anything essential, but because he loves her so much he cannot resist her.

We will not doubt Mary's power through love if we analyze the familiar events of the marriage feast at Cana. (John 2:1–12) It would be natural that Mary, if she were helping to look after the serving, should notice the shortage even before the steward. So she approaches her son. Now, to understand this exchange of words, we must recall that the mother and son had been together for thirty years. When we live that long with anyone, we get to know them, and the more we love, the deeper is the knowledge. So Mary merely makes the statement, "They have no wine." No details, no formal request. Just that. But our Lord understands her immediately and also understands the enormity of what she is asking: not merely a miracle, but that his first miracle, which by divine eternal decree had been reserved for some auspicious time and place, should take place now, and merely to save two people from embarrassment. So our Lord refuses, using the public form of address for all women, "What wouldst thou have me do, woman? My hour has not yet come."

Mary's response is extraordinary. She does not plead; she does not create a scene of recrimination; she doesn't even say another word to him. She merely turns to the waiters, "Do whatever he tells you," and apparently walks away. She is that sure of him, sure that he will refuse her nothing.

Even the best of us go to God as sinners. How much will we not be encouraged if we have on our side the help of this woman? It is foolhardy to think that we can do better without her. Refusing this help would be as impractical as learning the violin without a teacher. The long experience of the Church with the spiritual life bears this out. Those of us who have reached closest to God are the saints, and yet universally they love God's mother with a love that sometimes embarrasses us. When the minimizers of Mary begin to grow saints who do not deeply love Mary, perhaps then their words will sound more reasonable.

And if anyone wants it, there is a personal proof, a challenge if you will. Let anyone who doubts Mary's power to influence his life put himself seriously under her immediate protection, give her *all that he can give her* according to God's will, and then set aside some time for her in prayer. Let him do this for a trial period of six months, and he will see what we have been talking about.

Practical Reflection

Can I now see into the fullness of your plan, O God, and see that you have given us an insight into your love for us through the gift of your creature, Mary? Can I not trust your gift enough to see that she will not lead me away from you, but always closer and closer? While never forgetting that all our hope is from your goodness and from the cross of your Son, in the restricted sense that we can look to creatures for help, can I not place in her care my hope of perseverance, my desire to belong to you completely? Even when my sins and failures make me feel uncertain of you, can I still not grasp certainty because of this mother's love? For, can a true mother do else than love?

CHAPTER 46

Guidance for Love

Perseverance in the spiritual life is guaranteed somewhat by our traveling companions, as we said when speaking of friendship. But, although friends are of an inestimable value, there is always the danger that the blind will try to lead the blind. In our spiritual life, just as in climbing a mountain, there are certain points where we will need more expert assistance. The usual name for this is spiritual direction.

When speaking of confession, we omitted one of its most important advantages, and this is the seeking of advice. Often this advice may be about questions of conscience or about situations which have a bearing on the Christian life. But the proximity of the open soul to someone who can help will also make it an opportunity to receive advice on things which pertain to the spiritual life.

There are, of course, some excellent priests who will discourage any spiritual direction in connection with confession for fear that the principal aim of the sacrament, which is the forgiveness of sins, will be obscured. But many people have no other choice, and besides, the confessional has advantages too. The situation itself, charity to the priest and to those waiting, will confine the matters to an efficient exposition of the problem, rather than chatting one's way into it or all around it. This situation will also help to avoid many of the trivial problems which were discussed earlier as an abuse of friendship. But of course, there are problems and circumstances which will recommend direction outside of the confessional, and the priest should be the judge of that.

It is, however, necessary to distinguish between the functions of confessor and spiritual director, at least in theory, although the two often overlap. Whereas every authorized priest can forgive sin, not every confessor can give good advice. Nor, of those who can give good advice, is every priest fitted to give advice to every person or at every stage of spiritual development. Obviously then, much care and prayer, and perhaps some prudent experimentation should usually precede the decision to put oneself under the direction of a particular priest.

The qualities to look for in such a man are listed by St. Francis de Sales as principally learning, prudence, and charity. As to learning, it is usually an indispensable condition. Souls are sometimes disorientated, stunted, or even broken by ignorant or narrow men. St. Teresa, who went through such an ordeal herself, tells us that if she had to choose between a holy but unlearned man and a good but learned man, she would choose the latter.

But learning is not enough. An enormous amount of knowledge does not make a good director. All that has been said about the virtue of holy prudence applies in a superlative manner to him who exercises what is justly called "the art of arts." The director must be able to distinguish the right path from the wrong one, what will help or hinder the soul at its particular stage of development. He will not try to direct souls according to his own enthusiasms or prejudices but will try to bring about the particular perfection that is being indicated by the promptings of the Holy Spirit. He will not endlessly disturb or distract the person by questions about the past, about prayer, or other delicate subjects. He will not urge greater haste than the soul can manage in peace, and he will restrain too ambitious a haste if the soul itself falls into this deceit of the devil.

The final quality to look for is charity. One might almost say that any priest who undertakes a work so time-consuming and full of hardship, danger, and disappointment could be nothing but a charitable man. But unfortunately it is sometimes undertaken by those who wish to aggrandize themselves by having a following or who wish to propagandize their one-sided approach to the spiritual life. These will sometimes even be recommended to the searcher for God, but God will soon make it apparent that his peace is not there, and therefore he is not there. The sincere person will become aware of confusion and emptiness.

The love of a good priest for those whom God gives him does

not fall on unresponsive stone. Especially in the case of women, though not exclusively, a return of love is almost inevitable, and to some extent desirable. If there is not a certain bond of affection, the director will usually not be able to do very much good, and the spirit of God will not be able to do very much either. A famous doctor was once asked about his rather remarkable success. He replied that it was to a large extent due to the fact that these patients liked him. When asked what happened to those patients who did not like him, he replied simply, "They die."

An obvious but erroneous conclusion about the fact of this affection is to jump at once into the making of a spiritual friendship. After all, it is grandly assumed, this is what God must want since he wanted it for many of the saints. Yet this assumption is gratuitous; spiritual friendship, even more than any other kind of friendship, must be proven rather than assumed. Even a bond of deep and holy affection as to a father does not mean the sacred hold of two souls on each other called friendship. The truth is that few people can take it; too few can take the equality that friendship implies. The most obvious result is likely to be an emotional attachment. This, although it promises obedience, will be used by the penitent to avoid obedience. If the unfortunate priest is captured in this orbit, he will shrink from imposing any burden or hard decision. And in a basic sense he is right; here is not a strong soul seeking God, nor a weak soul seeking support and counsel, but a weak soul masquerading as a strong one in sentimental self-delusion. In short, the penitent is using the freedom of the friendship to dominate the direction.

Spiritual people have to be reminded of what they are: human beings with normal impulses and normal attractions to each other. In general these attractions are a father-son/daughter, a mother-son/daughter relationship, or the attraction between the sexes, or the companionship between equals of the same sex. There is nothing wrong with these attractions as such, and many times they are the initial ground upon which God builds a great spiritual edifice. But spiritual people should realize that our natural impulses are like the enormous amount of water held back by a giant dam. Our will, fortified by the grace of God, prevents certain emotional and physical results of our attractions; the water behind the dam is allowed to escape only through certain restricted channels. Between spiritual people these channels are very limited; all the water must come out through the spiritual life. This is the danger. We may think that we want God and direction in the spiritual life, when really the pressure is from the great sea of water behind the dam.

The principal things to be discussed in spiritual direction will be the problems that come up in the spiritual life. Yet as we have already indicated when speaking of friendship, not every problem needs the help of others. And if one's first thought, when faced with a problem or difficulty, is to "ask Father," one should know that there is already too great a dependence or attachment. A similar attachment can be discovered if one finds oneself talking about the director or his advice. In general, the advice given in confession or in direction is personal, and binds the penitent as well as the priest to secrecy, although not in the same absolute degree.

In direction it is not necessary to make a day-by-day description of our spiritual life. The result of this is usually too much introspection; we watch ourselves instead of God. This can be especially damaging in the matter of prayer.

A word of caution about being open and honest would seem to be unnecessary. But people will waste the priest's time for long periods over minor details, and never come to the real problem. They should make it a point to tell what they know they must tell, and even to bring this up at the beginning of a particular meeting. If anyone has been thus far made insecure by this necessary exposition of unsuccessful direction, it may be well here to give a practical rule whereby anyone may test his sincerity. If we are honest and open to the director, see him for no longer than useful and about things which really need his advice, and finally give him intelligent obedience, then there is no reason to doubt the sincerity of seeking direction.

We should be careful about presenting problems which do not pertain to the spiritual life. For instance, financial difficulties, frictions between husband and wife, or problems with the children may occasionally need spiritual direction, but sparingly. The priest is not a financial expert, and spiritual direction is not marriage counseling or child guidance. A priest may be a very good director, but only mediocre or even poor in things not pertaining to the spirit.

Furthermore, in the case of women, they may easily seek advice for decisions which properly belong to the husband and father. Such invasion of rights helps no one, especially the priest and the cause of the spiritual life. There is, besides, the danger that real direction will become secondary to the sweet sharing of domestic problems. This is all the more certain if there is frequent discussion of interminable problems of the sexual life. Beyond doubt these sometimes have a legitimate place in moral counseling and even in spiritual direction, but not always as much as is thought necessary.

A crucial point of all direction is obedience. This obedience is based on trust in God rather than on any human quality the priest may have, no matter how excellent. We trust that God will guide us by means of this man. If we have chosen him as prudently as we can, we must give his advice the presumption of at least a prayerful trial. Even if the advice is mistaken, God will not allow those who trust him to suffer loss. Our ideas and aspirations may not always coincide with what we are directed to do. But here, as in many other situations in our lives, we must solve our dilemmas by the principle, "Obedience is better than sacrifices." (I Kings 15:22)

In some cases it may be necessary to change directors, especially if something were counseled contrary to the teaching of the Church. But there is a great difference between a change resulting from a definite lack of progress or understanding, and the grand tour of different priests until one gets the particular advice one has decided on beforehand. Similar to this is undue pressure to get one's own way. An open exposition of the difficulties which stand in the way of obedience is desirable, but frequent insistence amounts to self-direction. If that is what is wanted, why waste the time of the priest?

The primary question, who should seek direction, has been purposely left until the matter itself was sufficiently discussed for the beginner to feel at home with it. To some this question is purely academic, because all direction is impossible to them under their present circumstances. For these especially, this book has been written. It contains much that could be acquired under an experienced director. For what cannot be contained in any book, the Holy Spirit must and will supply. In any case he is always the real director of each soul.

Concerning those for whom direction is possible, not even all these should seek it regularly at stated intervals. There is always a danger of overdirection, by which the subject is overloaded with advice and practices. Ideas need time to mature, to influence our other ideas, and therefore to change us. Or the subject can become overly dependent, and will hardly put on his shoes in the morning without the advice of the director. The excuse is sometimes given that there is a special merit in obedience. But God will give no merit for what will make us less mature men and women. If the director does not build up this maturity, or try to, he is failing God and the soul entrusted to him. Direction is almost by definition a steadily decreasing process. Like all fathers, the director must see his children grow up, able to make most of their decisions.

It is sometimes thought that only very advanced souls need direction. The opposite is sometimes true. In the first place there have been saints who apparently needed very little of it. On the other hand it is surely necessary for many who are merely good and are having a hard time being that. It is for anyone who encounters problems, questions, or uncertainties in the spiritual life. It is for anyone who wants to possess God in the end by total transformation into what God wants.

21. Beginnings

CHAPTER 47

Reading and the Love of God

The practice of daily reading in a spiritual book is an insurance policy on perseverance. What we read, largely determines what we think, and what we think determines what we are. If we do not feed the light that now burns in the soul, it may die of lack of fuel. Surrounded on all sides by ideas which do not harmonize with God, it will be smothered.

For the beginner there are many difficulties in the matter of reading. The first one is the question, what is a spiritual book? Obviously it is not just a book written by a Catholic, such as the recollections of fifty years as a bishop. Much of this kind of Catholic literature may be interesting and informative, but it is not spiritual reading. Nor is a spiritual book any book written on a sacred subject. For instance, a scientific analysis of some recently discovered manuscripts of the Bible may be of the highest scholarship, but it will do little to move us toward God. Similarly, any book of straight theology is likely not to be spiritual reading either. Rarely it can be so, but in that case it must move the heart as well as the mind. All such theological books, provided they are written by solid authors, are important for background to the spiritual life, since ignorance is the mother of many evils. But in themselves they do not build up the spiritual man into the stature of Christ.

A spiritual book is one which moves us to God, or to the virtues, or which gives us a better understanding of ourselves. Usually it must feed the heart, that is, the will, as well as the mind. Not that we must be emotionally moved by it, but we must find that the fruit of reading is some relevant insight or a determination to persevere in our spiritual journey.

But even spiritual books must undergo a further limitation when we seek the kind of book which is suitable for the individual. Here the criteria become exceedingly personal. A book which sets one person on fire will leave another cold. A book which might be read with profit a few years from now seems impossibly abstruse. For such reasons no list of books is being provided here. However, a few general cautions can be given.

The first rule is not to read a book out of a mere sense of duty, unless, of course, the choice be of not reading at all. There is an old proverb which fits the spiritual life: "Minerva [the goddess of wisdom] is not forced." If we have to push too hard at a book, the presumption is that it is not for us, and we had better start looking for another.

Another rule is to be selective. Even among books professing to be spiritual, there will be some which are not only useless but can even do harm. It is a matter of human experience that putting ideas into print gives them a sort of canonization, a quasi-divine authority. What we would dreamily endure if it came from the pulpit, we are inclined to take seriously because it is in print. History usually buries such books, but we cannot await the judgment of history. The beginner must read what the ages have bequeathed us, but he must also not lose the insights which contemporary works written in contemporary language give to him living in his own age. The solution goes back to what we said: he must learn to read selectively. This is not an easy art to acquire, but if he keeps his mind on what he is really looking for, it is not an impossible feat.

This is not to say that we read as critics. If we do, we stop the ordinary action of the Holy Spirit. We should read to be taught and to be moved. If we find neither effect, we probably have the wrong book. But we should not give up reading a book because we disagree with some one idea or another. Often these ideas can be adjusted to our profit. For example, the anti-intellectualism of the *Imitation of Christ* can teach us to avoid vanity and superficiality in our intellectual pursuits. This is, of course, the basic intent of the author.

Another reason for reading selectively is based on the fact that there are many good books which are not meant for every individual. Perhaps nowhere else is the truth so strikingly illustrated, that we do not all travel the same road to God in the spiritual life. Books may be well recommended in reviews, by friends, or even by a spiritual director, and yet cause mountains of internal opposition. Occasionally people become discouraged in the spiritual life or feel inferior because such books do not move them. But the real truth is very simple: this is not their way to God. Selective reading helps us to find and hold to the way God has designed for our personal vocation.

Some people are helped in their reading problem by a provident God. He leaves them so little time that they are forced to read only the best. It is the measured judgment of intellectual observers of our age that we read too much and reflect too little, and that we grow shallow roots because we seldom reread a book. The output of books is so great and the inducements as well as the inclination to read something new is so pressing that few people reread what was once acknowledged to be important to their development. Consequently they never learn lessons fully or deeply, and they never acquire a solid basis for thought or action. They are constantly at sea without a rudder, pushed this way and that by the latest book they have read. This is not to say that we do not outgrow books. We do, but we should sometimes make certain of it in regard to books that were once important to us.

There is one book, however, which we will never outgrow and this is, of course, the Bible. The longer we live and the closer we get to God, the more it tends to become the only book. The Second Vatican Council (*Constitution on Divine Revelation*, No. 25) "earnestly and especially urges all the Christian faithful . . . to learn by frequent reading of the divine Scriptures the 'excellent knowledge of Jesus Christ.' (Phil. 3:8) 'For ignorance of the Scriptures is ignorance of Christ.'" [St. Jerome, *Commentary on Isaiah*, Prol.: PL 24, 17].

A part of the difficulty with reading the Bible comes from starting at the first page and attempting to read straight through. Those who have survived past Leviticus are not many. In the Bible, as well as everywhere else, we should read where we wish. There is a suggestion, however, that the New Testament receive more attention than the Old. We are blessed with the fullness of the revelation and the example of the Son of God. We should therefore spend most of the time in the full light of the day rather than in the dim light of the growing dawn.

While, of course, there are in the Scriptures "certain things difficult to understand, which the unlearned and the unstable distort . . . to their own destruction," (II Pet. 3:16) there is greater danger to the spiritual life in not reading them at all. In using the Bible for spiritual reading, we do not read it as a theologian or an archaeologist might read it, nor do we need several commentaries at hand to collect opinions on the meaning of every text. We read it principally for the spiritual lessons and inspiration which anyone can draw from them.

In ignoring the New Testament, we can acquire a spirituality not built on the full gospel. Spirituality strangely seems to vary with each age of mankind. One age sees things too severely; another is overly sweet. This results not only from the temper of the age, but also from pulling principles out of the context of the full Christian message and building a distorted spirituality around them. But by frequently reading the sacred pages, we can avoid much of this. For instance, if we find no inspiration in the saints because of the pious tales we remember about them, we can meet one of the greatest, St. Paul, and we find out refreshingly that he is a *man*. If we are puzzled by books which seem to want us to eliminate all feeling and desires, we are reassured again by this man of deep feeling, deep love, and great desires. If this present book accomplishes nothing else, it will be successful if it implants a determination, for instance, to read a book of the Bible in between every two other spiritual books that we read.

Not only should we be careful in regard to what we use for spiritual reading, but we should be even more careful of our other reading. Some people make a brave show of being able to read anything, but often their bravery is foolhardiness, if it is not actual cowardice in trying to impress others out of human respect. Reading, whether we are honest enough to admit it or not, fills our minds. And if we fill them with trash, the obvious conclusion is that they thus become trash barrels. God has not given us freedom to have it abused. We do not have freedom to act rashly against the prudent judgment of those who have to account for the care of our souls. True freedom implies the right to choose between the various good things, not between good and evil, and generally not the absolute right to choose dangerous things. We do not, for instance, have the right to choose to eat rotten food in the hope that it will not hurt us. Similarly, if we are at all serious about the spiritual life, we cannot, without relatively serious reason, put into our minds what will react against the spiritual life, or what can only with difficulty be assimilated by it. A weakened or sickly spirit cannot have much energy to want God.

Practical Reflection

In organizing my daily life, can I not find some time each day when I can spiritually feed my mind and heart? If I cannot do this for ten or fifteen minutes, can I not at least read enough to turn a page at night, or until I come upon a thought that is important to me? Is not the love of God, and all that it promises, worth this investment of time as an insurance of perseverance?

CHAPTER 48

Daily Life and the Love of God

One of the most frequent excuses for not pursuing the spiritual life is the lack of time. Obviously this cannot be a valid reason; God does not want us to be so busy that we neglect all but the spiritual minimum, even when we do not neglect that. He has called us to perfection, and furthermore has most probably called us to perfection right where we are. In other words, he wants the love we can give him, and wants us to grow in his love, precisely in our present circumstances. The conclusion is then that we cannot wait for extra time to drop from heaven; we must make time now for the spiritual life.

We must, however, be practical in our solution to this problem. We know that we cannot spend long hours in prayer. We also cannot devote a comfortable leisure to stacks of spiritual books. If we can, we should look around for some constructive work. But here again, we cannot work for God to the neglect of our temporal and spiritual duties. If we have not as yet seen the value of the virtue of prudence, we surely will when we try to put order into our life.

There is one preliminary error to avoid in arranging our life to include the spiritual life. This is the error of categorizing. We should not divide our lives into God's part and God's non-part. The whole of our lives should be for him, even though one part may find him more directly. Our whole daily life should be a prayer of praise, love, and service. This is what so many of the saints also did, and St. Paul was one of the first. Contrary to an overly prayerful image of sanctity, most of them were very busy. St. Paul had to earn his living as a tentmaker in order to offset the lie that he was preaching the gospel for his own profit.

Perhaps it was this triple necessity of working, preaching, and praying that so impressed on him the lesson which in turn he teaches us: "Whether you eat or drink or do anything else, do all for the glory of God." (I Cor. 10:31)

This is the way to fulfill the Lord's command "that we ought always to pray and not grow faint-hearted." (Luke 18:1) In this way our whole life becomes a prayer, and perhaps as with St. Paul, there will be days in which it is almost the only kind of prayer we can offer. The small details of our life become great in the eyes of God when they are done with the intention of accomplishing his will out of love. If we are faithful in little things we can become a saint, as our Lord has told us. (Luke 19:17)

But as we have said, we ought not be satisfied if most of our days are so busy that we do not have any time to give to God directly. No matter what the apparent obstacles, God will help us to clear a way to him if we seriously ask him. He wants more of our time than a hurried prayer in the morning and one filled with yawns at night.

Yet these morning and evening prayers are important, and if we do not have this habit, then here is the place to start. Most of us have good will about this but still we may consistently forget. A reminder will be helpful. Some object, such as a crucifix, laid on our pillow will remind us at night. And while we are on our knees, how simple to slide our shoes or slippers under the bed so that we must get on our knees to get them out in the morning. Perseverance is often a matter of building walls to bump into.

Not many prayers should be said in the morning and, depending on one's taste, probably not many at night either. We can exhaust our willingness by too great a battle to get them said. But each night one thing should be done without fail. This is a short examination of conscience.

There are two kinds of examination of conscience, and it is better if the two are made at two different times during the day, but for the ordinarily busy person, this probably is impractical. The first kind of examination is the usual one, of looking to see how we have sinned during the day. The second is called the particular examen, and consists in examining ourselves according to some particular predominant sin or imperfection, or better, some particular virtue we are trying to acquire. This subject should be changed from time to time so that we do not grow weary by mere tediousness and can attack our problem from different angles. Also we do not only look for failures, but we note our successes as well. All this should be done briefly, ending with a practical resolution, a prayer for help and, of course, an act of contrition. One of the consolations of this practice of daily examination is that the ordinary act of contrition is an act of perfect contrition.

This habit of prayer suggests a further organization of our lives, and this by the careful adoption of a daily program. Such a program may seem like harsh regimentation, but it is a way out of the labyrinth of inconsequentials. It is advice recommended by many who are not particularly interested in the spiritual life but only in acquiring freedom. As it has been said, it is perhaps not so much a device to live twenty-four hours a day, but a help really to live for one hour a day. Obviously no attempt can be made here to formulate a program to fit everybody or even a majority. But in the course of this book many suggestions have been made for the spiritual life. These, and others which may occur to the individual, can be fitted by trial and error into the general framework of the many things which must be done each day.

But even though such a program is an assurance of perseverance, it has its own dangers. The mechanics of the system can get in the way of the basic purpose, which is freedom to go to God and to do his will. The program must be stable enough to bring a practical meaning into our life, but resilient enough to allow for God's will when it means an exception to the program.

Some lives are too orderly for their own good; everything must be done at its allotted time or there is distress. But the golden thread which gives a meaning to many detail-ridden lives is not an ironclad regime but the ever-present and often unpredictable will of God. As an example, everyone who writes knows that he cannot depend on a schedule to give him all his ideas ideally expressed. He is a slave to his moments of inspiration. These he must learn to cherish, and these ideas and words he must faithfully record. They are here now with a clarity and flow that may never come again. Similarly in the spiritual life and in our daily life, God does not always conform to a schedule, even to the best of schedules. We must learn to seize the moment. The moments may mean consideration for some unexpected need of our neighbor, or as we said when speaking of the presence of God, they may be those moments when God wants nothing but our absorption in himself.

A further bulwark to insure perseverance is the suggestion of a retreat made once a year. Another is a day each month when we shut out or get away from the daily duties as much as we can and give ourselves to God in prayer, reflection, and reading. Obviously this does not have to be done on the pinnacle of some lonely mountain. We can sometimes manage it by doing only necessary work, and postponing the other. Or it may be done on a Sunday, if this is not inconvenient to others who are involved in our lives. These, usually our family, are not to be pushed aside by the spiritual life. One of the resistances one meets to any kind of supra-minimum spirituality is the fear which these others have of neglect or a growing loneliness. The spiritual life is not a call to isolation but rather an incentive to do better with the duties of our state.

Finally, as a suggestion in a daily program, there should be a word on the rosary and, where practical, the family rosary. A devotion so warmly recommended by so many popes of modern times should not be lightly relinquished on the grounds that other forms of prayer are more official. Although some other prayers, notably the liturgy, are of a higher order, this humble prayer will nevertheless bring many graces. God is free to give as he wills, and the prayer of the humble always moves him. The man who is faithful to the rosary will find this true in many striking ways.

The rosary keeps us close to the essentials of the Christian life. Sometimes when we go afield into the esoteric, we can go astray from God. But here, our subjects of meditation are intimately associated with Christ and our redemption. The constant recollection of these basic truths cannot but be fruitful in the spiritual life. Besides, the threefold division of the rosary insures us that we will not emphasize exclusively the suffering part of the Christian life. There is also the joyful side of religion and our eventual glorification.

Practical Reflection

Am I concerned enough about my continued and growing friendship with you, O God, to give some thought to putting order into my life? Is my conception of love broad enough to include both the flights into the heavens and the patient treading of the earth along definite paths? Do I want my love to become like water lost in the sands, or will I make a definite channel for the spiritual life throughout my day?

CHAPTER 49

Unending Love

There is only one way to finish a book of this kind and that is to suggest that it is unfinished. If the impression were given that all things have now been successfully totaled up and all accounts settled, the reader might think that in making a beginning, he has accomplished the whole work. He may have won many battles. He may have glimpsed the peace and love that God is. But although he has fought well and found much, he has only partially achieved, and is in danger of being washed back into the ocean by the next large wave unless he moves forward.

This book is meant to be put aside, but only to be taken up again, perhaps again and again, after a period of maturation of the ideas and their practical effects. Through the new insights he then receives, it will almost seem as if he is reading it for the first time. He will discover a truth which all of us must learn, that even though we are advancing, it seems that we are constantly making new beginnings. But he will really be deepening the roots of these ideas and habits until they are no longer something he merely read about, but something that is his.

He will begin then to see that the ideas and habits are personal to him in that he will find his own way of expressing them in his life and attitudes. They will not be chapters in a book, but will cluster around the core of his own personality, thus giving them a vitality and meaning that is distinctively his. In this way he finds out what he is as a distinct human being. And by seeing this, he also sees more clearly the particular way God has chosen for him to his personal perfection and to come to God himself.

This individual road, though surely included in the broad map of the terrain which all must traverse, is partly a matter of the interior life and partly one of the exterior. But it is much more interior than exterior. It is the basic attitude that the soul has toward God, who wills to be found in the various ways that he has created us, in a variety of beauty and usefulness. Each soul must find this for itself, and it will find it primarily by finding its deepest instincts in its association with God.

But a personal vocation is more than an attitude, even the deepest of attitudes. Each man must also find out how he is destined by God in regard to the exterior world: what form of life, what work in life, even what compromises he must make with life as he sees more clearly the limitations it places on him through God's providence. For only a few of us will this external life be more than ordinary. For many it will be only the small corner of Christ's kingdom which God asks us to work and influence, even if it be only by prayer and example. We are present-day extensions of Christ's redeeming work in the world, but for all of us the most important thing will not be the extent of our influence but the God we do it for and do it with.

This book is incomplete primarily because love is incomplete. A writer once said that the true love story begins at the marriage altar. Thus it is with the soul and God. A beginning has been made only to want more, and to see that more and more can be had, more in the only thing which can fill the heart. This more of love is waiting for everyone with the heart to take the further steps into the full embrace of God.

333